AMAZON FBA,

DROPSHIPPING SHOPIFY E-COMMERCE

AND

SOCIAL MEDIA MARKETING:

3 BOOKS IN 1

DISCOVER THE BEST STRATEGIES TO MAKE MONEY
ONLINE IN 2019 AND REACH AT LEAST 10.000$/MONTH

BLAKE DAVIS

AMAZON FBA 2019

2019

BLAKE DAVIS

TABLE OF CONTENTS

INTRODUCTION

A question that is on many people's mind is "What Is Amazon FBA"? To help me explain what Amazon FBA is, let us look at a little tale, of how Amazon FBA can help you take your online trading business to the next level.

Amazon FBA or to give it full name Fulfilment By Amazon is a program set up by Amazon that allows you to use Amazon to warehouse and then send out your purchases (but always let you sell your items on the Amazon Site). Amazon FBA is very straightforward, but at the same time very persuasive and can take your trades to the next level for very low costs.

Imagine the scene: you are working on your product sourcing and have chosen some books, CD's DVD's, home and Beauty items and few new toys (items sold via Amazon FBA have to be either new or collectible). Now normally at the back of your mind you have a thought "I wish I could buy more stock" but there is no more room in your home; This is where the Amazon FBA comes into play. You can just test the water out by using the basic Amazon selling account or you can be a Pro-Merchant, it doesn't matter.

First: You go home and scan or list the items as usual into your Amazon selling account and a few clicks later, you print out some bar codes which you must put over the original bar code on the item (Items will need to have a bar code or listed on the Amazon site). A few more clicks and you print out a packing slip which goes in the box or boxes. You then book a pick-up from a carrier (this does depend on where you live and how you pay for it - each country is different)

Second: you complete the order and wait for the order to be picked up and within days your item will be in the Amazon warehouse being sold for you then you can sit back and bank the money. Amazon FBA deals with payments, shipping and customer emails, you just need to source more stock and bank the money.

Yes there are some extra costs that Amazon charges but these are low, and the savings you make on the postage is fantastic - remember you are using Amazon's buying power and no more queues in Post Offices and no more having to buy bubble wrap and boxes.

Something else people do not realize is that you can use Amazon FBA to ship out to your eBay and other buyers. Amazon store the items and send the items out for you, for a very little cost and in most cases a lot cheaper than you can think. All the pricing information can be found on your countries Amazon site, just do a search for Amazon FBA.

Go on and give it a go, you have nothing to lose and a lot to gain.

WHAT IS THE AMAZON FBA PROGRAM ALL ABOUT?

FBA is a service Amazon arrange to allow online and offline sellers to send their goods to Amazon. Amazon will pack and send the products to individual customers on your behalf. You may not know how big the Amazon marketplace is, if you don't use regularly. They have grown from just selling books to now selling just about anything.

You may also sell products on Amazon and do not use their FBA service, shipping your own products. As you see there are many advantages of using the FBA system which will give you more free time and provide a more automated business solution.

There are similar services that other drop shippers provide but Amazon hold your own goods in one of their fulfillment centres. The service will send your goods anytime and anywhere on your behalf. This system can be further integrated with your website to create a virtually fully automated system to send your goods through Amazon and for Amazon shipping them to customers. The costs for the service are very competitive and you only pay for actual storage and shipments at discount Amazon's rates as they don't charge a fee to use the system.

So why should you consider using Amazon's system?

Here are some of the key points to the FBA system:

-You can sell almost anything on Amazon or through your own website and have them pack and sent.

-By automating your website with Amazon, the business can run on autopilot and you can take time away if you choose and your business still functions.

-Send all your stock to Amazon and they will handle everything all you have to do is collect your profits.

-Amazon is now outranking eBay on Alexa for traffic they are indeed a major competitor to eBay.

-Some eBay sellers are using the Amazon FBA to ship goods sold through eBay.

CHAPTER 1
WHAT IS AMAZON FBA?

As a business maker or individual who is looking to trade products on Amazon, having the opportunity to take FBA can be quite beneficial. With the ability to cut off the amount of time that you would spend selling and shipping your products, Fulfillment by Amazon does most of the business for you. If you're presently interested in these services, below is information and how it can be useful for your selling needs.

The Fulfillment Procedure

The entire process is relatively easy. You will be provided with the opportunity to store your items in one of Amazon's fulfillment centers. Once a client purchases something that you have for sale, they will surely pick, pack, and ship it for you. Also, customer service will be provided to each product that you are wanting to sell. That means that if your buyer has any questions, customer service will answer and help.

Fees

Another large benefit associated with using Amazon FBA is that you will be able to take advantage of their services for a minimal fee. As a more cost-effective solution than opening your own warehouse and packing/shipping your own goods, you can eliminate this time-consuming task without having to pay outrageous fees. You will be able to pay as you go when you start working with Amazon. Each company will be charged by the space that you use in the warehouse and the amount of orders that Amazon fulfills.

What to Sell Using Amazon FBA

One of the biggest advantages associated with using Amazon's Fulfillment to sell your goods is that there are dozens of different categories that let you know what to sell. The majority of sellers list their products in the "Open Categories" section due to the fact that listing products under these categories does not require approval. Some of the open categories available to companies include:

- Kindle by Amazon
- Any Book
- Baby and children items
- Photos and cameras
- Cellphones
- Garden and home items
- Electronics

The other lists available for people looking to sell using Amazon FBA are known as "Professional sellers Categories". In order to list your products here, you will need approval. Some of these categories include:

- Powersports and Automotive
- Beauty products
- Memorabilia Coins
- Clothing and accessories
- Beaux arts
- Bonus cards
- Food and grocery

HOW AMAZON FBA HELPS ENTREPRENEURS

Amazon FBA is an amazing way to ensure you have products sold and shipped directly to customers therefore you don't have to worry about the shipping and handling procedure. It can also be quite useful for businesses who are unable to have a enough amount of storage space for their goods, as they house your products on-site. With that being said, Fulfillment By Amazon is essentially the perfect component for every seller. Prior to signing up, it is advised that you ensure that it is the right offer for you by determining how your products reach your customers, how you can have control of the process and the scalability of the program.

How Your Products Reach Amazon Prime Customers

The number one component to consider when selling with Fulfillment By Amazon is how your products will reach Amazon Prime customers. When you use Amazon FBA, all of your customers that have an Amazon Prime account will be provided with the opportunity to select two-day shipping for free. Alongside Prime customers, regular Amazon customers will be able to take advantage of the free shipping with orders of $35.00 or more. One of the largest benefits associated with listing with FBA is that your products will be listed without a shipping cost for Amazon Prime customers, allowing you to increase your sales.

What is Amazon FBA Seller Central?

Amazon FBA Seller Central is the aspect of the Amazon website that you will be able to use to have full control over what warehouse your items will be stocked in, how you want to list your items, and how you will display the selling features of your products. It is essentially an entire dashboard dedicated to your products and how they will be seen by the public. You will be able to search for your products once they have been added, look at the other prices of competing FBA sellers, and determine what steps you want Amazon to take during the sale such as shipping the products. Seller Central is imperative to the selling process as it will provide the "first impression" that your customers receive when they find your products.

What is the Scalability of Amazon FBA?

Amazon FBA scalability is another important factor to consider when working with Amazon. As your business grows, you will want to ensure that Amazon will grow with you to make sure that each order is fulfilled efficiently. With scalability offered by the program, you can rest assured that Amazon will be able to assist you during peak seasons and offer more resources when you are selling more products. With the ability to pack and ship either a single unit or thousands of different units, the options are endless.

CHAPTER 2
14 RULES BEHIND AMAZON'S FIERCE WORKPLACE

Many of Amazon's competitive tricks are guided by what the company calls its "Leadership Principles".

The 14 rules are a summary for how employees are expected to think through new ideas and constantly improve their trades.

Customer addiction: Leaders start with the clients and work backwards. They work strenuously, to earn and keep customer trust. Although leaders pay attention to contestants they're addicted over customers.

Ownership: Leaders are holders. They think long term and don't sacrifice long-term value for short-term results. They act on behalf of the whole company, after just their own team. They never think or say "that's not my job."

Invent and make more intelligible: Leaders await and require transformation and invention from their teams and always find ways to simplify. They are outwardly aware, look for new ideas from anywhere, and are not limited by "not invented here." As we make new things, we accept that we may be mistaken for a long period of time.

Leaders are right quite a lot: They are indeed. They have stable business judgment and instincts. They search different perspectives and work to disprove their beliefs.

Appoint and develop the Best: Leaders promotes the performance bar with every hire and promotion. They perceive exceptional talent and willingly move them all through the organization. Leader's develop leaders and take seriously their part in coaching others. We labor on behalf of our people to design mechanisms for development like Career Choice.

Reiterate on the Highest Standards: Leaders have relentlessly high standards — lots of people may think these standards are inappropriately high. Leaders are continually raising the bar and driving their teams to provide high quality products, services, and processes. Leaders ensure that faulty products do not get sent down the line and that problems are fixed so they stay fixed.

Think Big: Thinking small is a self-fulfilling prophecy. Leaders create and communicate a bold direction that inspires results. They think differently and look around corners for ways to serve customers.

Bias for Action: Speed matters in business. Many decisions and actions are reversible and do not need extensive study. We should value calculated risk taking.

Frugality: Accomplish more with less. Constraints breed resourcefulness, self-sufficiency and invention. There are no extra points for growing headcount, budget size, or fixed expense.

Learn and Be Curious: Leaders are never done learning and always seek to improve themselves. They are curious about new possibilities and act to explore them.

Earn Trust: Leaders listen attentively, speak candidly, and treat others respectfully. They are vocally self-critical, even when doing so is awkward or embarrassing. Leaders do not believe their or their team's body odor smells of perfume. They benchmark themselves and their teams against the best.

Dive Deep: Leaders operate at all levels, stay connected to the details, audit frequently, and are skeptical when metrics and anecdote differ. No task is beneath them.

Have Backbone; Disagree and Commit: Leaders are obligated to respectfully challenge decisions when they disagree, even when doing so is uncomfortable or exhausting. Leaders have conviction and are tenacious. They do not compromise for the sake of social cohesion. Once a decision is determined, they commit wholly.

Provide results: Leaders focus on the key inputs for their business and provide the right quality and in a timely fashion. Despite delays, they rise to the occasion and never relax.

FBA GLOBAL SELLING

We're all aware of how difficult international business can be. Apart from fulfilling your orders, careful thoughts such as import taxes, customs duties, currency conversion, regional laws or rules, language barriers and local cultures can all add more difficulties for selling your products in international markets. For small businesses with capital restrictions and lower risk tolerance, Amazon's Global Selling, joint with FBA services, allow them to enter a new market and test out products with little investment and risk.

Before you make the choice to enter a target market, you must conduct some market research to make sure your product is sellable in the region.

Amazon Global Selling is intercede to help companies find the information they need to sell to the right markets.

"Sellable" generally means your product is in concession with the target country's regulations and specifications, but that's not enough. Say you're a North American corporation of electronic devices, and you decide to sell your items in Japan. You re-work your actual products to meet Japan's electrical specifications, only to discover there is no request for that product in the region.

CHAPTER 3

BENEFIT OF USING FULFILMENT BY AMAZON

How does FBA look like and how does it work? Can you redeem money or enjoy other benefits with this offer or procedure?

FBA is a process through which Amazon keeps a stock of a seller's items and then list them on their site for sale. Apart from this, the company receives payments for each order placed online and the delivers the specific goods to each client.

Along with this process, a lot of stores have enjoyed a good deal of growth in their sales. Some stores have Amazon complete the orders for their items. Typically, the goods are sent directly to the buyers by the sellers that sells directly on Amazon. Sometimes it happens by the sellers on other websites, such as Etsy, eBay that move to the FBA. So, it's interesting to know how this offer by the big store has helped people all over the world.

According to many sellers, they have experienced a significant rise in their sales volume. On the other hand, buyers believe that they are purchasing from a trustworthy company instead of an individual. In other words, buying directly via FBA adds to the trust of the buyer in the supplier therefore they may buy again down the road.

Aside from this, sellers can make use of this offer in order to achieve many other benefits. If you use this service as a seller, you won't have to worry about the promotion of the product. Moreover, it will be Amazon's responsibility to deal with buyers and fulfill orders. On the other hand, you can focus on other tasks, such as getting new products and do other tasks that may make your business even bigger.

Additional benefits:

If you are a product owner, you can take some days off without worrying about who will take care of your business while you are away. Your business will keep running while you are having a great time with your friends in Paris. So, you can stay away from your office for as many days as you want. As long as Amazon has your products in their stock, you are good to go and you don't need to worry about anything.

Some people just don't like to deal with buyers directly. They find it hard to deal with difficult customers. Dealing with stress is not their cup of tea. All of these things will be handled by Amazon.

3 Reasons to Use Fulfillment by Amazon

1. Buyers will know that your products are in stock. When a buyer sees an FBA listing, they know the product is in stock and it will be shipped directly from Amazon's warehouse. Non-FBA sellers may cancel an order for different reasons, but with FBA, the buyer can be assured that this will not happen. This is particularly important during the holiday season when buyers count on receiving their order on time. There is nothing worse than a buyer who is disappointed because they did not receive their item in time for the holidays. By using Amazon fulfillment,

buyers know that the product will be professionally packed and will arrive in a timely manner.

2. FBA products are eligible for Amazon Prime. Prime is a service which allows unlimited free two-day shipping on all Amazon purchases and costs $79 dollars per year. In addition to Amazon's own items, FBA items from third party sellers are eligible for Prime as well. This means that your business has access to some of Amazon's best clients. Prime customer's purchase a lot of items, particularly during the holiday season. Prime customers enjoy the free shipping! When you use FBA, you have actually an advantage over other sellers who do not use it, since a buyer who has the Prime service will usually choose your item over you non-FBA competition. They can get your product with free two-day shipping, which they cannot have from you non-FBA competition.

3. You will spend less time on customer service. FBA takes care all customer service for you buyers. This means that if your buyer has any issue with their order, they can get in touch with Amazon Customer Service directly. You will save an enormous amount of time and afflictions when you do not need to manage your own customer service.

If you are a third-party seller on Amazon, using FBA will give you more time to spend on the most important aspect of your business: finding new inventory. With more time to find good inventory, your business profit should greatly increase.

CREATE YOUR OWN AMAZON SELLER ACCOUNT

You've done all the thinking, market research, and ordering of your new items. You've even got a smooth business plan. Since you've decided that opening a Fulfillment by Amazon's (FBA) business is right for you, now you're probably asking yourself how to set up your store so you can start selling your products.

It might seem a little intimidating to set up your Amazon Seller account, especially if this is your first online retail business. Luckily, it's really simple, and as long as you've got all the pieces in place, you'll be selling in no time.

It's important to take the time to prepare your store for customers, but once your account is all set up, you can add your inventory and get your store up and running!

Before diving into the step-by-step process of setting up your Amazon Seller account and your Seller Central space, there are a few things you need to have completed ahead of time to make sure the setup process goes as smoothly as possible:

Figuring out what you're selling and how you're sourcing your product are the most time-consuming parts of setting up your FBA business. Make sure you've already done these tasks before you go through the effort of setting up your account so you can start selling right away. If you haven't done this step yet, make sure you do your research on what products will help you excel as an Amazon Seller.

Besides knowing what product you're selling; you should probably decide on the name of your store before you create your account. Are you going to use your individual name, or do you have a business or brand name already decided on?

Most importantly, you need to know if you're going to be creating the account as a business or as an individual. Amazon has two different account options for sellers depending on their situation, but you'll also need to have this decision made ahead of time for tax purposes, since you'll need to fill out tax forms while setting up your account.

Once you have these things squared away, you'll have all the key background information that will help you set up your store in a super-streamlined fashion.

Your Choice: Professional or Individual?

It might sound like a no-brainer question ("Of course I'm a professional!"), but these are Amazon's choices for your seller account plan. It's worth exploring your options before you start the process of creating your account, since there are pretty big differences between the two.

Either way, you'll be able to sell your items and run your FBA business; the major difference has to do with whether you think you'll be selling more or less than 40 items per month (and whether you want to pay a monthly fee).

The Individual seller plan doesn't have a monthly fee, and this plan is pretty appealing if you're just starting out and in a more experimental mode with your products.

If you're feeling pretty confident that your item's going to sell like hotcakes, however, it might be worth it to pay $39.99 per month to be a Professional seller. That way, you won't have to pay Amazon $0.99 for each item sold, which is the fee that Individual sellers have to pay.

If you want to wait and see how your FBA does, you can start as an Individual and upgrade your account to the Professional selling plan at any time. There's a lot of overlap between the two plans: Both Individuals and Professionals have to pay shipping, referral, and closing fees, all explained on Amazon's website. And both Professional and Individual sellers can list their products in more than 20 categories, but Professional sellers can include their products in 10 extra categories.

Form Your Amazon Seller Account

Before starting your Amazon's website in the thrilling rush to open your new FBA business, make sure you have these important items right next to you: 1) a credit card that can be re – charged internationally, 2) your banking data, such as your routing and account numbers, and 3) your tax ID either for yourself or your business.

CHAPTER 4

PRODUCT RESEARCH TOOLS IN AMAZON

In surveys, Amazon FBA sellers say that items research is the most time-consuming – and most discouraging – aspect of the selling process. These days there are a number of dissimilar research tools available to sellers.

1. Jungle scout

The very popular Jungle Scout is a firm favorite among Amazon sellers.

Available as a web app or Chrome extension, Jungle Scout it's well known to take the guesswork out of product research in order to minimize the risks and maximize the possible profit.

The web app allows users to search through thousands of products, pinpoints the most profitable and keep an eye on the competition.

2. AMZ Scout

AMZ Scout is known as one of the most reliable and accurate product research tools on the market, and it's a great Jungle Scout alternative.

With a tagline of 'The Smart Choice for Making Smart Decisions,' Amz Scout is a comprehensive and competitive way of finding products and keeping track of sales.

3. Unicorn Smasher

Everybody loves a unicorn and, the Unicorn Smasher product research tool earns its place on the leaderboard of the best available.

Features include comprehensive data and accurate sales estimates and allows users to move quickly and easily between product niches.

4. AMZ Base

Amz Base is a great tool to help sellers to quickly search and identify the right products to sell on Amazon and, one of the best things about it is that it's free!

Sellers can quickly and easily use the tool to find descriptions and ASIN numbers of products on Amazon as well as calculating FBA fees.

5. Amazon Best Sellers

Amazon Best sellers is an extremely useful way of quickly getting an idea of the kind of products which sell well on Amazon. Categorized by product genre for easy filtering and searching, the page is great for those who do not yet know what they want to sell on Amazon. Clearly laid out and easy to understand, the Amazon Best seller's page allows users to make an informed choice based on price and popularity.

6. Amazon Hot New Releases

Amazon Hot New Releases is a regularly updated catalog of new and trending products on Amazon. Set out in clearly defined categories, the page allows Amazon sellers to browse all products or to navigate straight to a particular product genre such as electronics, children's products, popular books and movies and clothing and accessories.

7. Amazon Movers & Shakers

Perfect for FBA Sellers, the Amazon Movers & Shakers page is updated hourly and is an overview of products with the biggest sales rank gains within the past 24 hours. Listed by category such as books, electronics and toys, the page shows the sales rank and percentage increase for each product, allowing users to see at a glance the products which are performing particularly well.

8. Amazon Most Wished For

The Amazon Most Wished For page is an overview of the products which have been added to Amazon wish lists the most times. This is a really good tool for giving sellers an indication of the products which buyers find interesting.

9. Kickstarter

Kickstarter is a crowdfunding site which allows people to raise money for personal projects and causes such as the development of a new clothing range or a charitable project. Although not specifically a selling site, Amazon sellers can browse through current projects to find out the kind of products that are being developed for sale in order to plan ahead for future sales.

10. Indiegogo

Another crowdfunding site, Indiegogo allows users to raise funds to develop anything from clothing lines to new innovations in electronics. By raising money on the site, the developer is able to buy the materials and services necessary to get their project off the ground.

Not only can Amazon sellers use the site for product ideas but may even want to get involved with a campaign with a view to a future partnership.

11. Watched Item

Watched Item is a quick and easy way of identifying and tracking items on Ebay which have the most interest without having to make hundreds of individual searches.

Ebay's 'watch' option allows potential buyers to bookmark a particular sale and to receive updates on how the auction is progressing in order to be able to wait until the last moment before bidding on that item.

The Watched Item site allows Amazon sellers to search by country or product or by the products with the highest number of current watchers in order to see which products are the most popular.

5 WAYS TO FIND THE BEST PRODUCTS TO SELL ON AMAZON

With the event of the internet in the 90's, Ecommerce has blowout like wildfire. Consumers have passed from traditional shopping to ecommerce.

Today, Amazon has become synonymous with ecommerce. Apart from being a very good online store, it is known for its user personalization attributes. A study by Internet Retailer says that in 2016, Amazon accounted for 43% of all online sales in the US. That alone is a good reason for you to thinking of selling on Amazon.

In fact, people have been known to make as much as $5000 in an hour by selling on Amazon. However, this can be a little tricky. Keep in mind that Amazon sells more than 300 million individual products. And only by selling the right products you can become a successful seller.

Here are five ways to find the best products to sell on Amazon.

1. Start by Discovering Profitable Products

You can find the most profitable items to sell on Amazon without much experience. Amazon provides you all the necessary information to understand market trends and products that sell.

You need to understand what makes an item profitable. Criteria like, shipping weight, popularity, category, and competition all play a major role here. You need to identify products that meet most of the criteria.

Research the Shippable and Sellable Factors

While looking for products you need to first consider three things: Shipping cost, wholesale pricing, and Amazon Seller fees.

Try to buy products considering the following specs:

- The price should be 25% to 35% of your target selling price
- Your target selling cost should be in the range of $10 to $50
- The products should be light in terms of weight i.e., around 2-3 lbs. including box and packaging
- Simple and durable items that would reduce the risk of loss from damage

- Evergreen or everyday use items, meaning they can be used for the whole the year
- Better quality products when compared with competitors.

2. Check For competitors.

To bring in returns, you need a product that is rightly priced found and shipped easily, and in demand.

Below are the key factors that determine whether your products meet these criteria.

- Products that are not usually being sold by major brands and Amazon sellers
- Similar items that have Amazon's Best-Seller Rank (BSR) of 5000 or less.

> ➢ Items that can be searched under different product categories and keywords
> ➢ Leading items keywords having not more than 10,000 searches/month
> ➢ Similar items listings having less than 50 reviews
> ➢ 3. Acquiring knowledge From Amazon Product Listings

Here's an Amazon bestselling game called What Do You Meme. In the product description, you can find all the information on what makes it a seller's goldmine.

In the product description, you will find various information about the product, such as product dimension, weight, etc. From there, you can determine if your product is an evergreen one.

Lookout for the following criteria to find the most sellable and profitable items:

Item pricing: The item is sold at $29.99. The costing is perfect as it falls under the pricing bracket of $10 to $50.

Product measures and weight: There you can find that the product weighs 2.78 pounds and measures of 6.5 x 4.5 x 3 inches. This size and weight will help in reduce the shipping cost.

Overall characteristics and sales ranking: You will see that the Amazon BSR of this product is 3. This is way lower the BSR 5000 rank. Also, it can be found in the toys and games category easily.

Customer analyses: You will find that the item has more than 2000 reviews from consumers. This is way above the

500+ reviews rank making it a well-trusted product. This also indicates that the product has a lot of requests in the market.

4. Find Out What Others are Selling

Do you know that small-scale sellers are making it big by selling niche items? From handmade items to custom and unique jewelry items and even live bugs. In this way, they reduce the competition from large sellers and from Amazon itself.

Amazon is really good when it comes to upselling products. It keeps a section showcasing recommended products underneath a product's description. This encourages buyers to consider the products that are being showcased.

Here's an example:

Notice how Amazon suggests product pairing with the above-mentioned best-seller. Here, suggested products may not be "bestsellers" themselves, but as a seller, you can determine what are the products other sellers are selling.

5. Select Your Source For Products

Once you are done researching on which products to sell, you should start thinking about sourcing them.

Here are two places from where you can start your search:

Alibaba: If you are planning to sell on Amazon, Alibaba is a good place to source your products. It is a place where you can source inexpensive imports. A good thing about

Alibaba is that it helps you learn about product sourcing. This is extremely helpful if you are new to the business.

Wholesale marketplaces: Wholesale buyers markets are another way of sourcing your products. Wholesale markets are situated in every major city in the US. And the best part is, they focus on every imaginable industry. To locate your nearest wholesale market just google it. Also, don't forget to add the product name or category you are interested in.

CHAPTER 5
A FIVE-STEP GUIDE TO COMPETE WITH AMAZON

Competing with Amazon is attainable. I'm not saying you can overthrow the ecommerce giant from her throne, but you can surely rank for keywords, sell amazing stuff, and not get absolutely beated by them.

I want to tell you how to do that in actually 5 simple steps.

First, let's talk about what you cannot do. Admitting your errors is the first step to maximizing your strengths.

You cannot have the same size of inventory. Amazon basically owns every consumer product in the world, therefore yeah good luck with that. You're going to need some bigger places to store the stuff.

You cannot have Jeff Bezos. Unless you have a real good offer for him.

You can't have the name amazon.com. It's already been taken, and is not on sale. I have checked for you.

1. Tighten your niche.

Amazon's weakness is in its greatness. It has everything for sale. Amazon can be good at everything.

What about You? You don't sell everything. You just sell a few things. (At least you should.)

You will have a much harder time trying to rank for a lot of different keywords, even if they are all sort of in the same niche. Whatever you sell, Amazon probably has a few more variations, sizes, colors, and features.

2. Do something radical with shipping.

One area that Amazon has completely dominated is the area of shipping. It is, in fact, one of the company's greatest successes.

Members of Amazon's Prime service can get two-day shipping for free, and next-day shipping for just a few dollars on each order. And same-day shipping? Yep, they offer that, too.

3. Create a subscription service.

Another way that Amazon has increased revenue is by creating subscription services:

- Subscribe and save (repeated shipments)
- Amazon Prime (fees paid annually)
- Amazon Simple Storage Service (AWS)

Because they're so good at this repeating payment thing, Amazon actually launched a new service called Amazon Payments with what they can help other companies keep charging customers on a daily basis. You might start seeing more of that quintessential yellow button on the web:

The subscription service is one of the smartest ways to sell a product. You don't just get a one-and-done transactional experience with your customer. Instead, you get a relationship, and revenue every month or year.

You don't have to be a software provider to make the subscription model work. Any form of recurring deliverables warrants recurring payments.

4. Boast the best customer service experience on the planet.

I mean no disrespect to Amazon, but they can't do customer service the way you can. They're too big.

This is a sandbox that Amazon can't play in. But you can.

One of the best ways to compete with Amazon is to provide something that they can't. They can't provide personalized, one-on-one service to human beings like you can.

Your brand can achieve viral spread ability through passionate brand evangelists.

5. Build a fanatical fan base.

Building a jumping, screaming, raving, fanatical fan base is not easy, but it is possible. The strategy is to stay small, at least as it pertains to customer interaction. Everything you do as a brand — from social media outreach to content marketing efforts — must have this personal and close-connected feel to it. It's about cohesion, connection, and knock-out service.

TIPS TO STAY COMPETITIVE ON AMAZON

To say Amazon is a competitive marketplace is a litotes. In order to be successful when selling on Amazon, you need to make sure your product is noticeable to the people who might want to buy it and that your listing grabs their attention enough to make a purchase.

Invest in advertisement: High-volume seller's surely make use of Amazon sponsored ads. These ads ensure that your product is noticeable on the pages your potential buyers are already browsing. Simply put, sponsored ads gives you the chance you to purchase space at the top of Amazon search results and category listings.

Offered on a pay-per-click (PPC) system, you only pay when someone clicks on the ad. If that click converts into a sale, it can go a long way toward helping you improve your BSR and increase the visibility of your brand across the entire channel.

Use A+ pages or enhanced brand content: A+ pages and enhanced brand content (EBC) give you a greater opportunity to display your product to people who are viewing your listing.

Both of these options offer more room to describe your product and post additional pictures, allowing potential buyers a more in-depth look at your product.

This additional content provides clients with a deeper understanding of not only the product you are selling but your brand as well leading to an increased likelihood of a purchase.

Choosing A+ or EBC depends on your store sort. EBC is designed for third-party sellers and is available through Seller Central whilst A+ is for first-party sellers or vendors using Vendor Central.

TIPS TO STAY COMPETITIVE ACROSS E-COMMERCE

To be a truly fruitful high-volume seller you need to be able to move your product outside of Amazon, as well. It may be a prevalent marketplace but there are other options available that can undoubtedly increase your sales and boost your profits.

Social media also gives you the opportunity for you to grow brand awareness and trust. People are more likely to purchase from a seller they feel like they have a relationship with. By staying active online and appealing with your followers, you are amplifying this relationship.

When operating on so many channels it can be hard to keep track of customer information and which efforts you are making and where, but it is important that you try. Social media followers and their responses to your posts give you that social proof you need to convert a sale from someone who may have otherwise been sitting on the fence.

Sell on another marketplace: Increasing the number of places you sell your product can only increase the number of sales you stand to make. Amazon is massive. That's why it's an obvious place to list your products.

But no matter how much the marketplace continues to grow, it is still only part of the wider e-commerce space. And with so much competition, it makes sense to try less crowded spaces as well.

Similar to Amazon, eBay sells just about anything and has a wide-ranging customer base. If you sell handcrafted items, Etsy may be the place for you or Newegg for electronics. For every niche product, there is a niche market so do your research and list your product anywhere that makes sense.

When establishing yourself on these other channels, make sure all of your listings are different. The purpose of doing so is twofold. First, when you write a custom listing for each marketplace, you can speak directly to the customer that shops in that space. Using language that is not appropriate for the audience will alienate potential buyers and make them less likely to purchase your products.

Secondly, writing the same thing in all your listings can hurt your results in a Google search. The first result Google returns will be the most popular page. The vast majority of the time, that first hit will be your Amazon listing. Some customers will be happy to visit your Amazon listing to learn more or purchase your product but not everyone will.

If you are using different language in each listing, you increase the chances of returning multiple results on the first page and that makes it more likely that the person who initiated the search will end up clicking a link that takes them to one of your sales channels.

To be a competitive, high-volume seller, you need to use properly the tools that are available to you both on and off Amazon. Following the tips listed above may increase your brand recognition and position you to not only keep pace with the big sellers but move ahead of your direct competitors.

AMAZON COST STRATEGY

Price on Amazon is changes continuously and unless you own your private label or custom-built bundles, you need to keep your listings' prices repeatedly in order to stay in the competition. Amazon dynamic pricing helps to win Amazon buy box and to increment your sales. Employing the suitable repricing strategies for your aspirations is important, nonetheless unearthing the right ones is challenging. When selling on Amazon, you must have a united Amazon pricing strategy for backing the price you decide to charge for your items.

Here are three traditional pricing strategies you can use for your products, later we'll discuss repricing strategies.

1. Market Penetration Pricing for Amazon Startup

Also known as penetration pricing strategy, this pricing policy is mostly used by startups looking to break into the Amazon market.

What it is: Penetration pricing involves charging an amount lower than your competitors to attract customers when you're new to the Amazon world.

Initial Losses: At the beginning you can expect to cumulate some losses as your sales figures will not be big enough to cover the discount you're willing to offer to your customers. As sales grow, you can choose to stick with these sales if the general sales figure is covering costs.

Increase Prices: Most sellers don't keep their initial prices. When they think they've developed a good enough engagement with customers and have built a good standing, they usually raise their prices to match their current standing in the market.

A Warning: In the online world, charging extremely low prices usually leads customers to believe your product is of a low quality. Therefore, lower your prices by just a dollar, or a few cents, so customers don't see you suspiciously.

2. Price Skimming for Innovation

This Amazon pricing strategy is usually for those sellers who are looking to introduce something new to the amazon marketplace.

What it is: Price skimming refers to initially raising prices when you introduce a new invention or a non-existent item to the Amazon marketplace. As more players enter the market, you gradually bring down your price (while still charging more, preferably).

What it does: Charging higher prices initially means that you'll attract early adapters and lowering them eventually makes more price-conscious customers come your way. If your innovation is good enough, you can generate a lot of money by initially charging more.

Illusions: By charging an initial higher price, you will create an impression of exclusiveness and high quality. By the time competitors arrive, you'd have built a brand, already.

A Warning: Charging too high price may push customers away, even early adapters. If you have to charge a higher price, make sure your marketing for the product matches it.

3. Bundle Pricing

Bundle pricing is perhaps the most relevant for Amazonians. This Amazon pricing strategy not only do increase amazon sales, but a great way to increase visibility for your business.

What it is: It's selling multiple products together at a lower rate than what they would cost if purchased separately.

What it does: It attracts customers by making them think they are being offered something for free. You can also get rid of items that are holding inventory space and/or aren't selling well lately. Bundles work great during holiday seasons and can even increase exposure for your other products.

A Warning: if you don't offer something good to customers (something they can actually use) or include products that don't really complement each other, you'll end up generating a lot of bad PR.

Repricing Tips to Compete Amazon Dynamic Pricing

Tough competition drives sellers to reprice their items frequently in order to compete with Amazon dynamic pricing. It is not easy to continuously change the prices of your items especially when you have several products listed. In such a case, Amazon repricer tools are the best options to keep watch on competitor's and match their prices. But you can't just rely on an automated repricing software, you also need price tracker to track the prices of several competitors in order to learn about their pricing trends and history.

Take a look below on the repricing tips:

Controlling Price

Monitor Manually – Check each listing separately and modify prices as required. Doing it yourself gives you the unparalleled control, but also consume heaps of time. If you're dealing with limited number of listings, the manual handling is a good option, but in-case of large quantity it would become unworkable to do it this way.

Incorporate Automation – This basically refers to using any repricing software to automatically adjust your prices. This salvage a lot of your time and energy and even helps maintain competitiveness of your listings. However, like all other things this method isn't safe from risks as well. Keep in mind, an effective Amazon repricer not only reduce prices but also raises it, if needed.

Selecting a Repricing Strategy

Whatever pricing management mechanism you pick, it's still unavoidable to determine the price of your product. The interpretation of this will differ from seller to seller contingent upon number of aspects. Scroll down to unveil some of them.

Add Delivery in your Price Estimation

Amazon classifies listings on the basis of price delivery. For Fulfillment by Amazon program, there are no delivery charges. While pricing your products compared to other sellers, make sure you're setting it on the total cost.

Avail your FBA Benefit

If you trade through FBA, customers will usually pay extra to have a free of cost shipping advantage. Make sure to fix your rates on the basis of your FBA competition. You can even try asking for 10% more than your Merchant Fulfilled competition if you're the only FBA seller on the listing.

Select Pricing

 With The Help of Amazon Price Tracker

While using an amazon price tracker for tracking prices, you can easily decide about the product price. Calculate the incurred cost of your products with fee depending on which you can fix your least possible rates.

Price isn't something that makes all the difference

Keep in mind that by just reducing your rates doesn't necessarily increase your chances of making more sales. Especially, if your product is in a low-demand niche, reducing the price will not increase your possibilities of making quick sales. One of the ways to deal with this problem is to hold your price and wait till the right customer comes up. In addition, try to include relevant keywords to the listing to optimize and improve your product visibility.

Don't post Your Strategy in Stone

Determine to opt for a flexible Amazon price strategy according to the best sellers on Amazon and don't forget every exclusive product demands unique treatment. In case you aren't content with the present results, don't be scared to try something more effective and newer.

Use Amazon Repricer Software

To effectively reprice your listings and match prices with the competition, try to put into effect Amazon repricer tool. It will help you to smoothly automate the cost changes as per your set minimum and maximum limits.

CHAPTER 6
3 SUREFIRE TIPS HOW TO CHOOSE THE BEST PRODUCTS TO PROMOTE ON AMAZON

Making money with Amazon is a very well-known method for creating a good additional online earning but if you do not know the best items to promote or how to find them, then you will issue from the beginning to make any decent money.

In the next chapter you will discover three great tips how to choose the best items to promote on Amazon

Tip 1 - Always only choose products from the bestsellers list

If you only select from items in the best sellers' category then you can be confident that those particular items already sell. Amazon is telling you that those are the hottest products in that category and people are already buying these items. This is important information and by using this single tip you will be ahead of 99% of other sellers.

Tip 2 - Always check out the product ratings and price

After you have found a product in Amazon in the best sellers' category you need to make sure there are good ratings for the product. Good being a 4 star or above as an average rating. If you only select high rated products you can be sure that customer's like the product and returns will be minimal. Also, you must make sure the product has high priced items, the higher the items the more you get paid in affiliate commissions.

Tip 3 - Always check out the product reviews

The 3rd thing you must also check for this technique to be effective are the reviews, especially   searching for how many reviews have been left for the particular product that you are looking at. A product may have a 4 or even 5 star rating but if it only has 5 reviews then it is not very convincing when people look at it and consider buying the product. The best thing to do is make sure there are a lot of reviews. A good number is around at least 50+ reviews. Also, you need to scan the whole page in the category and get an average amount of reviews, ratings and price, if the page looks good and meets these 4 pieces of criteria then you have found a great product to promote.

HOW TO BUILD YOUR BRAND ON AMAZON

There are so many sellers on Amazon, set yourself apart is key to getting ahead. You may be rolling your eyes and to overthink.

Understand What Your Brand is made of.

Before you can start building a brand, you have to know what you'll be creating. Jot down on a piece of paper the categories of products you sell, the demographics you're trying to reach, and what you want to achieve.

Build in Small Blocks

You'll want to take the same approach with building your own brand. Focus first on creating something of quality, then be patient while it'll grow (this can/will take years). Put your brand/logo on everything so that, in time, consumers will soon begin to associate it with your products.

Don't Go to Bat with the Big Boys

It can be tempting to have visions of grandeur, of competing with the likes of the world's biggest brands and products. But even if that happens (and we certainly won't discourage you of trying to reach those heights), it's going to take some serious time.

Instead, a better, smarter and more efficient strategy is to look at the really popular ideas out there, and make them your own.

Get Other People to Spread Your Word

When you first started selling on Amazon, you bought from other suppliers, suppliers with their own brands. But now that you've started to create your own brand, it's time to put the shoe on the other foot. Start soliciting to small shops to see if they can carry your brand, say yes to anyone and everyone who wants to buy in bulk from you, and set up supplier-only specials to encourage business. And think a bit outside the box, too, in trying to establish relationships with brick-and-mortar shops instead of just solely looking online.

Start squeezing Your Prices

Do you want to know one of the awe – inspiring things in dealing with your own brand? You get to cut out the intermediary, which means more money left in your pocket. And while there are a load of ways you can spend it, here's an effective one: cutting off your competition.

This technique works if your competitors are buying from already existing brands and have to pay a wholesale fee. That way, you can merrily skip over that step and cash the money for yourself, then use it as a buffer to decrease your prices to lure more clients to you.

CHAPTER 7
4 STEPS TO FIND THE BEST AMAZON SUPPLIER FOR YOUR PRIVATE LABEL BUSINESS

You've chosen a private label product niche, and now it's the moment to find the best Amazon supplier that suits your private label business' needs.

To make your product idea come to life, finding an advisable Amazon supplier that fits your production type and is open to assembling a lasting work relation is demanding to your accomplishment as a private label auctioneer.

Here are 4 steps to find the best Amazon distributor to work with:

Step 1 – Assemble a Possible Output List

It is imperative to jot down a few product ideas and devise a list of the ones you're most attentive to. Your cultivated product search will help your fixation and registration accordingly.

Step 2 – Search for the Most Suitable Amazon Supplier

Search for Amazon suppliers by using the following resources:

Google: Start searching on Google by entering the name of the product you wish to sell followed by the term "manufacturer" or "private label supplier" as well as your location.

Alibaba: This website has a simple platform in which you can find manufacturers of various products.

Reddit: Many seller focused subreddits are incredibly active. Search for posts related to your product(s) and look for manufacturers there.

Amazon/eBay: You can check out the manufacturers' names for the products you're most interested in; however, it should be noted that Amazon may be more saturated than other platforms, so it may not be the best choice to find low competition products. Search eBay for products you're interested in to dig up more supplier options.

Indiamart: Similar to Alibaba, you can find all types of household, sport, tool, apparel, accessory products, and more.

Global Sources: This is another great source to find private label suppliers that can import for less than many US-made goods.

Attend Trade Shows Abroad: There are trade shows around the world each year that show off the work of different manufacturers and offer a chance to speak with a representative personally to get a true sense of how the supplier functions.

Step 3 – Assess Potential Amazon Suppliers

Having some basic guidelines in mind when assessing potential manufacturers will make it easier for you to find the right supplier.

As you explore various suppliers and speak with them, consider the following factors:

Price

Find out the cost of the raw materials needed for your product, average labor wages, and other manufacturing costs typical of your kind of product, then compare with the supplier's proposed pricing to see if it is fair and not exorbitant.

Reliability

Large suppliers tend to be more reliable due to their well-structured systems and well-trained staff to serve many clients at once.

Small suppliers can often provide more individualized attention, foster stronger relationships, and give you a stronger sense of prioritization.

Retention rate, especially after Lunar New Year celebrations when workers often do not return to work, should play a crucial role in your decision since skilled workers are not easily replaced and can lower the quality of your product.

Versatility

If you're considering new product launches in the near future, find out the supplier's capabilities in producing different products concurrently.

Stability/Competency

- How long has the manufacturer been in business?
- What do customers say about this manufacturer?
- How is the company's overall reputation?
- Does the manufacturer keep up with the latest products and services?
- Does the company provide excellent customer service?

Location

- How close is the supplier to you?
- How close is the supplier to the nearest sea freight port or airport?
- How close is the supplier is to your desired fulfillment centers?

Government Compliance

Ensure that the manufacturer's production facility is compliant with government regulations and environmental precautions with a third-party inspection company; independent inspectors will often provide detailed reports without bias on the state of the manufacturer's facility.

Step 4 – Request a quote and Sample Products

Once you've narrowed your choices down to a chosen few Amazon suppliers, it's time to request a quote. The quote should include the following items:

- Private label and packaging fees – Some Amazon suppliers will charge for starting a new private label and packaging your products
- Shipping fees to your fulfillment location
- Product prices for quantities ordered
- Import requirements and/or duties that must be met or paid

Afterwards, you will want to demand sample products so that you know what kind of traits the Amazon supplier can administer.

Most suppliers will implement you with a sample at a low cost. Study the sample and make notes as to how it can be enhanced if the supplier has at least proven itself to craft a quality product. If you are unsatisfied overall, you may be better off looking at another Amazon supplier. If you're serious about having your own private label, this will be a worthwhile initial expenditure.

CHAPTER 8

HOW TO PREPARE AND LIST PRODUCTS IN AMAZON

Once you've explored, found and purchased products to sell on Amazon, you're only an inch away from making your first sale. Listing products on Amazon lawfully makes them available to millions of people across the world. Before listing products, you need to gather some information about them. There are two methods to list your products on Amazon: individual or bulk.

How to List Amazon items Individually

Listing products individually is advised when starting out. It gives sellers a better idea of information is behind each product. To start listing items, visit the inventory tab of Seller Central, and click "Add an Item." You will be showed a search bar and the option to create a new item. The easiest way to do this is entering noticeable information within the search bar and searching Amazon's catalog for the item information. If you find your item, there is definitely an option to sell yours.

The three required pieces of information to list your items are item condition, price, and item quantity. You may also indicate sale date and prices, restock dates, and select shipping items. Lastly, you can create a SKU for your product, which is a unique identifier for managing your products. Amazon creates one for you if you don't specify one.

The "Create a New Product Tool" is used if you're unable to find your item After selecting the button, browse to the category that your item best fits under. Keep in mind that some items require approval from Amazon before they can be sold; for example, jewelry or automotive parts. The "Create a Product" page requires more details than if you were to find it in Amazon's catalog. This is to make sure you provide a complete listing for buyers. You are required to fill in the manufacturer, product name, and UPC of the product. The UPC is necessary because it helps buyers identify products easier, even if you've accidentally mislabeled them.

Take a Picture of Your Amazon Product

Uploading pictures of the product is paramount, because buyers usually won't make a purchase without seeing the product. On this page is a drop-down box labeled "Variation Theme." This gives sellers the ability to list products of different colors or slightly varied designs without listing them one-by-one. You will need a picture of each variant listed.

How to List Items in Bulk on Amazon

The ability to list items in bulk is a convenience for Amazon sellers who have large inventories. Amazon provides templates of various types of stores. For example, a clothing-related store would require the clothing template. If you have existing inventory that you listed individually or any time previously, its recommended that you make sure that all the information for those products is entered correctly. If it needs changes, you can do that in one step while you're listing new items.

If there is existing inventory, select everything and then "Export to File" under the action tab. If you don't select all items, your store will be incomplete when you update your inventory. Copy all existing items to the template, and add new items as well. Once this is done, upload the new inventory file under "Manage Inventory" in Seller Central.

BRANDED SCANNERS AT AMAZON

A scanner is a device which is used for the purpose of scanning images, objects, printing text, hand writing, certificates and other such kind of material. Scanners are widely used in offices to scan their important documents in order to keep record of the activities performed in an organization. These scanners convert the scanned image into digital form which could be then saved in the computer for further use. Most of the people use branded scanners for their personal and office use, as they are not only efficient but rather effective as well.

Amazon also offers a huge variety of branded scanner including Fujitsu, Epson, Cannon and a lot of other branded scanners. The scanners offered by Amazon can be seen on their website along with their picture, specification and cost. In addition, differentiation of different kinds of scanners in term of their cost & qquality is also very easy because all of them are exposed on the website of Amazon along with the required details.

Buyers can not only buy new scanner but also used scanners are offered by Amazon. Buyer can also pick their favorite brand from the website which will then expose all the models offered by the selected brand.

CHAPTER 9

WHY BRAND SHOULD FOCUS ON AMAZON ADVERTISING

Different factors come into play when trying to file your products in Amazon search.

Also, Amazon has been constrained reviews and rank manipulation.

To accommodate a lot of marketing energy that was hitherto focused on gathering reviews has shifted to advertising on Amazon.

Instead of focusing on discounted products for reviews – or, even worse, encourage reviews – you can use Amazon Advertising to start initial conversions.

This leads to product reviews as your sales velocity increases.

This allows you to get the traffic and conversions you need for your product to be ranked organically.

When working with products on Amazon, the ranking problem is solved by combining Amazon advertising with different promotional offerings that Amazon offers (e.g., clippable coupons).

Initially, after launching a product, you will heavily rely on Amazon advertising to rank your product on the first page.

However, if your product is optimized correctly, your reliance on Amazon advertising will decrease with time.

Nevertheless, you might still need to carry on some advertising even after your products have ranked high to protect your digital real estate or from competitor's who might still be using Amazon advertising.

The more niche your product is, the less you will likely have to spend on advertising on Amazon's platform.

However, for most products, I have found that at present the cost to advertise on Amazon is significantly less than other advertising platforms like Google Ads.

Should You Advertise on Amazon?

If you already have a product that can sell online, then you can advertise on Amazon.

Amazon offers you a way to get your product in front of shoppers at a much lower cost than competing advertising platforms.

You can start with a product that already sells well and measures your ROI before adding other products.

Over the last several years, Amazon Advertising has had a variety of changes, and recently, they renamed some of their products.

Here are four ways to advertise on Amazon.

1. Sponsored Products

This is the most popular method of advertising on Amazon.

Brands have used this powerful tool for many years to automatically and manually target shoppers.

Here, you can use different match types that are familiar to you as an advertiser – broad, phrase and exact match, as well as negative keyword matching.

Any seller on Amazon Seller Central, Kindle Direct Publishing, or Vendor Central platform can participate in the Sponsored Products program.

Amazon has been rolling out additional targeting options on its Seller Central platform such as Product, Interest, and Category Targeting.

It is rumored that even more match types might be available to advertisers in the near future.

While the match types mimic Google's advertising platforms, there are some nuances to Sponsored Products.

Before setting up your campaign, check the following to make sure that your campaign will run:

Own the Buy-Box

Your ad will not run if you do not have the buy box for that product.

This means if a brand is selling a product directly and there are third-party sellers in the buy box, the brand will be unable to run any Sponsored Products Ads for that product.

Amazon SEO Tips to Boost Your Listings and Sales

Amazon accounts for 43% of all online sales. This retail giant is one of the largest and fastest growing retailers on the web. Many businesses sell products on Amazon, so if you want to help your business stand out and reach more customers, you need to use Amazon search engine optimization (SEO).

How does Amazon SEO work?

Before we dive into our Amazon SEO tips, it's important to understand how Amazon ranks products. The way people search on Amazon is different than Google, so there is a slight learning curve.

When people search for products on Amazon, they can only find your products if their search queries match your keywords. This creates a challenge because you must use keywords that your audience uses to find products like yours.

The important thing to note is that Amazon's A9 algorithm focuses on displaying products first that increase purchase likelihood. The algorithm focuses on two factors: performance and relevance. Performance is based on how well your products sell and relevance is based on how your keyword match the search query.

Therefore, keyword selection is challenging. It isn't enough to choose the right keywords to get your products to rank. You need to offer products that consumers will want to buy or one that consumers already buy frequently.

Amazon thinks about the buyers. They want to expose products that best fit their queries. When you optimize your listings, you need to base on the buyer's experience and how you can make it even better.

6 TIPS FOR IMPROVING YOUR AMAZON SEO

If you want your market to find your products, you need to improve your Amazon rankings. It will help you reach more valuable leads that are focused in your products.

1. Conduct keyword research

If you've used SEO before, you probably know about conducting keyword research. With Amazon SEO, keyword research has some similar qualities to traditional SEO, but with a few more buyer-focused qualities.

Just like traditional SEO, you want to focus on long-tail keywords. These are keywords that contain three or more words. When people search for products on Amazon, they use long-tail keywords to find products.

Long-tail keywords will help more interested leads find your product listings. It is important that you focus on all relevant keywords. You don't want to miss out on potential leads because you didn't include certain keywords in your Amazon product listings.

To help you figure out the right keywords for your Amazon SEO campaign, you can use a free tool called Sonar. This is a keyword research tool that focuses specifically on keywords that people use on Amazon. It helps you see the search volume for each keyword, which enables you to prioritize them in your Amazon SEO campaign.

Once you select your keywords, you need to integrate them into your listings. You need to use them in places like the product titles and descriptions. This will help your products appear in search results for those keywords.

2. Manage your reviews

Reviews are a crucial part of any business. They can be the reason a person buys your products or decides to pass. It is important that you manage product reviews to help improve your Amazon SEO campaign.

For the most part, the products in the top of Amazon's search results generally have four or more stars. These are products that have great reviews and people enjoy. You want to encourage your audience to leave feedback about their experience with your products.

When your audience leaves feedback, there's a good chance you'll receive negative reviews. As part of managing your reviews, you need to take the time to respond to negative reviews. It will prevent you from deterring future customers.

Your response to negative reviews allows people to see how you handle negativity. If you address the issues, offer to replace broken or damaged products, and respond to questions, you'll encourage more people to buy your products. They will feel more confident that your company takes issues seriously and that if they have an issue with your products, they know you will respond.

This will lead to more conversions and positive reviews. It will improve your rankings in Amazon search results.

3. Optimize your title

The way you format your title will affect where you appear in the search results. It's important that you include all vital elements into your title.

The general format to create a product title is:

This is the general rule of thumb for how to order your title. These categories may not all apply to your products, but you want to use the ones that do. The order of your title impacts how your audience finds your listings, so it is important that you stick to the proper order.

When you optimize your title, you want to place your most relevant keyword first. This ensures that people always see your most important keyword, regardless of how short or long the title appears in the search results. It also helps your listings appear in the most relevant search results.

4. Follow image guidelines

Images play a vital role in the purchasing process. People need to see products from different angles to get a better sense of how the products look. It's a key component to help build confidence and trust with your audience — especially since they can't physically see the product in front of them.

Amazon encourages you to use product images that are larger than 1000x1000 pixels. This is because they have a zoom feature that allows users to zoom in one image when they are above that dimension. If you want to provide a more positive experience for your audience, you need to use images that are larger than the dimension stated before.

The ability to zoom in can possibly increase sales for your business. People can look at your items more in-depth and get a better sense of how they look. It becomes even more helpful when you post multiple photos with different angles where an audience possibly use the different zooming characteristics.

Adding zoomable images doesn't directly affect your Amazon SEO, but it does improve your conversion rate. When you earn more conversions, you increase your listing's ranking. It can also help you earn more reviews, which also impacts in a positive way your product listing's performance.

5. Think about your price

Pricing is an important factor for customers. They want to get the best product and spend less. When you expose your product on Amazon, you need to look at how your competitors' pricing.

If you're selling your product for $100 and all your competitors have a similar product for $20 - $30, you won't help your Amazon SEO campaign. In fact, your product list won't rank because it is too expensive. Your audience will choose a cheaper product that suites their needs.

To have competitive listings, you need to see how your competitors are pricing products similar to yours. This will help you get a better idea of how to price your product and see if your product can even compete amongst the competition.

6. Use bullet points in your item descriptions

When you post a new product, you probably have a lot you want to say about to describe it. After all, you really want to sell your public to beneficial your products compared to the competitors. When you do this, it is vital that you break down your information so it is manageable for your public to read.

The best way to do this is to divide your product descriptions into bullet points. It's an easy way for your public to digest the information. People like when information is short and easy to read.

Products with bullet points usually convert better, as well. People read the information more and feel more informed to buy. This helps improve your Amazon SEO ranking because you get more conversions.

CHAPTER 10
HOW TO LAUNCH A NEW PRODUCT ON AMAZON

Even if you're a first-time private label seller on Amazon or are already established and looking to improve launching a new product takes time and careful planning. After all, you don't want to end up investing all your resources in a new item that doesn't sell or give you high allowances. You rather want something that will win you the Buy Box and set your private label business on a path for long-term production.

To help you get there, follow these five advises for launching a new item on Amazon:

1. Choose an alluring Product & Price

It goes without saying that you want to sell a product that will actually, well, sell. If you've been selling on Amazon for a while, you likely have an idea of what's in demand. But in case you need a refresher or if this is your first time selling do some research. You can look on Amazon (or even Alibaba) to see what the top-selling products are or consult a product research tool to do the heavy lifting for you.

Once you decide on what you're going to sell, you have two price-points to think about: the sourcing cost and the selling price. For the former, you want to pay the lowest possible price to have your product made — that means comparison shopping and negotiating with suppliers. For the latter, you want a price that will attract sales, win you the Buy Box, and give you high margins — that means researching competitors prices, looking up the price history for a similar product and/or using a repricer tool.

Your last step here is to create a stellar product detail page that includes everything a customer needs to familiarize themselves with your product: high-resolution images, product demos, accurate and thorough descriptions, etc.

2. Manage Your Inventory/Supply Chain

Once you've chosen your product and price, you need to stock up so you can avoid a stockout. That means developing an inventory management strategy to determine how much product to order at the start plus how much to have on hand at any given time in the future.

Understanding this information will not only prevent you from running out of stock, it will also keep you from buying too much at one time. Not only that, you'll know when and how much to reorder as business picks up.

As important as it is to manage your inventory, it is fairly important to be on top of the supply chain as well. That way, you can establish the reorder process and not run up against any surprises or delays when it's time to place a new order. Nonetheless establish an agreement with your suppliers and stay in frequent communication with them — i.e. don't just reach out when you need more items.

3. Create rumors

Generate interest in your items before it's actually listed so that when your listing is actually live, you don't have to work as hard to get clients. You can do this by advertising its release on social media or your own website if you may have one.

Then chase the pre-release marketing with a Sponsored Product campaign on Amazon. To really create a lot of "rumors", you can offer a new special item or for example a discount for the first 150 customers.

4. Create Reviews

Since online shoppers can't preview or test your items in person, they trust on feedback from previous customers before making a purchase decision. But you can't consequently launch a new product with reviews. Unless, that is, you have a separate ecommerce channel you can launch on first.

In other words, if you have your own ecommerce website, consider launching their first and running a marketing campaign on social media and other channels outside of Amazon. From there, you can solicit feedback from your customers and build up reviews on your website.

Then, use those reviews in your marketing campaigns for the Amazon launch, directing people to your Amazon listing. After your Amazon launch and as you start making sales, you can solicit feedback from your Amazon customers.

5. Get money

Initiate a new item isn't cheap, especially when it's a private label product. After all, you have packaging and branding expenses to budget for in addition to anything else.

Find the best Amazon Bargains – 4 Secrets to saving up to 65% on Amazon

Amazon has always been a main player in the e-commerce industry. There are a huge variety of items categories listed on their website, with available products numbering in the millions. Along with all these items come several ways to save money while shopping on Amazon. We'll look at a few of these methods and see just how easy it is to save money and find Amazon deals.

Amazon Discount Codes

Amazon sometimes provides coupon codes that you can apply to your purchases to save money. Although these are not regularly advertised by Amazon, a quick Internet search will reveal a plethora of coupons. One of the great things about these discounts is that they are deducted from the total price of your shopping cart. This will sometimes allow you to get free shipping on items which cost less than $25. Amazon coupon codes usually apply to certain products or categories only.

When you find a coupon code for a product you are interested in, all you do is enter it in the "Promotional Codes" box when you're checking out. The discount will then be applied directly to your shopping cart and you'll see the savings instantaneously.

Cash Back Rewards

Another way to save money on Amazon is by using their new Platinum credit card. This will allow you to save money on every purchase you make. For every dollar you spend at Amazon you will obtain three points on your card. These points can be accumulated and transformed into Amazon gift certificates which you can use towards your purchases. For every 2500 points you collect, Amazon will provide you with a gift certificate valued at $25. If you do the math, it turns out you get about 3% cash back on all your purchases. This is a great reward especially considering most other cards only give you 1% cash back. On top of that, your first purchase with the card will receive an immediate $30 discount. All the gift certificates you earn with the card can be used during your checkout process.

Free Shipping Offer

One of the fantastic things about Amazon is its Super Saver Shipping. What this means is that most items purchased directly from Amazon or from one of its third-party retailers are eligible for free shipping as long as the order total is over $25. Although the Super Saver Shipping is generally slower than other shipping methods available on Amazon, in our experience orders still arrive very quickly. Because the shipping costs on many online purchases can normally be quite expensive, this is a fantastic way to save money.

Amazon Price History Tracker / Price Drop Alerts

Another excellent way to find Amazon deals is by being aware of upcoming sales. If you are like many other people and lead a hectic life, this can normally prove to be a very difficult task. Fortunately, there are Amazon price tracking tools available which will keep an eye out for sales on your behalf, and alert you when prices drop. How does this work exactly?

Well, suppose you are looking to purchase a new color printer. You would visit a price tracking website and enter the name of the printer you wanted into the search box. This would bring up a list of printers available on Amazon. You could then set up a price drop alert for the particular printer you are interested in and the price tracking website would send you an e-mail the next time that printer goes on sale. This is a brilliant way to save loads of money on those big-ticket items you're saving up for.

Adding it all up

Now that we have explored some of the ways to save money on Amazon, let's take a look at a real-world example of how much you can save. Suppose that color printer you are looking to purchase normally sells for $300. The first step would be to track the price of the printer on an Amazon price history tracking website. When the printer goes on a 1-day sale for 50% off (which you'll be alerted to immediately, lucky you!), the price drops down to $150. Next, doing a quick Internet search we'll see that there is a $25 coupon code available for all color printers on Amazon. Using this coupon code along with free shipping and 3% cash back (obtained when using the Amazon Platinum credit card), here's what the savings would look like:

- Normal retail price is $300.
- Get it at 50% off by setting up a price drop alert. Subtract $150.

- Subtract $25 using the Amazon discount code.
- Subtract $30 with the first purchase on an Amazon Platinum credit card.
- Subtract $2.85 for the 3% cash back.
- Get free shipping on orders over $25.
- The total: $92.15 - a total savings of 70% off the retail price!

Obviously, if you make a lot of purchases on Amazon these savings will really add up. Fortunately for us, Amazon makes it really simple to save money. It's just one of the many ways they like to reward their valued customers.

COMMON MISTAKES TO AVOID WHEN SHOPPING WITH COUPONS

Coupons are supposed to make you incredible savings on your purchases. However, if you are not wise with how you use the coupons, you could end up making little payoffs. Shoppers who hunt for coupons to make the big savings on items need to come out with some sort of strategy to ensure they get maximum deals possible with the coupons they have. If you are among shoppers that like enjoying discounts using coupons, here are some errors you should try and avoid if at all you want to enjoy maximum benefits using the coupons.

Mistake 1 - Sticking to one brand

To enjoy great savings with your coupons, you really do not have the luxury of being loyal to a particular brand. Sure, you may love the brand for a number of reasons, but you will not save much if you choose to stick only to products from that brand. If you are really inclined to making savings, then do not let great deals pass you by just because you prefer a particular brand over another.

Mistake 2 - Buying any item on sale

As much as items on sale offer even better returns when using coupons, not every one of those items will be a good sale for you. Evaluate what is in the sale for you so you can decide to go ahead or to wait for a much better sale that offers you greater value with the coupon. It is not always worth to use coupons on every item on sale because it may not save you much in the end. Do your calculations and choose the most rewarding sales.

Mistake 3 - Using coupons on items that are full priced

Whereas coupons are supposed to make items you want more affordable by saving you some money, you will enjoy greater price cuts when you use them on items that are on sale rather than on items that are full-priced. When you use coupons on items that are on sale, you end up getting the items almost free, but when you choose to use on full priced items, then you only manage to save a few coins on them. Whenever possible, try not to use coupons on full priced items and instead look for sales on items you are in need of.

Mistake 4 - Using Every coupon you find

Not all coupons represent real savings and you consequently do not have to take advantage of every coupon that you find. A good coupon is one that offers you real discounts on items that you really need. So instead of picking up any coupon you find along, access its value first and determine that it is worth. You should also only use the coupon on items you really will use and not just any item you can enjoy the markdown on. It does not make any sense to be hurried in using coupons on products you never use or will never end up using otherwise you end up wasting a possible good offer.

CHAPTER 11

HOW TO HIT YOUR TARGET ACOS ON AMAZON

ACoS on itself is just a number. In order to optimize your Ads and increase your margins, you need to understand how it works and what it means in practically.

What does it mean a low vs. high acos?

The lower your ACoS is the better your Ad is working: a theoretical ACoS of zero would mean you spend nothing, yet make a sale.

A high ACoS means an underperforming Ad. You are spending more to reach your target audience and are in danger of losing margins on your Ad.

But just how low or high must your ACoS be?

How to figure the right acos for your ad campaign

In order to determine the right ACoS for your Ad campaign, you need to first understand what Break-Even ACoS and Target ACoS are.

Break-Even ACoS is the point where an Ad neither makes nor loses money. Any ACoS lower than your Break-Even ACoS is profitable. Conversely, any ACoS higher than that is costing you money.

Of course, merely breaking even is rarely an advertiser's

goal, unless used as a short-term strategy—for example, to raise brand awareness. What you normally want is to make a profit?

Your Ad's profitability is determined by the Target ACoS. This is your ideal ACoS—how much your profit should be for a particular product. If your Break-Even ACoS gives you an upper limit above which your Ad is no longer profitable, your Target ACoS lets you know how profitable an Ad is.

Break-Even ACoS and Target ACoS are the keys to determining the right ACoS for your Ad campaign:

Any ACoS lower than your Target ACoS further increases your profit margin.

Any ACoS higher than your Target ACoS but lower than your Break-Even ACoS is profitable, but eats into your profits.

And any ACoS higher than your Break-Even ACoS is making a loss.

How to measure profit with acos

To better understand how ACoS can help you calculate your profit, you need to remember that your Break-Even ACoS depends on a number of factors beyond your Ad campaigns' cost.

How to lower your acos

Most advertisers start a campaign with the goal of reaching the Break-Even point. They then optimize toward their Target ACoS.

In practice, this means you need to lower your Ad's cost while increasing its profitability. This is a continuing process which can take weeks—or even months of optimization.

There are many factors which can impact on your success with reaching your Target ACoS, only some of which are within your control. For example, your ACoS depends on your target audience, the market your product belongs to, who your competitors are, and how much they are investing on AMS. You can't control any of these.

However, there are also a number of things you can control in order to improve your campaign's success and optimize your Amazon ACoS.

The Importance of Ad Ranking

The first thing to do when striving to reach your Target ACoS is to put yourself in Amazon's shoes. Amazon prides itself on its customer-centric approach, so the company prioritizes a relevant and helpful shopping experience for their customers. They want to ensure that their search results are helpful and that any advertising shown will improve their shopping experience instead of being an irritation.

Furthermore, a successful Ad is also in the company's interest in other ways as well. The company makes its money in two ways:

- By selling you advertising space on its pages, and
- By taking a percentage of each sale.

WHAT IS AMAZON PRODUCT ATTRIBUTE TARGETING?

The Amazon Product Targeting is the newest targeting mechanism that allows you to build a targeted campaign based on the characteristics of the target product you are able to specify.

In simple words, the Product Targeting Beta allows you to set your Amazon ads to appear on other people's ASIN pages and the category search results.

It allows refined targeting options to display your product ads alongside other product ASINs, brands, categories with refinements in the price, brand, and ratings.

Product Attribute Targeting is twofold,

1. Manual Product Targeting with granular refinements
2. Enhanced Automatic Targeting Options

Best Strategies to employ with Product Attribute Targeting

1. Maximized Attention for a Product Launch or for Increasing Brand Awareness.

A new product launch could do good with a lot of visibility. Especially since it's a new launch it's hard to predict what keywords could work the best.

The main aim during the launch phase is to generate the maximum sales during this period, product targeting can be an advantage to target popular brands and similar products, while you benefit from their visibility.

This strategy could be a great benefit for products with upgraded and reinvented features from the existing products. Eg. If you have invented a better sunscreen, it makes sense to target the top-selling sunscreen brand.

2. Explore into Competitors' Market Space

The most obvious use of Product Targeting is to attack your competitors and capture sales.

Do thorough research before you target products. Look through your Automatic campaign Search Term report to discover ASINs you are converting the most. Think twice before targeting a better product that has better ratings or a lower price than yours.

3. Defend your Market Share

Remember, just like you, your competitors are also going to take advantage of the product targeting ads. So, build brand awareness by showcasing your entire product line by targeting your own products.

Targeting your own product will ensure that buyers will not stray towards your competitors' products

Direct the most attention to products that have good ratings, reviews, are lower priced, which could be tough for your competitors to steal from.

While advertising your products against your other products, ensure that you pair products that are a good buy with the targeted product.

Understanding the Manual Product Attribute Targeting types

Amazon allows sellers to choose the target where you want your ads to appear by choosing the targeting option from the following.

1. Category Targeting
2. Individual ASIN Targeting

1. Category Targeting

This is where you can target a category of products as a whole. The category can be chosen from the search bar and also by the brand name, price range and the review rating.

Word of Caution: Since this option allows targeting the entire category of products that are of relevance to your product, it can be leveraged as advantage by-products that fall into the are frequently bought together and by brands trying to build brand awareness.

Brainstorm and carefully consider product categories that could be your best target audience. For each category that's selected, refine the category to target products based on a particular brand, price range, and star rating to choose the best target.

2. Individual Product Targeting

In the products tab, you can target suggested individual products that are similar to your products or search/upload specific ASINs.

Category targeting VS Individual ASIN targeting – When and what to use

The Category Targeting is a nice way to get a lot of visibility, a benefit when you are trying to build brand recognition or a product launch. Nevertheless since you are eligible for a broad reach, the ad is likely to show up on a lot of searches, resulting in a lower conversion rate, with a high ACoS unless you have an faultless brand with a very desirable product having chosen the right set of categories.

The Individual Product Targeting is a much restricted reach compared to the former, nevertheless it is a more mature way of targeting products since you are likely to choose items at which point you stand an upper hand in winning the sale, or products that are trying to eat up your space in the marketplace.

CHAPTER 12
WHICH FULFILLMENT OPTION IS BETTER FOR AMAZON SELLERS?

If you're an Amazon seller, one of your most important decisions will be whether or not you ship using Fulfillment by Amazon (FBA), Merchant Fulfilled Network (MFN, or sometimes FBM, as in "fulfillment by merchant"), or even both.

Amazon sellers have strong opinions about each method, and each has its own points of strengths and weaknesses.

FBA vs MFN: What's the difference?

Sellers who use FBA pay fees to store their products in Amazon's fulfillment centers as well as for Amazon's world-class fulfillment services.

When an order is placed for a seller's FBA product, Amazon receives the information, picks the stock from the shelves, packs it, and ships it.

Amazon also provides the customer service for all FBA products. These services are covered by Amazon's FBA fulfillment fees, which are based on the size and weight of items sold. Amazon also imposes short- and long-term storage fees, so the longer an item stays in FBA inventory, the more fees a seller will incur.

MFN simply refers to sellers shipping their own products directly from their own homes, businesses, or warehouses after receiving orders through Amazon.com.

This means that locating the stock, packing the orders, arranging the shipping, and providing all customer service is the direct responsibility of the seller.

There's also Seller Fulfilled Prime (SFP), a relatively new fulfillment option that awards MFN sellers with excellent metrics. Those who qualify for Amazon SFP enjoy the benefits of FBA without having to send shipments to Fulfillment Centers.

Amazon SFP sellers also seem to get the same royal treatment as FBA sellers from Amazon's Buy Box algorithm. That means stellar sellers with their own fulfillment systems in place can win the Buy Box just as often as FBA sellers pending their seller metrics remain high across the board without having to incur FBA fees.

Advantages of using FBA vs MFN

There are many advantages to using FBA, especially for sellers with high margins who can absorb Amazon's ever-evolving FBA fees.

One major FBA perk is that you become eligible to offer Prime shipping to your customers. On top of being able to tap into Amazon Prime customers, you'll also increase your odds of winning the Buy Box because "fulfillment method" has heavy weight in Amazon's algorithm, with preference given to FBA listings.

As an FBA seller, you can offer all of the shipping options that Amazon does, no matter the size of your business. You also gain access to Amazon's remarkably efficient shipping and distribution network, along with access to Amazon's discounted shipping rates.

Faster shipping especially pleases Amazon Prime customers, who are accustomed to taking advantage of free Prime 2-day shipping.

Another FBA advantage is that many Amazon customers know what they want and are willing to pay for it. According to Amazon, almost half of their customer base refuses to buy from seller's who do not use FBA. This makes sense, considering that not just shipping, but also customer service, are so important to those who subscribe to Prime.

Using FBA vs MFN is a way that even the smallest sellers can set themselves apart from the competition. You'll be listed higher in Amazon search and be more likely to have your listings chosen by customers.

Cons of using FBA

As any FBA seller will tell you, the major disadvantage to FBA is the cost. Because Amazon holds all the cards, the company can tack on as many fees for its service as it deems appropriate.

As long as FBA remains a cheaper fulfillment option than MFN for a large portion of sellers, Amazon can continue increasing FBA fees.

Amazon also charges long-term inventory storage fees for sluggish products. These fees are an effort to discourage sellers from shipping stagnant inventory to FBA Fulfillment Centers that take up precious inventory space.

Pros and cons to fulfilling via Amazon MFN

One clear advantage for MFN sellers is that they can ensure their packaging is perfect for their products. This leads to fewer damaged products being reported by customers, and, as a result, fewer returns.

MFN sellers can also create custom packaging to differentiate their Amazon store from competitors. To take this even further, MFN sellers can create custom receipts and even include hand-written thank-you notes to customers.

Of course, having to handle the packaging and shipping is a clear disadvantage to using MFN. Worse yet, MFN sellers have to deal with customer service issues and returns. These are time-consuming and, at times, difficult tasks, and the fees paid to FBA is often worth it.

The other main disadvantage to MFN is that buyers aren't always as happy to use it. How much this impacts your business isn't always clear, but Prime users spend more than non-Prime shoppers on average. And, they also tend to purchase Prime products over non-Prime ones; that's what they're paying for, after all.

Using MFN may also decrease your chances of winning the Buy Box versus FBA competitors.

Some sellers test each fulfillment method with limited inventory using both MFN and FBA listings so they can see which works better for them. Sometimes, MFN and FBA fulfillment have different advantages for the same seller, depending on the products being sold.

For example, if there is a particular packaging issue for or a target buyer who isn't picky about shipping speed, MFN may be a better option. And, for heavy or bulky items, sellers may also prefer fulfilling via MFN so they don't have to incur extra shipping fees.

On the other hand, FBA would work better for high-volume Amazon sellers who can't afford to spend time (or money hiring staff) to handle packing and shipping an excess of orders.

The typical seller that would benefit from FBA vs MFN

Amazon sellers poised to make the most of MFN are those who already have storage and shipping systems in place. If you've got a warehouse (or several), staff, and a logistics network you trust, consider using MFN and reaping higher profit margins.

Better yet, if you have exceptional seller metrics, apply for Amazon Seller Fulfilled Prime and enjoy the benefits of FBA without paying FBA fees.

If you have an operational eCommerce website or a brick and mortar store, you're also in a much better position to successfully fulfill orders. If you can handle it, you'll save yourself a fortune in storage and fulfillment fees.

On the other side, if your business can't rapidly and effectively fill orders, FBA is probably the better option. Small-time sellers can benefit from FBA since many buyer's actively look for stores with items that feature Prime shipping.

Bigger sellers can also benefit from FBA by strategically fulfilling orders with MFN and then using FBA on listings where it makes more sense. And any seller that lists items with high sales velocity can benefit from FBA, as they'll avoid getting hit with long-term storage fees.

CHAPTER 13

HOW TO GET A LOAN TO START AN AMAZON FBA BUSINESS

It wasn't so long ago that starting a retail business would cost tens of thousands, at least. You needed pay rent for store, hire staff and pay thousands in manufacturing just to start.

In 2006, Amazon revolutionized small business with Fulfillment by Amazon (FBA) and now anyone can initiate their own brand and sell it to the world. Starting an Amazon FBA business costs a fraction of what you'd pay to launch a traditional business and you've got the world's biggest ecommerce website in your corner.

The opportunity is incredibly amazing. Amazon FBA sellers report an average profit of 66% and monthly sales of $10,000 or more between 18 months. Even smaller sellers can make a few bucks a month within the first year of business.

While costs to start an Amazon store are much lower, they can still run into the thousands. Even with the reseller strategy, costs can reach $2,000 to start your business.

How Much Does It Cost to Start an Amazon FBA Business?

Starting an Amazon FBA business isn't as inexpensive as starting a website or some of the other work-at-home businesses. Then again, you wouldn't expect to be able to start your own retail brand with just a few hundred dollars.

Even so, starting an ecommerce business through Amazon is still millions cheaper than the traditional route of renting commercial space and buying all the manufacturing inputs necessary to a private-label brand. This is the real opportunity in Amazon FBA, to be able to compete with the biggest brands and get started for just a few thousand.

Let's walk through the costs of getting started on Amazon FBA as a private-label first then as a reseller of other products.

I like the private-label business model because you can create some real brand strength in your products and grow your business. The reseller model means you're always on that hamster wheel of buying and selling.

Manufacturing costs for a new Amazon FBA Business – Manufacturing is by far your biggest cost with an Amazon FBA business. This goes for startup costs as well as ongoing production. Sites like Alibaba make it easy to connect with low-cost, Chinese manufacturers that can provide consistent quality but it's still going to cost some money.

Your first step here is to find a manufacturer and order samples. There are hundreds of providers on Alibaba for every product and quality can vary quite a bit even from what is listed on the website. Research at least three manufacturers to send you a test sample of the product.

This is usually going to cost a nominal fee of $100 per sample but is well worth it to find a reliable producer.

Once you've chosen your Amazon supplier, you'll need to order initial inventory. You'll get discounts for ordering in bulk and most manufacturers have a minimum order quantity (MOq). Don't be intimidated by a minimum order that means putting down a few thousand. This is your biggest expense and can be hugely profitable if you've done your planning beforehand.

The average product sold on Amazon FBA costs around $20 and can usually be manufactured for less than $5 each. Ordering a batch of 500 for your initial inventory means costs of $2,500 to start your FBA business.

That means producer testing and inventory will cost you around $3,000 to get started. Note that these are estimated costs for a small product costing roughly $5 to manufacture, package and ship to Amazon's FBA warehouses.

You can relax now that the biggest cost is out of the way. It gets easier on the budget from here.

Photography and Video: You'll need professional images for your product and a video demonstration can really help your marketing efforts. I'd recommend looking on Craigslist for these services but make sure you check out a few providers and their past work. You can get all the photos you need plus a couple of short 45-second videos for $500 or less.

Amazon Professional Account: You can sell your FBA products through an individual account but it costs about

$1 per item. Starting an Amazon Professional account costs $40 a month but you don't pay the per item fees. Hopefully, you're planning on selling more than 40 items a month so the professional account makes more sense.

With the professional account, you also get bonus features like promotional codes and better tracking.

UPC Code for your product: You need a barcode, a Global Trade Identification Number (GTIN) for each product you sell. Many Amazon FBA businesses are still using third-party UPC codes even though Amazon has change their requirements stating you need a code from GS1.

It's more expensive at $250 for registration and a $50 annual renewal for up to 10 barcodes but go the safe route and stay in compliance. The last thing you want to do is go through all this work only to get your store shut down by Amazon.

Amazon Marketing: Next to manufacturing, marketing is your next biggest expense and may even be a bigger cost for some products. Amazon doesn't disclose how many FBA stores there are but the world's largest ecommerce platform ships more than a billion sales every year. So yeah, that's a lot of competition no matter what's your product.

You can market your product through Facebook, Twitter or your own website but the best marketing channel for most FBA businesses is through sponsored ads directly on Amazon. That's where your potential customers are most ready and willing to buy.

Once sales and reviews start coming in, your product will rank on Amazon and your business will have a life of its own. Starting those initial sales means, a marketing budget and I know a lot of FBA sellers that spend money on Amazon ads continuously to keep their products ranked.

Even a small budget of $10 a day can be enough to start seeing significant sales for your product. It won't take long before you know exactly how much it costs per sale in marketing and can adjust your continuous marketing budget accordingly.

Graphic design and copy writing: Most of the budget items for starting an FBA business are something you probably can't do yourself. Graphic design of logos and copy writing your sales material is one place you might be able to save money with a DIY strategy.

I would still get a professional logo developed from a freelancer on Fiverr. You can try a few freelancers for $5 each and then pick the best idea. Even if you go the inexpensive route and write your own marketing material to launch your store, consider hiring someone to review it after sales start coming in.

Trademark for your brand: This is more of an optional cost to start an Amazon FBA business but totally necessary for the future. You're going to be putting thousands into developing your brand and how customers see your company, you need to protect that investment with a trademark or someone can just start their own company under the same name.

How Much Does Starting Amazon FBA Cost as a Reseller?

Startup costs for an Amazon FBA reseller business are simpler but more uncertain than the private-label business model.

With the reseller strategy, you're simply looking for things you can buy cheaply and resell at a higher price on Amazon. There are apps you can use to instantly compare prices of something on Amazon but it's still a very time-intensive business.

Inventory Costs and Shipping: This all depends on what you're buying to resell but can easily reach $1,000 to buy an initial inventory and ship to Amazon's warehouses. You want to buy in large quantities if possible. It's difficult enough finding things for sale on Amazon with enough markup over your in-person costs to make it worthwhile, you might as well buy as many as you can when you find something.

Photography and Video Costs: You usually won't need custom photography or video for the reseller business model. Check the manufacturer's website for product images or look for other Amazon pages selling the product.

Amazon Pro Account: You'll still need to open a Pro account for $40 but this is relatively minor.

Marketing Costs: Marketing costs are still a big expense in the reselling strategy. You're usually going to be competing with other FBA resellers in the same product so you'll need to rank your store with those consistent sales. A marketing budget of $500 will usually suffice here as well.

On the upside, you probably won't need to spend quite as much in on-going marketing because you'll be selling products that already have some brand recognition. Customers will be more familiar with the product versus your private-label business and won't need quite as much convincing to buy.

You won't need to register your items or get UPC codes because they will already have these from the original seller. You can seemingly also just reuse and rewrite a lot of the advertising copy from the original seller's website or find pages of the product already for sale on Amazon.

You can truly start an Amazon FBA reseller business for less than $1,000 if you're buying less expensive products. The reseller strategy is simpler than creating your own branded products but it's more time-intensive in the long run and I believe more limited on profit.

CHAPTER 14
TIME TO THINK BIGGER? SCALING YOUR AMAZON BUSINESS

I'd all like to create the kind of business which grows sustainably, provides us with a solid income and gives us the freedom to make the lifestyle choices I'd wish to have. There are many stories circulating of sellers who are unquestionably killing it through FBA and jetting their debt-free selves wherever they please.

What is the difference from these highly successful sellers and the rest? What factors provide an edge when it comes to climbing your business? Here's what I've found:

Stay above Your Numbers

Successful sellers sell huge volumes and make a profit from them; wildly successful sellers are those who stay firmly on top of the vital numbers of their business.

This includes having a good grasp of exactly what they are making on every product they sell. Many people focus too much attention on metrics which are really only vanity. This means that they are only paying close attention to measures which may make them look good on the surface, but become meaningless when you dig down to the truth.

For example, there are sellers who will gaze starry-eyed at their gross revenue; "I sold $500,000 worth of products!" Pure vanity. It's quite possible to sell $500,000 worth of products but be operating at a loss. Obviously in this case, you should be more concerned with net profit.

Margin is another one to be careful of. Have you got the right measures in place? This means you should be focusing on your adjusted gross margin — the amount that is left over once you take out all overhead costs.

On average, FBA seller's usually make 15% – 20% adjusted gross margin, but the high volumes of sales which are made possible by the Amazon platform help to keep their businesses doing well. If any of your products are making less than this, you're giving yourself very little room to move, especially if you want to stay competitively priced. If that's the case, you may want to investigate either raising your prices or moving on to a different product — one which you can make a reasonable margin.

Inventory Management

If you want to be able to scale your Amazon business, you need to have a good grasp of inventory management for each product you have. Are you losing valuable sales to stock-outs? Do you have inventory languishing in the warehouse, costing you storage fees and effectively tying up your cash on the shelf?

The bigger you grow, the more products you have to manage, so knowing these details can become more difficult. This is where having good inventory management software for FBA (such as forecastly), can help you to grow your business.

Do Something You Enjoy

This is just from the point of view of your own motivation to grow a business. Some people are motivated by the idea of making money, but for most this is not a strong enough factor to keep them going when it comes to putting in the hard yards for a business.

Selling products, you are actually interested in is a great start if you want the motivation to continue, as is selling something where you have good connections who can help to promote or grow your business in some way.

Improve Your Best Seller Ranking

The best way to improve your best seller rank is simply by outselling your competition, though of course this is easier said than done. There are several factors which go into how you are positioned on Amazon and whether or not customers are enticed to buy from you. We've written about a few of them previously. You could:

- Look for ways to boost your hourly sales.
- Incorporate the right keywords into your product listings.
- Encourage more reviews of your products on Amazon.
- Spice up your product listings with better descriptions and enticing product photography.

If you're trying everything to improve sales but you're not getting the growth in your category that you'd like, you may need to look at a less competitive category or for some other factor which will give you a competitive advantage.

Have Good Systems in Place

One of the keys to scaling any business is the systems and processes you put in place. Most FBA sellers don't want to have to hire on a lot of employees, for example, that's usually a reason why they opted for FBA. No matter how big you grow, Amazon can handle your fulfillment.

So, if you don't want an entire team of staff (or, if you want to make it easier to hire on one or two people and quickly get them up to speed), having simple, scalable systems is the way to go. This includes having the right tools to automate your processes as much as you can.

18 BIG MISTAKES NEW AMAZON SELLERS CAN'T AFFORD TO MAKE

Notwithstanding if you're selling on Amazon as a beginner, there are some mistakes you could easily make without realizing it. There's a lot of small print in those requirements, and Amazon put them in place for a reason – everything they create is driven by the shopper experience.

Having said that, below are some of the leading avoidable mistakes Amazon sellers make when setting up accounts, selling on Amazon, and managing Amazon orders.

Amazon Account Setup Fails

The Amazon Seller Account is the place where Amazon sellers spend much of their time (varies based on agency or management automation).

This is the place where Amazon sellers have a holistic view for ongoing orders, items purchased, and what is getting listed on Amazon. This is also the place where sellers manage inventory, product performance, and define campaign settings.

Be sure you set up a solid foundation for your account and products by avoiding easy blunders.

1. Registering for More Than One Seller Account

One seller account per Amazon seller- it's that simple. And it happens to be an Amazon policy violation to have two accounts. Don't get greedy.

2. Pointing Amazon Shoppers to Your Website

Several sellers have tried including a URL in their product or seller information (such as their product inventory file or business name. This is an Amazon policy violation.

Amazon is a closed ecosystem, which can be a disadvantage for retargeting (remarketing) and branding opportunities. Amazon's marketplace design and notoriety grant your store to a large shopper base- but that comes at the price of losing the ability to point shoppers back to a seller website.

Take advantage of other selling channels and strategies to increase site traffic and retarget customer's rather than trying to game Amazon.

3. Copying Another Seller's Setup

Remember selling on Amazon is difficult, and your competitor's may be violating Amazon policy and or may not have an optimized account. Constantly review Amazon best practices, audit, test, and refine your seller account.

4. Choosing the Wrong Seller Account Type

Be sure to research and choose the type of seller account that's best for your online store.

5. Misunderstanding How Amazon Works

Don't treat Amazon like eBay or Google. Amazon operates on a fundamentally different structure than either of those shopping sites. Be sure your store is capable of handling selling on Amazon, and that your strategy is aligned with Amazon policies- so you get the highest ROI on the Amazon Marketplace.

It's also very important to calculate your Amazon spend, and forecast profit margins before you go full throttle on Amazon.

6. Including Sales or Coupons in Your Product Title

It can be exceedingly tempting to include a coupon, sale or store marketing message in your product title to make your store stand out on Amazon. However, this is a clear Amazon policy violation, and Amazon will hurt you more in the long run than any short-term benefits.

Avoid any title information with: "20% off", "Lowest Price", your URL or other information that may be construed as promotional. Amazon will eschew any product information which isn't descriptive of the product itself.

7. Using Non-Amazon Sanctioned Categories

Amazon stresses that product categories match Amazon's (Amazon.com) browse tree. Review Amazon's inventory file templates for correct product information formatting, including product title information. (Templates vary based on seller inventory)

8. Including Information in Your Product Titles Amazon Doesn't Allow

Amazon titles should follow Amazon's policies to the T. Product titles should be 100 characters (max), start with the product brand if possible, and include numerals.

9. Adding Promotional Text in Images

If you haven't caught on Amazon doesn't much care for any of your trading promotional material- anywhere near its marketplace. Avoid   any messaging or product information which Amazon might view as a violation. Avoid any messaging which includes "Sale", "Free Shipping", or a similar promotional feel.

Realistically, including that type of information in an image is a bit distorted anyway.

10. Using Main Images Featuring Colored Backgrounds or Lifestyle images.

Common pictures best practices advocate using a white background. Amazon's image policy for the main image follows this guideline. On look at some of the product pictures on eBay and you can understand how this policy benefits your bottom line and Amazon clients.

11. Incorporating Image Borders, Watermarks, Text or Other Descriptions

Amazon image policy is strict. Amazon isn't playing around with its user experience, which is impacted heavily by product images.

12. Expensive Shipping

Nothing sends an online shopper running faster than over-priced shipping. Remember your Buy Box share and Amazon selling status rely (in part) on your reviews- those for your online store and your products. Bad or expensive shipping policies may mean more immediate profits, but will negatively impact your Amazon selling success.

13. Late Shipping

Amazon customers generally note that they appreciate the ease of shopping on Amazon, but prize Amazon's cheap, and fast shipping policies. Your competitors (and Amazon) will feature fast and reliable shipping speed. Be honest with your shipping dates, and realistically consider what speed and shipping price your store can manage.

14. Sneaking in Marketing Collateral with Packing Materials

Usually, I recommend using Fulfillment by Amazon (depending on your store, fulfillment needs, and budget) to benefit from Amazon's shipping speed and customer service. In which case there's very small chance that anything promotional will get by Amazon. Nevertheless, if you're handing your own fulfillment, anything featuring your store may likely confuse or worse disappoint Amazon shoppers.

Review Amazon's Seller Shipping Rates, Fulfillment by Amazon (FBA) and fulfillment policies before choosing a fulfillment method. Remember to consider the cost of shipping to Amazon, returns, and related fulfillment variables.

15. Managing Your Account Based on Email Notifications

If you're using email to make Amazon changes, you're not managing your Amazon account effectively. Remember emails can get lost, deleted, or missed easily.

Proactively respond to customer needs, manage inventory and handle account activity. If you're in over your head, consider leveraging agency resources or outsourcing data management.

16. Paying for Positive Feedback

Amazon relies heavily on user trust–a metric they value dearly:

"Customer satisfaction is one of the most important performance measures we use to determine how well you are doing as a seller on Amazon. The Customer Metrics page provides reports that give you greater insight into how you are doing with respect to customer satisfaction."- Amazon

It's vital that you monitor and improve the variables which influence your customer metrics score, including shopper reviews for your store. However, gaming the system isn't going to push the needle in your favor enough to warrant the risk.

17. Getting Upset with Customers

Sometimes Amazon customers are unreasonably demanding or argumentative. You're guaranteed to encounter an overly-needy or irate person more than once when selling on Amazon. Avoid arguing with these shoppers at all costs.

18. Thinking Amazon Shoppers Read

Your Amazon clients aren't thoroughly reading (if at all) your policies. Even more likely, many people who have bought your items haven't read the product description entirely.

State your policies clearly, and in multiple places. Kindly reiterate policies in customer interactions, but don't forget its unlikely shoppers have read your store policy or the product description for what they've purchased.

CHAPTER 15
USING AMAZON FBA FOR EBAY FULFILLMENT

Did you know that Amazon FBA can be used to fulfill orders across several channels? Using Amazon's state of the art fulfillment network could be just what you may need to provide faster shipping for you.

Did you know that Fulfillment by Amazon (FBA) isn't just for Amazon traders? If you sell on eBay or your own web store, you can also benefit of Amazon's fulfillment network.

Using FBA could allow your selling to grow by giving you access to immense logistical expertise, but it does come at a price. Amazon charges premium rates for FBA and, if you don't pay attention it can be expensive especially if stock doesn't sell.

Order fulfillment is a major headache for multi-channel sellers. Getting it right is crucial if you want to succeed. There are benefits to using FBA—but does the service and its costs suit your business?

I break down the practical implications and discuss the pros and cons of mastering eBay fulfillment by using Amazon FBA. I'll also look at how the recently changed prices of multi-channel fulfillment will affect online sellers.

How does an eBay seller go Amazon FBA?

You'll need an Amazon Seller Central account to begin. Once you're registered and logged in, follow these steps:

- Go to Multi-Channel Fulfillment in the FBA settings.
- Submit your order fulfillment requirements with either a simple online form, upload a bulk file or integrate Amazon with your web store.
- Lastly, ship your inventory to an Amazon fulfillment center.

There are no minimum requirements and you can send as many items as you want. It is worth noting that as this is not a product sold through Amazon. Customer service will be handled by you.

Amazon decides which fulfillment center you use based on factors like size, product type and storage needs, as well as location. You can select your own courier or use Amazon's discounted service.

When your item is received, Amazon scans the FBA barcode sticker. These stickers are inexpensive and can be purchased easily. When you get an order and place it with Amazon, the company picks, packs and ships the item. You can monitor its progress using Amazon's online tracking system.

TOP 5 BENEFITS OF AMAZON FBA

1. It's giving you free time

Have you ever tried doing the order fulfillment by yourself? You have to speak to the potential buyer, pack your product and prepare the package for shipping. Then you have to physically drop it at your local post office. (And more often than not, there's a long queue there!)

2. It is a steroid for your business

This point is on e-commerce in general but it drives home a point that you can leverage FBA with.

Not only are more people putting items and buying from their e-cart, the proliferation of online shopping is still rapidly growing in USA. (This is also true world-wide and we will explore more about this soon.)

3. Tagging onto Amazon's perks!

Treat your customer's right with the added bonus of delivering your product the next day or two.

Amazon is also a household brand which your customers love and trust. There's a report that states that half of millennial today would rather give up sex and alcohol than to give up Amazon!

4. Win the Buy Box and qualify for Amazon Prime!

The Buy Box is akin to a competitive sport where various sellers selling the exact same item will compete for the coveted prize; which is winning the Buy Box.

While there are many factors that affects the chances of winning the Buy Box, one of them is using FBA.

By using FBA, the chances of you winning the Buy Box spot over other sell-fulfilled sellers are significantly higher.

It has become a new norm for sellers to head to FBA just to get the Buy Box.

You will also be automatically qualified for Amazon Prime shipping – Prime members can get free 2-day shipping for your products.

These Prime members are customers ready to buy and when they see that they can get the free 2-day shipping on your product, you will be viewed as a trusted seller. This in turn helps bring in the moolah!

5. Profits Kaching!

Since Amazon have taken care of all the heavy lifting in your business for you, you can focus on areas that matters.

Think that the fees are too high? Think again.

The cost that you would have spent on setting up a large and efficient logistics machine is no small investment. On top of that, the amount of advertising you will invest is minimal as they are all congregated in a single platform which Amazon have spent years building. In short, your customers are already on Amazon.

It is an absolute privilege to be selling on Amazon as you are paying less labor and administrative cost on the warehousing, shipping and customer service.

CHAPTER 16
10 TIPS FOR SELLING ON AMAZON

1. Perfectionate Your Product

Fastly in 10 words or fewer, describe what you're selling. You need to be an absolute expert on your product or else your buyers will sniff out that you don't know what you're talking about. Take all the time is necessary to learn everything you can about your items so that when the occasion arises, you have an answer to all questions asked.

2. Register as a Professional Seller

There's a bit more involved than simply signing up with Amazon, uploading product descriptions and calling yourself a merchant. You can technically do that, yes, but it won't pay off in the long run. Not only will you save money on the commission on each item sold, but you can also upload items that aren't available anywhere else on Amazon and sell in previously restricted categories.

3. Keep Prices Flexible

There are two ways to create a cost for something: the price you want to sell it at, and the one it will sell at. Sometimes, the two intersect, but it doesn't happen very often. For the rest of the times, you should look at repricing software to compete with the best of them.

4. Sell What People Want

You may think macaroni necklaces are just the best thing in the world, but if enough people don't agree with you, then your sales will be kind of meagre, to say the least. I am not saying to completely abandon your dreams and passions, but to complement it with sure-fire money-makers. For example, sell the macaroni necklaces along with other types, diversifying and offering a decent selection of what people want.

5. Automate Your Listings

There's no doubt being an online merchant will mean a lot of tough work, but you can create several handy shortcuts for yourself that will add plenty of time back to your life. One of those is to use an API to automate your listings, letting technology do the heavy lifting for you. There are plenty of software programs out there, so it's just a matter of finding the one that works best for you.

6. Sell in the Middle Ground

If you've been reading so far, it may be tempting to think that selling the most popular items on Amazon is a surefire recipe for success. But when you think about it, how many merchants out there are selling Xbox systems and iPods? Plenty, which makes competing with them pretty tough. Instead, widen your horizon to the top 1,000 items or so, giving yourself a big middle ground to deal with but still with plenty of profit potential.

7. Optimize Product Listings

This is probably easiest if you're just starting out on Amazon, as everything is still a blank slate. If you're an established seller, it can be easy to lapse into bad habits and forget about optimizing your listings. Don't spend a day or two going over the quality of images, writing, keywords and everything else.

8. Play by the Rules

Yeah, Amazon's really big and there are going to be several cases all the time when something slips by. But if you continually skirt under the radar. It's just not worth it, as it can result in bad reviews, fewer sales and even being booted off Amazon.

MEDIA SELLING - FIVE STEPS TO RUNNING A SUCCESSFUL AMAZON BUSINESS

When starting a media trading business, just like any other kind of business, you need investment capital. Depending on how quick you want your business to take off, you will need more money. The bulk of your spending will be in the beginning, as you will need to purchase the proper equipment.

If you are not the kind of person who is willing to go 100 miles from home to get inventory, you probably will not be nearly as successful in this business as you could be.

1. Years ago, media scouts used to guess the price of the items by site, and buy what they thought they could sell for a good price. If you try that now, you will be losing out on

incredible amounts of money. Now, an amazing piece of technology is used, called a scanner. By scanning the bar code of a media item, it gives you the prices of the items on Amazon almost instantly. I recommend using the $400 scanner from ASellerTool.com, as it is cheap, but efficient. This service costs $30 per month to maintain.

2. Sign up for FBA (Fulfillment By Amazon), at Amazon.com. It is $40 per month, but this service will pay itself off incredibly fast, you don't have to spend hours packing, and the shipping is fast. Buyers prefer buying something from FBA, as there is fast shipping and great customer service. With FBA, you can price your items lower than the $3.99 + 1c, allowing you to get an edge on your competition. Never sell something below $3.25.

3. FBAPower (FBAPower.com) is a service that will increase your efficiency of FBA that much you will not want to go without it. Using a $70 USB laser scanner, you can scan fast your items into the system. This lets you box up 50-70 pounds of media products taking about 40 seconds per item. In these 40 seconds, you need to examine fast the item, click its condition, and stick the special bar code sticker on it. This type of service costs $40 per month.

4. You will need a thermal printer. A printer, that prints with heat. I recommend getting a Dymo Thermal Label Printer. This will allow you to print without ink, and very quickly. These labels hold the bar codes of each item you send to the FBA warehouse. This printer costs about $100, and the rolls of labels tend to cost around $12.50 per roll. This seems to be cheap, as label rolls tend to have a lot on them.

CHAPTER 17
THE ADVANTAGES AND DISADVANTAGES OF USING FBA

You pay a small fee each month and in return, Amazon takes care of packing and shipping your orders. You send your inventory to Amazon so that every time you get a sale, they send pickers through their warehouse to select the items and send it to its new owner. If anything goes wrong with the order or delivery, Amazon takes care of all. They also offer help in the way of 24/7 customer service in the languages of the marketplaces it sells in and provide tracking information.

With that being said let's now take a look at what the advantages and disadvantages of FBA are.

Advantages of using FBA

Frees Up Time: You can't put a price tag on having time to grow your business and focus on strengthening it.

Storage Space: It's entirely taken care of, and you don't have to worry about stepping over boxes to reach your bed or kitchen.

Reputation: Amazon's got a solid name and buyers trust it. When you back up your line with Amazon, you increase your chances of landing a sale.

Shipping Protocols: Don't want to hassle yourself with complicated customs regulations and shipping practices? You don't even have to make it a whisper of a thought.

Amazon Prime: FBA translates into automatic qualification for Amazon Prime, which your Amazon Prime buyers will be very happy about.

Returns: Amazon will take care of all of that for you, from talking to the buyer to sending them a new product.

Sell Volume: The FBA fees, along with Amazon's commission, may seem like it's hard to get a profit until you see just how much more your sell rate has increased.

Listings: Yup, you can use other people's listings for your own, adding even more time saved by using FBA.

Money-making Tips: Bundle and multipack your items for even bigger profits.

DISADVANTAGES OF FBA

Cost: FBA isn't free, and can eat up your profit margin if you sell large, heavy and/or inexpensive items.

Co-mingling: Your inventory is sorted by like, and the product that goes to your buyer may not necessarily be the one you sent Amazon.

Order Volume: It can be tricky to ascertain how full you need to keep your inventory, particularly around busy times like holidays.

Control: You give up a lot of it because Amazon packs and ships their way, so you don't get to suss out cheaper materials or routes.

Sending to Amazon: You have to follow very specific ways of sending your inventory to Amazon, like labelling products individually.

Competition: I don't want to say you'll have to start sleeping with one eye open, but you should definitely be aware of Amazon cutting into your potential revenue.

Part-Time vs. Full-Time: If selling on Amazon is your sole occupation, it can pay off to use FBA. But if you're a casual seller, then the costs may cut into your profit margin too much.

Patience: It may take time to see a profit, and the trial-and-error period where you may be in the hole for a while can be uncomfortable to bear.

What to Sell? Market research is necessary to know what the efficient-selling items are and which ones to steer clear of.

CHAPTER 18
HOW TO BECOME A TOP-RATED AMAZON SELLER

From its humble roots in 1994, Amazon has grown from a small online retailer to become one of the world's largest online stores with outnumbered individuals, businesses, and companies using its platform to sell their items.

Some traders do not know the most effective and efficient ways on how to make money selling on amazon. Some of the best ways to sell your products on Amazon and become a top-rated seller have been mentioned above.

Ensure You Have Enough Products

Though it is important to have a few products when you start selling on Amazon, it is important to have enough products to cater for demand in case people like your products and you begin getting more orders. This ensures that return customers and those who have been referred do not look for alternative sellers

Your Products Should Be Affordable with Flexible Pricing

The best way on how to make money selling on Amazon is by selling your products at affordable rates. Check your competitor's prices and adjust accordingly. Though this might not get you a huge profit margin at first, it is the best way to get and retain more customers.

In addition, you should be flexible in pricing. If you are the only seller of a given product and there is increased demand, you can slightly push the prices up to increase profitability.

Use Amazon Marketing Tools and Amazon Seller Central

Another way on how to make money selling on Amazon is by utilizing existing Amazon marketing tools including Tags, Listmania and Likes which will help your products get more visibility. Additionally, Amazon seller central provides regular reports that can help you analyze your sells, know potential customers and find out the effectiveness of your marketing and promotions

Become an Amazon Featured Merchant

Being a featured merchant on Amazon will not only get your products noticed, but will also make you reputable and trusted among potential customers? Though Amazon does not say how sellers become featured merchant, you can easily get to that list by having good sales, little or no customer complaints and excellent customer reviews. You should also ensure that you adhere to all Amazon selling rules, regulations and policies to avoid getting banned.

Understand all expenses and fees

The most effective and efficient way on making money selling on Amazon is by understanding all associated fees and costs. If you are a seller who buys products then sells them on Amazon, your selling cost must be able to accommodate all your costs and amazon fees. Amazon charges fees for trading and referrals.

HOW DOES SMM HELP TO INCREASE YOUR AMAZON SALES?

If you are a seller on Amazon, it is e important to do right marketing for getting an increased number of sales. There are some established marketing methods, which give amazing results if applied. Due to huge competition on Amazon, every seller tries to apply peculiar strategies to get valuable customers to his/her product listing. To get a hold of this unconventional change, many sellers have followed an extraordinary way of media marketing to boost their Amazon sales.

The media marketing services are the most excellent way to generate real impact on ones' business. Due to rapid and efficient results, a number of Amazon sellers are taking help of social media marketing experts. Media marketing basically means an approach to endorse a company or business website via various social media channels such as Facebook, LinkedIn, Twitter, etc. This method of business development has redefined globe of communication. Furthermore, with right social media services, you have all chances to drive a massive amount of traffic to your listing on Amazon.

Hiring an Amazon SEO Company who is well-familiar with social media marketing techniques can promote and provide all information related to their products within huge series of networking. They can help raise various ground-breaking proposals through such broad networks to reach your potential consumers in a big way.

Benefits of Media marketing

Social Networking Sites

Regular updates and information about your Amazon products can be posted on different social networking web sites. In fact, these sites are frequently visited by millions of visitors every day. You can also integrate appropriate pictures, content, coupons, and even videos for selling promotion.

Accordingly, there is no shortage of social networking websites to popularize your selling business. On the other hand, it is recommended to hire a professional marketing company for the same to handle things perfectly for your product advertising and increase your returns all together. You should make social connections and facilitate your business reach your budding customers' world-wide by hiring an Amazon SEO Company.

Blogging

A reliable Social media marketing agency takes up the assignment of creating a blog for your Amazon products and updating it frequently. Blogging can be highly informative that is utilized to drive massive traffic to your product listing. Therefore, it is extremely important to make sure if the Social media firm does this task professionally.

CHAPTER 19
MAKE MONEY SELLING USED BOOKS ON AMAZON

First of all, look for all the books around your home that you no longer need. Once you have your books ready then register on the Amazon site which will literally take ten minutes or so.

Register the books on the site is extremely easy as you enter the international book standard number and it will automatically bring up your book. You then can see the market cost applied for your used book.

I would recommend entering your book price at one penny less than the nearest person which ensures you get a low-price tag next to your book. You then just click and complete your listing. Amazon will then send you a sold dispatch now email when the book is sold and you mail the book to your customer.

Once you need more stock, I recommend looking at the local charity shops and libraries. Also, car boot sales and fairs are very good too. I have bought books for 25p and sold them for 20 pound and this happens weekly.

Not every category of book will sell extremely well so it is very important to avoid modern fiction titles. There are literally thousands of used books in this category on amazon and you will not be able to generate income with these types of books.

You should really be looking for older books with a hobby connotation. Good examples of these could be music, religion, self-help, military, arts and crafts, sports and poetry to name but a few.

It is very easy to get the hang of and in time you will easily be able to identify what sells and what does not sell. I also personally sell DVD's online too but you must make sure that your DVD works before sending out to a customer because good customer feedback is very important in this business. Having said that DVD's are fast moving items and can easily make you a lot of money.

If you have an amazon library online of about one hundred books or so then you can be expecting to sell about 30 books or so a month. When you reach this level of sales then it makes it worthwhile to become an amazon book seller. This costs 25 pound a month but also cuts the 85p charge that amazon puts on your account every time a book sell. Of course, Amazon needs to make some income from the arrangement with yourself but as you can see the 30 book per month and over limit makes it a viable business decision.

Another top tip is to try and keep your books small to medium in size to save on the postage costs. Amazon are quite generous and will give you a good postage allowance when selling your books but on very large books you will actually lose out.

Having said that school textbooks and educational books are very good sellers and can attract prices over 20 pounds or so therefore I would make an exception for those type of books.

This really is an easy business to operate and amazon provide an excellent online forum so you can talk to other amazon sellers and also gets lots of good tips and advice.

PROS AND CONS OF SELLING BOOKS ON AMAZON

Have you published yourself as an author? If so, have you already decided where are you going to trade your books? What about auction books on Amazon? The idea sounds fascinating and you know that, actually thousands of traditionally and self-published authors have adopted this platform as their main point of sale for their books.

If you have still a decision to make, you should better evaluate the pros and cons of selling books on Amazon. Here are some ideas to get you started:

Advantages

• One of the main advantages of selling books on Amazon is that it can be really profitable for you. Amazon pays for part of the shipping costs and even this may not cover for the whole expense, it will definitely increase your profits.

• Many sellers also find fascinating the fact that they can add plenty of information on their books' description that makes them peculiar to the eyes of the potential buyers and, needless to say, also increases your chances of selling them. For example, if you have an autographed book from a popular author, it will definitely be much more attractive and valuable for some of his avid readers and fans.

124

• Other important advantage of selling your books on Amazon is that your Amazon gives you the email and physical address of the person purchasing your books. That is very valuable data as you can create your own clients' list and keep them updated on any new titles you have for sale or any main discount or treat you have to offer them.

Disadvantages

• Your customers won't receive free super saver shipping on orders over a certain amount. This may seriously discourage some potential buyers from purchasing the books directly from you if they are also sold by Amazon directly.

It's advisable to ship your books 48 hours after receiving the purchase order. This can make selling books on Amazon quite messy if your books are popular and you receive continuous purchase requests.

THIRD-PARTY SELLERS' COVERAGE FOR AMAZON SUSPENSION

More than product returns and cart abandonment, third-party sellers on Amazon fear losing sales and access to their accounts due to suspension whether it is valid or not.

Getting banned from Amazon can ruin not only your finances but your life regardless of how long the suspension is.

That especially holds true if you use the Amazon marketplace as your main source of income; you don't have an eCommerce site, a bricks-and-mortar shop or a regular job as a backup.

When you get banned, it's like you lost a limb as you lose the ability to pay for your everyday expenses.

Various reasons can lead to a third-party seller's suspension from Amazon: late response or shipment, high order defect rate, high cancelation rate, etc.

There are also painful instances when a seller gets banned not for their own doing, but as a result of their competitor's devious stratagems.

Did you know there are sellers on Amazon who would go to the extent of paying large amounts of money in exchange for fake reviews on their biggest competition's product?

It's a good thing you can do something about that now thanks to the Amazon suspension coverage which some insurance companies offer.

Protect yourself and your business

Anyone can be banned from Amazon without notice regardless of their seller rating or performance metrics.

It is an ordeal which you never want to suffer, but the odds are high that you can avoid it, so might as well find a way to protect yourself and your business just in case it befalls you.

Lloyd's of London, which has gained global fame by ensuring famous celebrities' body parts, is one of the insurance companies that are offering insurance plans to compensate seller's for lost sales and expenses during an Amazon suspension.

Businesses of all sizes can be insured; coverage limits range from $50,000 to $1,000,000 for a period of 30 to 180 days.

Monthly premiums depend on many factors, among them are your annual sales, and how long you've been selling on Amazon and your average feedback rating.

Even sellers who have been suspended in the past can apply for coverage, but this too will influence their premiums.

Be reinstated and receive payout

In case you get banned from Amazon, you can get your account reinstated within 72 hours aside from your payout.

The amount you will receive will be based on your midpoint gross sales volume plus regular day-to-day expenses.

Note that your coverage will only be effective after the waiting period which is stipulated in your policy.

During that length of time, you are expected to push your day-to-day expenses, hence classed as your insurance deductible.

If Amazon raises your suspension before that period is over, you won't be able to collect money from your policy.

Getting suspended from Amazon is no joke, so it's good to know that third-party sellers now have an option to preserve what they've strived so hard for.

CHAPTER 20
DON'T GET BANNED FROM SELLING ON AMAZON - IT COULD BE FOREVER

Amazon.com offers small businesses and entrepreneurs' ready access to a huge customer market for their products. Of course, sellers pay a price for the chance to trade on Amazon's good name, internet saturation and global market reach. Not only do private sellers often find themselves in direct competition with the internet colossus for products and services, but Amazon holds all the cards. To protect its own reputation and maintain a satisfied customer base, Amazon's sellers' agreement and many rules stack the deck firmly in Amazon's favor.

In order to sell on Amazon.com, sellers must follow an exacting list of expectations that dictate how and when they interact with their customers at every point in the sales process. Fail to meet Amazon's performance expectations and you could receive a not particularly cheerful "Hello from Amazon.com" letter notifying you that your account has been blocked and your sales listings terminated. And, by the way, Amazon will be hanging onto your money for the next 90 days to cover any unresolved financial issues.

For businesses that rely on Amazon.com as a primary conduit to customers and order fulfillment, receiving one of Amazon's computer-generated "Hello" letters can spell disaster. A big part of the problem is that the letters are computer-generated. Computer algorithms don't care if you didn't respond to a customer within the required 24 hours because you were hospitalized or on vacation. They're completely unsympathetic that your approval rating appears to be in the toilet not because you provide poor service but because the only customers who have bothered to offer feedback are dissatisfied ones.

Many Amazon.com sellers complain that they've been unfairly booted off Amazon because they've fallen victim to the "law of negative averages" in which a small number of negative comments can, if they outnumber positive feedback, result in a negative feedback score. For example, if out of 50 sales, 47 customers are satisfied, but only 1 post positive feedback while 2 dissatisfied customers post negative comments, Amazon's trackers will record a negative average and you'll soon be the recipient of a letter from alliance @ amazon.com, Amazon's enforcement department.

What sends sellers into a panic is the phrase "the closure of an account is a permanent action," implying that you will be forever banned from selling on Amazon. And the ban will not only affect you, but anyone Amazon's online trackers can connect to your name, street address or email address. All is not lost; however, sellers can petition Amazon for reinstatement and a number have done so successfully. The process is not easy; and, if reinstated, you can expect Amazon to scrutinize your account carefully for some time (and hang onto your money while they do so); but you can get back in the game.

1. Look carefully at the points made in the letter you receive from alliance @ amazon.com. Review your

consumer metrics to see if you're falling short of expectations.

2. Respond promptly via email, explain that you feel your suspension is unfair and rebut each charge with as much factual information as possible. Attach pertinent records or letters from consumers and offer your explanation of any negative feedback.

3. If you've failed to meet Amazon's performance targets, review your sales practices and provide an action plan to correct the problem.

4. Plead your case, emphasizing your sales and customer service record and pointing out how your product benefits consumers.

5. Monitor your email for Amazon's decision.

To prevent being terminated, keep a close eye on your email and regularly review Amazon's agreements and help pages as Amazon may change its procedures and guidelines at any time without notifying sellers. Monitor the customer metrics Amazon provides and compare your performance to the Amazon's seller performance targets to make certain you are hitting the expected benchmarks.

What Is Amazon's Choice?

So, you've received an email that one of your products have received an Amazon's Choice badge. What is it? How can it help your business?

WHAT IS AMAZON'S CHOICE?

Amazon's Choice is a feature that helps people save time and effort when looking for common, everyday items. Initially meant for Alexa-enabled devices like the Amazon Echo and the Echo dot, this feature has now paved its way to the website and the Amazon app.

The Amazon's Choice badge is a recognition given to select products that meet a certain criteria. The criteria are a closely guarded secret; however, judging from products that received the badge - highly rated products and well-priced ones with Prime Shipping are the ones usually selected.

Amazon's Choice vs Best Sellers

Amazon's Choice is mainly a suggestion for customers buying a product for a specific query for the first time. So, if you have looked for pet seat cover for the first time, this would be on top of the list. When you asked Alexa for a car seat cover for the first time, Alexa will suggest products with the badge first.

Best Sellers on the other hand, are rated by the volume of sales of the product (while taking into account the historical data), relative to other products in the category. The rank is based on sales, not reviews nor ratings. So, unlike Amazon's Choice you may find that some Best Sellers have low review ratings.

How to Get the Amazon's Choice Badge?

To receive such recognition, the seller must have an Amazon Prime, has received positive ratings from the clients and provide excellent service (mainly focused on fast delivery). These factors may or may not be the reason products get picked as we know that the reason a product is chosen is a closely guarded secret, but nothing changes if you try to improve on these criteria.

The badge cannot be bought like an advertisement would nor can it be suggested. There isn't any means to suggest your product to Amazon for suitability.

CHAPTER 21
WHAT ENCOURAGES PEOPLE TO BUY ON AMAZON?

Every seller who is having problems on Amazon wants to know the answer to this question. After all, if you make out how to stimulate people to buy your products on Amazon, then you should have no trouble boosting your sales, which is the leading goal. The golden rule is to offer people what they need, because that is what they will pay out for.

In case, if you have a product or service to sell, you are advised to present it to your potential customers as something they wish for. You should spotlight on the benefits of your products and make them feel like it is something they without doubt should have. Make them think like they can't live without your product.

Most individuals make a purchase on Amazon, because they get happiness from their purchase. Amazon platform offers the most convenient and easier online shopping experience in comparison to other e-commerce sites. While it is the most important factor, many other triggers can motivate them to whisk out their wallets. For example, if you can connect your product to consumers in a way that can facilitate them save more time, have comfortable experience, and increases their enjoyment.

As a seller on Amazon, you should take advantage of the opportunities that will benefit them in an optimistic way.

Only then you can encourage them to take suitable action. Once you realize what they would like, present your product or service in such a manner that makes them consider like they can't live without it. Consequently, you should have no problem in boosting your sales on Amazon.

VIRTUAL ASSISTANTS SHARE 6 BEST TIPS ABOUT AMAZON SELLING TACTICS

Amazon is a very large online platform, to do your business. To become successful, follow some tactics of selling in Amazon and make excellent profits. Virtual Office Assistants share few selling tactics that are easy to use and highly effective. These tactics will quickly increase your sales volume and profit, without increasing your expenses.

Sell your product in Bulk:

Increase your sales by combining 2 or more related products into a special combination package. Price them with a cost that should be low when compared to the cost of buying them separately. Promote it as a special offer. Another tip you can add with this is selling them for relatively low value with the warning comment that such an offer will never happen again. For example, you're selling a product for $50, normally. Create a onetime offer that will cut the price in half and offer this for certain period.

This would create a sense of panic on anyone who would get to know about your offer. The result would be a huge rush to purchase your item! At times this would initiate a fire sale.

Listing should be simple and informative:

Include your listing description in such a way that it should be simple and informative. Avoiding using exaggerated phrases during listing; this would make your prospective customers not to believe, even if it is true. One tip you can include, while listing is to state the numbers with fractions or decimals than converting to whole number.

Emphasis your product's price in a positive way:

Make sure that the cost you include for your product or service should not distract your customers though it is comparatively high. For example, "600 Rs per year" frightens many customers away. Instead present it as "Enjoy all of this for less than 50 Rs a Month" which attracts them to the low cost.

Use a Simple Buying Procedure:

Increase your sales by making your products or services to be easily available to your customers. It is because the method of ordering should be easy and convenient for everyone to buy. Potential customers will always like to buy your products only if the method of ordering is easy and suitable for them.

Make simple buying procedures and also ensure that you have more methods of buying. Offering choices of

HOW to buy increases your sales. Use simple order form instead of shopping carts when customers come for few items.

Expose yourself in the public:

Potential customer's like to buy a product or service from familiar and trustworthy sellers. Expose yourself in such a way let your prospective customers reach you.

Publicize your real name and personal contact information. Include your name, address and phone number and professional pictures on everything you use to promote business, like including it in your web pages and email messages. Also make sure that you are there to solve their problems whenever they face with your products or services.

Reply customer enquiries promptly:

Replying to customer's inquiries and questions will surely expand your sales. If you think it's vague to answer a lot of questions, then post the answers to your most FAq on a questions and Answers page at your web site. This would help in establish healthy relationship between you and customers, which in turn leads to profitable business.

CHAPTER 22
TOP 3 SECRETS TO CONVERT YOUR NEW CUSTOMERS TO REPEAT CUSTOMERS ON AMAZON

Amazon is one of the largest online platforms. To lead an endless successful business, you as a business maker should make your existing customers happy, so they become loyal repeat clients.

Here are some few strategies that our Professional Virtual Experts shares to make of your new customers a repeat customers on Amazon.

1. Follow up your client with more offers:

This is one of the best strategies of retaining the existing customers. Clients are very interested to more offers immediately after they buy from you. Offer them another item or service related to the one they just bought. Many will accept your offer, producing a smooth sale for you. If you don't already have additional products or services, try to find or create something for them.

By offering them additional offers thereby motivating them to become repeat customers, you are one step forward in becoming a successful and smart seller.

2. Encourage your customers with prompt replies:

Make sure that you reply to your customer's queries and issues quickly. Ensure them that you are there to solve their issues at any point of time. This will build a healthy relationship between you and your prospective customers.

For repeated multiple questions use FAq in your website. This will build confidence in your products and services there by increasing your sales.

3. Welcome issues from discontented customers:

Do remember that customers are the backbone of your business. Whenever they come for your products or services ask them to give a feedback on the same, so that it may focus you as a trustworthy seller in the public. Obviously, this would gradually increase your sales.

Pay more attention on unhappy customers. Resolving their issues helps you to find a solution to a problem to improve your business. Just think how great it would be for businesses if you take care of your customers. This will make your prospective customers to advertise for you through word-of-mouth advertising which would precisely increase your sales.

6 TACTICS ON DISCOVERING THE AMAZON WEB SITE FOR YOUR WEB BUSINESS EXPANSION

The official website of Amazon.com, Inc. Became operational i.e. went online in 1995. In just under twenty years the site has become the biggest online dealer and retailer of almost every type of product or service and covers almost all categories you can think of. Whatever item you name it, they have it including products and services. This is not limited to consumer electronics, retail items, digital applications and contents, customized and branded labels, cloud computing, content production, donations and charities. Mind that Amazon started online retailing with books.

If you're thinking of launching your own start-up or want to take your existing business to the next level by going online, then Amazon's own success story will really work as a morale booster. It was once an innocuous start-up and now it is providing a platform to countless others to get started up. You too can join the bandwagon of those who have already used the amazon platform for promoting their business online and countless others who are registered online members of the Amazon online club. Take stock of the following six strategies on how best you can exploit the portal of Amazon for your business gains: -

1. Promote your products or services on Amazon.com: - Although Amazon is the largest online stocker of all sorts of products and services; it will stand you in good stead if you start with just a single product or service hitching on their 'sell on Amazon' plan. Thereafter, you can graduate to becoming a small merchant seller selling more than 10 items. You will be required to pay either a proportion or a flat amount per sale apart from a fixed fee every month. In return you'll get the benefit of using administrative, creative and technical tools to help increase your revenues.

2. Use the Amazon platform as an advertisement platform: - You can use the site for listing images of your product with lucid product details and' how to instructions. This mode of promotion is much cheaper than using the 'selling

on Amazon' program as you pay on pay-per-click (PPC) basis. Using the advertisement programs also involving furnishing minimum of details as far as your product or service is concerned. You at least don't have to keep uploading price lists, inventory lists and other details.

3. You can make your online store a sort of store within a large store: - Amazon offers you the opportunity of opening a 'webstore' if you are a greenhorn and hence inexperienced in online marketing. It's your own virtual store.

4. Use the fulfillment policy of Amazon to the hilt: -The best thing about promoting and selling through Amazon is that they undertake full responsibility of delivering your products safely to your customers, dealing with returns, and providing customer support.

5. Capitalize from Amazon's data storage and cloud computing services: - Apart from using Amazon's portal as an advertisement and selling platform you can make good use of web facilities for storing your files or valuable business data.

6. Use checkout by Amazon: - Irrespective of the online platform you're using to promote your products or services, you can always proffer 'checkout by Amazon' as a payment alternative to your customers.

CHAPTER 23
IS AMAZON KILLING SMALL ONLINE BUSINESSES?

Most people think of Amazon as an online bookstore, which manages to be both true and incredibly incorrect at the same time. Amazon started life as a bookstore, of course, one that could potentially sell you any book ever printed, but they've grown business even bigger than that.

They are an incredibly powerful retailer with a highly refined sales funnel, and it might seem impossible for a small online commerce to compete with that level of name recognition and money.

The sad truth is that for too many online businesses, Amazon will eventually kill them, if it hasn't already. Small independent book sellers, for example were some of the first retailers to embrace going online. It was hard to find out of print and rare books, so there was a prepared group of bibliophiles ready and waiting, and for a couple of years the online booksellers did well.

Until Amazon steam rollered over the top of them, using its massive economy of scale to offer both a bigger selection and better prices. There are still online booksellers out there, but the vast majority succumbed to the Amazon huge force.

Something similar has happened to online music stores and online DVD retailers as Amazon has continued to expand the range of products they offer.

But in spite of that, there are more small online businesses than ever before. The world of online commerce is more refined and more vibrant than ever before, even with some powerhouse sites taking a huge chunk of the market share.

So how do you save your online business from becoming a victim of Amazon's seemingly unstoppable growth? There are two ways that you can carve out your own unique spot on the Internet; you can do it through having a laser focus on a very specific niche, or you can do it through personality. Or you can combine the best of both worlds and use both.

Amazon does many things well, but it is still fundamentally a giant corporation, and that means it can't even begin to have the same kind of one on one interaction that a small online business can have. If you make friends with your customers, they will stick with you and even pay a premium to do business with you. Personality is something that no corporation can beat you at.

FINDING AMAZON KINDLE ACCESSORIES THAT PROTECT YOUR KINDLE

When you get an Amazon Kindle, you will want to purchase accessories with it and if you know someone who owns an Amazon Kindle an accessory would be a great gift. There are a lot of different ways to customize it. Customizing a Kindle adds personality, color, and also protect it. The most common accessories are surely chargers, covers, and reading lights. The Amazon Kindle accessories come in all colors, shapes, and sizes and prices.

Finding the perfect Kindle cover for a particular person can seem easy but very easily becomes a meticulous task, contrary to what you might have first believed. The Amazon Kindle has become very popular amongst book lovers. When looking for the best Amazon Kindle cover for yourself or someone else you should look at how well it protects the device, your preference, and personality.

Accessories are available from various online sellers on the internet. When choosing the best skin for yourself or someone else you should check the reviews and ratings for durability and quality of the particular product that you are looking at. Since cases and covers are protecting it the durability is key to a good cover, and the quality plays into saving your Amazon kindle if it is dropped. There are various kindle covers flooding the market giving you sophisticated, elegant, dark colored, pink colored and leather look. You can also find added protection for the Kindle with a magnetic snap closure to protect the front and back of the kindle. The covers also are designed to give you access to the different ports and switches on the device.

TIPS TO PROFITABLY SELL USED MEDIA ON AMAZON

When most people believe of selling online many times they automatically think EBAY While eBay remains the largest online auction marketplace their main competitor which is Amazon is also an excellent place to sell merchandise of any kind This is especially if you are selling any kind of used media such as books, music and movies, DVD, vcr. Here are some important things you need to know to successfully make a money selling on amazon.

1. Since people who buy from amazon are generally looking for the best deal it is important to be able to compete to offer the lowest price or at least be very near the bottom. That means you will need to acquire items very cheaply.

2. The best places to find used media for very low prices that you can sell on amazon are thrift shops and garage sales.

3. If you are scouting for books you will need to be picky on what you purchase. The kind of books that do well on amazon are specific topical. Examples of good topics that do well are business and finance.

4. If you are scouting for music to sell your best bet is to stick to greatest hits or compilations.

5. Another area that is important to cut costs in is with your shipping supplies. Since your profit margin on the actual product sometimes is low you can make up for that by earning a profit on shipping. Amazon compensates you with a shipping credit. If you purchase your mailing and printing supplies at a discount wholesale store you should be able to make a profit spread between your shipping credit and your expenses.

6. If you sell more than 40 products a month upgrade to pro merchant. There is an additional 1-dollar fee on each product you sell that every pro merchant doesn't get charged so it saves a lot of cash for high volume sellers.

C0NCLUSION
HOW TO SHIP PRODUCTS TO AMAZONS

So, you've tracked your products, contacted suppliers and received samples you're happy with, and you're now ready to start trading them to your potential clients. Since this is your first time with Amazon FBA, you're all excited and electrified until you realize and asked yourself, how will you actually supposed to do it.

How exactly do you ship your items to Amazon in the first place? What are the steps involved in getting this step done?

Before we jump to the steps, its essential to note there are two ways to do this. You can either ship the product straight from China to Amazon or ship the product to yourself or to a US-based intermediate (presuming you're selling to the US), then send it to Amazon's warehouses.

The difference lies in communication and familiarity with Amazon's requirements. If you're shipping from China, you need to instruct your suppliers to prepare the product according to Amazon specifications. You see, Amazon can reject your package if it doesn't comply with their standards. Though suppliers are usually familiar with the process, there's always the chance of miscommunication or incorrect labelling.

Sending the goods to yourself or to a US-based middleman may put you in a safer position because there's likely clearer communication, knowledge of the process, and a quality inspection before they are sent to Amazon.

Now that we've got that out of the way, below are the steps you need to take to ship your product to Amazon:

1. Prepare your shipping plan

The first step is to get all the details ready for the incoming inventory order you will be raising in Seller Central. You'll need the following information to build an incoming inventory order:

Number of Units and Cases – There are two things you need to remember. First, Amazon has a limit of 150 units per case and that boxes over 50lbs need to be marked "team lift." As long as you follow these conditions, your shipment should be okay.

Universal Product Code (UPC) – new products require a UPC which you can buy and send to Amazon as a way of telling them that you'd be introducing new products to the market.

Who does the packing and preparation? – For this part, it will be better to have your supplier's handle the preparation. With Amazon's popularity, it's rare for these suppliers not to know the processes and guidelines for shipping products to Amazon FBA.

The only thing you have to make sure is that suppliers understand Amazon's fulfilment center guidelines specific to the goods you are sending (loose products, products with expiration, etc.)

Are you going to use Amazon's FBA Label service? – Each product you ship to Amazon requires a scannable barcode for storage and fulfilment purposes.

Who's your shipping partner? – You have 2 options to choose from if you are to use a local shipping partner. You either use one of Amazon's partner carriers who will provide you the tracking numbers and barcodes (UPS recommended), or any other carrier. Just take note of the tracking number and give them to Amazon.

Weight and Size of order – You'll need to provide Amazon with details about the weight and dimension of the product you're sending. Just make sure to specify weight in pounds and dimension in inches. If your supplier will be the one sending the goods, you have to get this information from them.

Location you are shipping your products from – For the last part, you just need to give the location where the shipment will be coming from along with the tracking number associated with it.

With a couple of fulfilment centers in each marketplace, it is worth noting that Amazon may require you to divide your products into a couple of shipments so they can send them to different warehouses. The reason is simply because the delivery will be much faster if the product is spread across different locations.

Inventory placement Service

Remember what we said earlier about how Amazon distributes your items across multiple locations? Well, you can now send all of them to just one fulfilment center (though you don't get to pick the one you want) via Amazon's new service called the Inventory Placement Service.

This option isn't really something I would advise for first timers but certainly it does offer some advantages. One of these actual advantages is that you'll be doing your customers a favor, especially those who order in bulk because they'd be receiving your items in one shipment instead of separate ones.

This will also help reduce the likelihood of errors like putting on the wrong shipping labels or sending to the wrong fulfilment centers in the case of sending your inventory to many fulfilment centers.

It's also worth knowing that the feature will cost you $0.30 for each standard size unit and $1.30 for each oversized unit.

Make use of Freight Forwarders

While Amazon allows the sending of inventory from an International Supplier directly to their fulfilment centers, it's important to know that they won't take any responsibility for the shipment should something unexpected happens therefore you need to talk to your suppliers to make sure that everything goes smoothly.

Your best option is to use a freight forwarding company for the reason that, apart from taking care of your shipments and sending them to Amazon, they will also take responsibility of the customs issues and be your onsite quality assurance checker, making sure that everything's in place on your behalf.

DROPSHIPPING SHOPIFY

E-COMMERCE 2019:

$10,000/Month business blueprint – A Step by Step Guide on How to Make Money Online with SEO, Social Media Marketing, Blogging and instagram

By:

Blake Davis

Table of Contents

INTRODUCTION

The whole spectrum of doing business has undergone a huge change in the last few years. One of the latest online business ideas is dropship services. This online business involves a process in which companies or suppliers deliver the products directly to the customers of the dropship business without the business having to purchase first or stock the goods. The best part of the bargain is that the business owner, or reseller, does not have to invent, design, buy, make the product, test the market, describing the product on the website, making the website attractive, or promoting the product.

The dropship services business owner has just to do a list of the products on eBay and get orders for the products by using its own or the supplying company's descriptions and graphics. When the orders are received the reseller gather the information regarding the buyers' and other details of the order, so that the supplier can send the products and the company will also collect payments.

The business of dropship services can obtain returns for the business owner and it's necessary to take care of all complaints and issues to build a good customer service.
Any negligence in providing necessary after-sales services and attending to complaints can tarnish the image of the company and lead to loss of income and future orders. In order to find an answer to how to dropship and how to start a dropshipping business, it is important to select a reliable supplier. The wrong selection can have disastrous results.

What is Dropshipping?

Drop shipping definition: a fulfillment model that allows you to buy products individually from a wholesaler and ship them directly to your customer.

Instead of purchasing a large amount of inventory, you simply partner with a drop shipping supplier and list their merchandise for sale. Then, once you receive an order you forward it to the supplier for fulfillment. The supplier will ship the product directly from their warehouse to your customer, and charge you only for the price of the shipped item.

How DropShipping Works:

No matter where you plan to sell products online (eBay, Amazon or even open your own online store) if you are starting a business selling products from home then you probably don't want to carry much, if any, inventory. Most people who are starting their first online business via auctions or online stores don't have a lot of money to buy a bunch of products or the space to warehouse and store the products they want to sell online. This is where working with a real Dropshipper will save you a ton of money.

A real Dropshipper is simply a Certified Wholesaler who offers dropshipping. Not all wholesalers offer dropshipping. In fact, it's quite difficult to find genuine certified Wholesalers who will dropship and work with online sellers.

For online sellers, working with a Dropshipper is pretty easy. You find the Dropshipper you want to work with (the one who has the products you want to sell.) They will then give you access to their product images so that you can post them on your website, auction, blog or however you plan to sell online. When a customer orders the product, you then order the product from the Wholesaler and they ship it to your customer.

Using a certified Wholesaler that dropships is a low-cost solution for people who work from home, don't have money to spend on inventory and want to sell products online. Drop shipping does work and it works very well but you do have to be careful with a few things.

You can't just sell any product you want and expect to be able to compete with drop shipping. When you have a product dropshipped, you are buying and selling 1 product at a time. That means your wholesale price is for 1 product when you have it dropshipped. Wholesalers always give discounts to retailers when they purchase in bulk. That means your wholesale price for 1 product (drop shipped) can be higher than a competitor who is buying in volume from the wholesaler...which means they can sell that product much cheaper than you can, and in some cases, even cheaper than your large scale cost!

So how can dropshipping work?

Easy. You have to pick the *right* products to sell; the right kinds of products to dropship. You can't assume that just because you might think a product is a 'good idea to sell' that you should jump in and start selling it, especially with dropshipping. Doing a little bit of market research before you start selling is critically important. You have to find the products you can have dropshipped that you can compete with in the current online market. But by doing a little bit of research first, you can be very successful with dropshipping!

Pro and Cons of Dropshipping

Pro of Dropshipping?

The drop shipping model has a number of advantages:

Reduced Risk

Without thousands invested in inventory, the risk involved with starting an online store is dramatically reduced. If things don't work out, you aren't stuck with thousands in inventory you have to sell at a loss.

Wider Product Selection

When you don't have to pre-purchase all the items you sell, you can offer a significantly larger number of products to your customers.

Highly Scalable

Because you don't need to manually fulfill each order, it's relatively easy to scale a drop shipping business.

Location Independence

Because you don't have to worry about fulfillment or running a warehouse, it's possible to run a drop shipping business from anywhere with a laptop and an internet connection.

Lower Capital Requirement

With drop shipping, you don't need to invest thousands of dollars in inventory. Instead, you only purchase a product when you have an existing order to fill.

Cons of Dropshipping?

Here are some cons of dropshipping

No control over supply-chain.

In standard ecommerce, if customers complain about product quality, fulfillment speed, or return policies, you can address the problems yourself.

In dropshipping, you're more or less at the mercy of your supplier — but you're the one who still has to talk to your customers directly.

Dropshippers are essentially trapped, doing little more than hoping the supplier addresses the problems while simultaneously reassuring the customer about something that's out of their control.

On top of that, there's also a delay in communication as the dropshipper goes back-and-forth between the customer and the supplier. If one answers slowly, all communication grinds to a halt and the problems take longer to fix.

Lower Barriers to Entry

Because you don't need capital or a warehouse more people dropship which increases competition.

Legal liability issues.

Although this isn't a common problem for dropshippers, it's worth mentioning. Some suppliers aren't as legitimate as they claim, and you don't always know where the merchandise comes from.

Even more deceptive is when suppliers illegally use a trademarked logo or another company's intellectual property, which happens more than average.

Whatever illegal activities your suppliers are up to, as their vendor you're automatically complicit.

This potential problem can be rectified with a solid Dropshipping Agreement Contract, but not every dropshipping upstart knows that.

It's something you'll want to keep in mind when choosing suppliers.

Lower Margins

Because there's more competition margins for drop shipping businesses are usually lower. This makes it harder to grow early on because you can't afford to advertise as much to acquire a customer.

Highly competitive.

There will always be overly optimistic entrepreneurs who focus solely on the "low overhead" part, ignoring the clear evidence above.

Because very little capital is required to start a dropshipping business, that low barrier to entry means a lot of competition, with the most popular markets suffering more than others.

Basically, the bigger a company is, the more they can reduce their markups to offer the lowest prices.

To make matters worse, chances are you don't have an exclusive deal with your suppliers.

That means any number of competitors could be selling your exact same products. And if you're just starting out, your rivals with years of experience have the resources you don't to undercut your prices.

That means customers can buy the exact same thing from someone else for cheaper — why would they buy from you?

Things to consider before starting Dropshipping business

In order to find an answer to how to dropship and how to start a dropshipping business, it is vital to select a reliable supplier. The wrong selection can have disastrous results. Follow the following steps before starting this type of business.

Unreasonable Subscription Fees

As a reseller, the dropship services business has to pay registration fees and in some cases ongoing subscription charges to access the supplier's catalogue, although for a limited time is normally allowed before registration. Fine print should also be checked well for any between-the-lines clauses.

Select Recommended Suppliers

The first step to start a dropship services business is that the procurement of the suppliers should be done with great care. Simply select the suppliers recommended by other people. It is possible to get lists of dropshipping companies on Internet directory sites. But be careful as some may give accurate information whereas others mightn't .

Beware of wholesaler sisguised as suppliers

Check whether the potential supplier holds enough stock of the products and they are not a wholesaler posing as a supplier. These may place orders with the real supplier and recieve orders from the reseller and, in this process, long delays can take place. These delays can result in losses to both the customer and reseller .

Check Business Terms

In case of disputes with the supplier regarding faulty or undelivered goods business terms and conditions of the supplier should be properly stated .Also figure out that the responsibilities of the business as a reseller are different than the responsibilities that the supplier would have toward the reseller.

Look for Web Reviews

After short listing a few suppliers, it would be helpful to seek out reviews and comments regarding the companies on the web from other dropship resellers. However that could be difficult as nobody wants other to know of any bad reviews.

Payment methods

Find out how the supplier prefers to receive payments as the most convenient mode would be the same by used by the customer to pay the reseller. This will save charges and time. It is also advisable to avoid having to pay by Wire Transfer or Telegraph Transfer because the risk is higher if there is no customer protection.

Beware of fake goods

While choosing a supplier, avoid those sites that offer branded goods in "to good to be true" low prices. Designer good are usually bound to be fake unless the supplier is trustworthy and acclaimed or if the goods are refurbished or Grade A returns. If the reseller sells fake goods, he can also be accused of selling counterfeits.

Check the Contact Details

Once a selection is made based on reliable recommendations, and after checking that the range of products that the business intends to deal with are sold by the supplier, check the contact details.Pertinent contact information such as phone number, email address, and a mailing address should be available on the supplier's website. Avoid any supplier with incorrect or with no contact information at all. Make sure that there is always a good communication with supplier as it may become handy later.

Team up with artists and showmen/ women

Teaming up with artists for their creative products is a unique way to do dropship services business. These creative people usually lack marketing savvy. Visits to local markets and fairs can provide unlimited opportunities to get creative items at good prices. The dropship business doesn't really need these items, but an arrangement could be worked out for working on commission. They will likely be happy to take payments and deliver the products to the buyer of the dropship business when a sale is made.

Reasons Why You Should Start Dropshipping

Do you want to start a drop shipping business? If you're still wavering back-and-forth, this book will help convince you why you should—along with the most important practices to ensure you can scale your business while keeping unnecessary stress at bay.

Successful Drop shippers

Some drop shippers have been very succefull:

Here are some notable ones:

- Irwin Dominguez grew his dropshipping business from $0 - $1m in under 8 months
- Aloysius Chay and Galvin Bay once sold up to $60k in a single day
- Justin Wong made $11,793.97 in one month and a host of other regular people making profits from this business model.

No doubt, some entrepreneurs are running at a loss, closing down or selling their dropshipping businesses, but those who know and follow the right strategies are succeeding.

Ability to Work From Anywhere

A dropshipper can operate from California, ship from suppliers in China and deliver to customers in Nigeria without moving an inch, just by moving computer mouse.

If you love an independent lifestyle, then drop shipping should be on your to-do list.

Now you can travel the world like you've always wanted to visit Everest, come down to Africa or visit your Grandma in Scandinavia.

The best part is that your business travels with you wherever you go plus you can discover new in-demand products you should be selling on one of your trips abroad.

Work From Home

This must be the best reason for having a drop shipping business. You can manage and run your business from your own home. There is no need to rent an office and commute to work everyday. You can put in as much or as little time as you want to your business, and your time is flexible.

Plenty of Options to Choose From

In all essential aspects of drop shipping there are plenty of options to choose from platform to suppliers to products

There are also so many niches to pick from. Whether you're interested in maternity, babies, toys or automobiles, there's something for everyone.

This means you have room to reasonably experiment with options new to you, as long as they're viable and have potential based on your research findings.

Low Startup Cost

How much do I need to start dropshipping is one of the popular questions one will ask.

According to reports, 82% of businesses fail due to cashflow issues. Another major challenge entrepreneurs face is startup funding, but with dropshipping, this barrier is either removed or greatly lowered.

Here are basic things you need to start:

- Platform e.g. Shopify (including domain name, hosting)
- PC or Smartphone
- Internet Connection
- Automation Apps
- Wholesale Suppliers Directory

These are some of the essential things you need to start dropshipping ecommerce business.

Low Running Cost

Drop shipping can be done from home in your PJs, from your smartphone, tablet or PC; you save on office rent.

Except you're growing fast and ready to scale you may not need to hire support staff just yet; you save on HR, staff salaries, retirement plan, and staff disputes.

Most of the ICT infrastructure you need like PC and

internet connection you probably already have and it will further lower your startup cost.

With Shopify for instance, you save on e-commerce website design and programming to get yours business running.

These and more to keep your overhead down so you can invest your funds where it matters more.

Focus on promoting your site.

The traditional way of selling involves buying stocks in bulk at wholesale prices and selling them at retail prices. Storing your products, packing and shipping them to customers involves a lot of work. This is now all done by the drop shipper. You will have plenty of time to work on advertising and promoting your selling site in order to attract more customers.

Zero Need for Stock/Inventory

One of the major investments in running a retail business is buying stock and keeping inventory.

Usually smaller retailers seek out loans or other sources of funding to finance this aspect of their business.

With drop shipping, on the other hand, all you need is the product image on your website. Stock images can replace actual stock, isn't that cool?

And since you don't own physical stock, you can't invent inventory either.

In any case, apps help to update your virtual stock and inventory.

It Sets You Up For Scale.

Most importantly, in order to truly run a successful business, you need to prioritize the important things. Getting your store up-and-running, while manageable, does take hard work, so it's important to try to automate tasks like adding products to your store, and to get rid of unnecessary to-do's, like fulfilling and shipping your own orders. With drop shipping especially, having the ability to delegate allows you to focus on what's most important: marketing your store, talking to your customers, and strategizing how to scale your business.

Wide Variety Of Products.

Just imagine a store where you can sell all sorts of products. If you had a storefront, you would need thousands of dollars to pay for stocks to display on your shelves. With dropshipping, you do not have to spend a single cent to be able to sell a wide selection of products. Drop shipping eliminates the risk of buying stocks that you may not be able to sell later. SaleHoo drop shippers can offer you a wide variety of products to dropship at no risk.

You're The Boss

Not only , you are the boss, you equally don't have to share space or cubicle with nosy or noisy coworkers.

Being the boss of your business means you're totally responsible for outcomes, which will require your best input.

Similarly, all the risks and rewards are yours to bear. It is both exciting and daunting to be a sole entrepreneur, but the benefits of running a successful drop shipping e-commerce business outweigh any drawbacks.

Who Needs a Warehouse?

Yeah, who needs a warehouse when your supplier already has one or more?

Storage is a major issue for small retailers but not dropshippers.

See some of what dropshipping saves you:

- Warehouse rentage
- Warehouse management software
- Insurance
- Warehouse staff salaries
- Cooling and other temperature control measures, etc.

Now you can run your business in space with zero worries about storage space.

Dropshipping Let's You Be Mobile.

Now, all you need is an Internet connection to run your store from anywhere! Not only is this a nice perk, but it allows you to work on-the-fly, especially when small emergencies or big orders come in when you're far from home.

Ability to Automate

Automation makes dropshipping even easier than you can imagine. Usually, product importation into your Shopify store, for instance, can be a real hassle if done manually.

Apps like Oberlo and others help you completely automate your entire dropshipping business so you can focus on the marketing.

With automation, costly avoidable errors like inventory or pricing mistakes can be prevented, you save time, money and improve efficiency.

There are also a host of other apps and plugins in the Shopify store that extends the functionalities of your e-store.

Start with your big WHY: A Success Mindset of Dropshipping

You often read all the good sides associated with dropshipping. Almost all are guaranteed success type of websites. They often sell dropshipping directories and related services but the problem is they do not show the real score behind the other kind of the coin.

Low Customer Loyalty

As a dropshipper naturally your prices as higher that your supplier. If your customers would know where to go, they can easily stop doing business with you and buy the same price from your supplier. Once your buyer is planning to order the same product again and in much higher quantity, it is more likely that they will order directly from the source. With the technology nowadays, there is a great chance that they will do their research and locate your supplier. This will cut you out from the scene.

Even if this happens to you, you should build loyalty with your customers.. As a dropshippers, you have no hold on the product. The product has no physical presence therefore you have to work hard to build the identity of your product and repeat-customer business.

Online Factors

Since most dropship sellers will be running the business through the internet, they are exposed to some risks . These includes copying of the content of your website without your authorization, increase in your advertising cost, increase competition from businesses that are larger than your business and unpredictable customer traffic if you are relying on search engines.

If your business is online, you will have a hard time in succeeding if you are a beginner of the web.

How to start Dropshipping

When you run a drop shipping business, you sell goods without buying them first. Instead, you contract with a supplier who will send the goods directly to your customer. Because a drop shipping business has no overhead, you can usually run one out of your home or office.

Choosing a Dropshipping Niche

A niche is a portion of the market as for example, "Bluetooth speakers" are a popular niche in the home audio market. You get the idea. The more specific your niche is, the better.

Choosing a niche is the first step to start a drop shipping business. The rising popularity of drop shipping means it's becoming harder to find niches that aren't already largely used . But new products and niches are emerging every week, so the opportunities are almost endless.

A common misconception about dropshipping is that you can be successful and profitable in any niche, but that is not always the case . If you choose a niche that's already saturated with sellers or dominated by major brands, you're going to face an uphill battle with your new business.

Here are a few guidelines and advises to help you choose a drop shipping niche that will make you money online:

Start with your interests and passions: Tap into your hobbies and interests. If you enjoy travel or hiking in the outdoors, you're going to have unique knowledge of the products and trends in those markets that can help you identify a viable niche.

- *Scratch your own itch:* The theory is, if you have a problem in your life then it's highly likely that others will have the same problem. If you can identify a product that solves that specific problem, you might have uncovered a great drop shipping niche.

- *Research the competition*: Is the niche you're interested in already largely used ? If so is there any competition? Better yet, is it worth to outpace it? You'll often find that the niche you're most interested in joining is the one that nearly everyone is already a part of, just be ready for some competition.

- *Ensure the niche is profitable:* The objective of business is to make money, right? Therefore, you need to check the profitability of every dropshipping niche and product idea that you come up with. Ideally, you want a profit margin of at least 40% after shipping costs, seller fees and taxes, but you should be aiming for margins of 100% or more.

Dropshipping Products that Work Well on Amazon and eBay

While it's possible to dropship everything from toothpicks to the kitchen sink, some products are more suitable for dropshipping than others.

The perfect dropshipping product is generally:

- Non-seasonal: Ideally, when you're starting out you want to avoid products that are only in demand for one particular season a year. For example, selling something you'd only use at the beach during summer or Christmas decorations really limits your selling power during the off-season. Choose drop-shipping products that are in demand all year round.

- Retails for between $15 and $200: This price range is known as the e-Commerce "sweet spot". Anything cheaper than $15 and you're not going to be making much of a profit margin and anything over $200 is going to be difficult to sell en large. While there are plenty of exceptions to this rule, following it will make your dropshipping journey easier to begin with.

- Not dominated by major brands: What's the first company that comes to mind when you think of the word 'smartphone'? Probably Apple or Samsung These major brands have the smartphone market on lockdown and it's going to be tough for any business to compete for a slice of that pie. A good drop shipping product isn't dominated by a major brand so that you can have a greater chance of capturing a chunk of the market.

- Small and lightweight: The general rule is that a good drop shipping product should be able to fit inside a shoebox and weigh less than 2kg (4.4lb), the weight limit for e-Packet. This is to save you paying extra for shipping.

Brainstorm Business Ideas

Now that you know the criteria for a good drop-shipping niche, you can start selecting product ideas for your e-Commerce business.

You should aim to analyze between 10 to 20 products ideas and then use the guidelines above to either qualify or eliminate them from your list.

Once you're done with that process, you might only have a few product ideas that are worthed to explore further.
If you have at least one solid product idea at this stage, you're ready to progress to the next level.

Use Google Trends And Google Research

Google Trends is great for knowing whether a niche is on an upward or downward trend.

This handy app proves the popularity of any given search term, suggests related keywords, and shows a keyword phrase's performance by location.
Some features:

Interest Over Time

You can graph searches by time and easily customize a timeframe, from years to minutes.

Interest By Region

Comparison of where searches originate from. Geographic areas are organized by proportion, so smaller countries may score higher than larger countries that technically produce more searches. The 0-100 score is relative compared to all searches globally.

Related Queries

"Users searching for your term also searched for these queries." A more specific variation of "related topics".

Top vs. Rising

This refers to the most popular related topics/queries of all time. "Rising" refers to the most recent increases.

Breakout

If Google Trends deems a topic or keyword "Breakout," it means it is currently receiving an "tremendous increase" in searches. These could be either a fly by night search or the early stages of a new trend, so be careful.

The practical benefits of Google Trends have made it a favorite tool of digital marketers, especially those whose budgets preclude paid SEO tools. It may seem off-putting if you don't know how to use it therefore we will give you some guidelines to follow.

How to Use Google Trends to Find Your Niche

Google Trends is easy to use, once you know what you're doing. Follow our three guidelines below to start using Google Trends like a professional.

Trial and Error

Much of Google Trends works by trial-and-error. You type in a search term, see how it performs, then type in another one and compare. You can repeat it until you find the right for you.

To start, you may want to make a list of potential search terms/product areas. These could be data-driven queries based on your own sales experience, or nothing more than a hunch. They could be products you're personally passionate about, or products you have overstocked. It's best to start with a full and open-ended list, and then narrow it down based on what you find.

Another tactic is to use the Related Topics and Related Queries features to see what the same users are also interested in. This is most effective when you already have an established customer base and want to offer them new products .Simply search for products you already know they like and check the "related" sections to see what else those same people are searching for.

The Two Things You're Looking For

You should also pay attention to the shape of the time

179

graphs. Namely, you're looking for two graph types that signify commercial viability:

Slow and Steady Growth.

These are your more stable niches, good for long-term strategies. The good news is that you can rely on a steady stream of business; the bad news is the competition grows with time .

Steep, Sudden Growth.

On the other end of the spectrum, you have products and topics that have suddenly become famous, perhaps because of a news event or PR stunt. If you act quickly, you can capitalize on the trend before other competitors latch onto it but it's hard to know for how long.

Finding a Niche with Google Search Tools

First of all, you will need to go the Google keyword tool and then click on the "Searched-based Keyword Tool" tab, see the image below:

The Search-based keyword tool is a free tool that is supposed to be used to enter your website into, and Google will provide some more related keywords for you to bid on in AdWords. However you can also use this tool to find untapped niches that you can market in as an affiliate, either using PPC or SEO. All I can say is that this sort of market intelligence is absolutely priceless yet free.

When you open the tool, you will then want to scroll to the bottom of the page and click the link that says: "or see top keywords across all categories"

Then you will be taken to where you can browse categories of potential niches

You will notice that Google has kindly categorized niches for us, and when you open one up, by clicking on it, you can then drill down further and see more sub niches inside these larger ones.

This is some extremely valuable data for us as marketers, because Google are telling us what the hottest niches are and they also show you, on the right, what people are spending money on these keywords, which is a healthy sign.

Now that you have a complete list of potential niches, that we know people are searching in, all we need to do then is go back to the Google Keyword tool and type some of these phrases in, and see what the results are.

What you then need to do is work out how competitive that phrase would be if you were going to build a simple website to promote it. You can do this by typing that phrase into Google itself in quotes and seeing how many competing pages there are.

How competitive is too competitive? Well that depends on your SEO skills, however as a rough guide if there is more 50,000 competiting pages when you type the word in quotes into Google, them maybe try another one.

Of course judging competition on the amount of competing pages alone, is not the greatest way to tell. Therefore you may also want to analyze the top 10 places in Google and in particular the top 5 and see what they are like.

Here is a quick checklist of what to look for: Page Rank, Back Links, Age of Domain, On Page SEO, and as a very rough guide, if you see a lot of authority sites like Amazon, and they are actually purposely trying to rank for that phrase, then that's not so good.

When I say purposely trying to rank, I mean they have that exact keyword phrase in their pages Title tags, H1 tags, and meta description. It is encouraging to be proactive and do a quick Google search and learn what these terms mean, as it is crucial to know these basics of SEO.

Once you have found a niche and some keywords that you feel you could target, you will then need to see if you can find an affiliate program that you can join to promote products in that niche. You can do this by typing the niche word + affiliate into Google, so for example: "GPS + affiliate", and searching this way. Or you can use the Amazon market place and simply place an Amazon widget on your site.

Use Google's Keyword Planner

What's the search volume for a keyword? If you're using the free version of the Keyword Planner you'll notice that you have big ranges which makes it difficult for you to know whether or not the keywords for your niche are worth pursuing. Ask a friend or your boss if they pay for Google Adwords to check out the competitiveness of your niche keywords. Using Google's Keyword Planner will help you understand the potential of your dropshipping business ideas.

Hunt Around On Social Media.

I've come up with dropshipping business ideas by doing competitor analysis. I'll browse Facebook ads within a niche and social media pages for top brands. How many followers do they have? How do they market their brand? How much engagement does their brand get? What can I do differently to stand out against them? What are they doing right that I should copy?

Browse Popular Websites Within Your Niche

For example, if you check out a fashion retailers website, they'll often organize their store into trend categories. This helps you understand what trends you should be adding to your store right now. You can also browse a store's best-selling products to help you find the best products to sell.

Check Out The Order Volume For Products

Inside of Oberlo, you can browse products based on their

order volume to help you understand how popular a product really is. Don't rule out dropshipping business ideas if they're not as high as other products, because those products could be newer.

The most profitable dropshipping business ideas aren't trends

Instead, they have trends within them. For example, denim apparel is a trend within the fashion niche. Artificial eyelashes is a trend within the beauty niche. Marble phone cases is a trend within the phone case niche. You'll want to have the trends as products but not as the entire store, especially if you're building a long-term business. So keep that in mind when you're working on your dropshipping business plan.

Select a profitable product

You probably don't have all the time in the world to experiment with figuring out which dropshipping products sell well and which don't. I hear you. It'd be ideal to already have some idea of which products sell well before using this business model.

For instance, you might want to know whether t-shirts sell better than toys. The answer is: It depends. It all depends on your niche, but there are certain product criteria you can keep in mind when considering which dropshipping products to sell to figure out if they will sell well or not within your niche.

THE BENEFITS OF DROPSHIPPING PRODUCTS

Though it started as a subset of retail, e-Commerce has grown into a burgeoning industry in its own right, and (as big as it is now), e-Commerce will only continue to grow. In fact, is expected to overtake physical retail sometime in the next few years.

But eCommerce hasn't been easy to get into. This has largely been due to the significant starting capital needed to establish an inventory and build infrastructure. As if on cue, drop shipping emerged, and offered a practical shortcut to e-Commerce success.

Dropshipping lets you focus on the customer-facing aspects of the online retail experience by deferring the more difficult aspects — like inventory management and order fulfillment — to your partners.

Because there is little upfront investment required, drop-shipping has become very competitive. In fact, many have been discouraged from drop-shipping by the fear of getting overshadowed by so many competitors. Then, can you be more competitive?

Choosing a niche, which involves picking the right products to dropship, is the key to being competitive as a dropshipping company. Here's how to do it.

HOW TO FOR FIND DROP SHIPPING PRODUCTS THAT SELL

Here are few steps.

Get the Right Profit Margin

Choose products that you can sell with a 30% or more profit margin. The more popular the products, the more likely you'll earn less because you'll have to keep your prices low to stay competitive. However, there are some products that allow you to make handsome profits, you just need to research more to find them and decide for yourself if the profit margin is worth it.

Find Popular Products

Popular products can be easy or hard to sell. A popular product on Amazon, eBay, and Etsy for instance, might not be that easy to market by a small retailer like you. Also, since popular products have too many competing sellers, it may leave you with a very slim profit margin. The trick is to find a popular product you can make unique to your own store in some way, and find a way to compete against other retailers based on price, selection, choice or availability. For example: T-shirts, children's toys and fashion products are all popular dropshipping products that sell well, but might be hard to compete against if you don't have a competitive edge.

Use Your Personal Experience

Consider choosing a product category that you have actual experience in using. This provides you with a competitive advantage because you can explain the technical aspects of the product and its various uses to prospective customers which will help you sell the product. For instance, if you're a professional drone operator, you can sell various types of drones online by teaching people how to use your products and help them choose the most appropriate type for them. Your experience will be the leverage that helps sell your products.

Online Marketplaces

When you've narrowed your choices down, or if you've otherwise decided to sell a particular product, you should check how they're performing in real time through online marketplaces.

At one point or another, most people who buy online have visited or bought from online marketplaces such as eBay and Amazon. Most online marketplaces are kind of cagey about publishing stats concerning transactional volume, but there are ways to find out.

A good resource for eBay sales stats would be the SaleHoo Market Research Lab. Members can search for specific products that get a good number of hits and find out how many people are selling them, how many sales there are, how easy the item is to sell, and what the average price is.

Immediately you have a snapshot of your chosen product's profit potential.

Find the Right Price Point

Recognize the best price points for each product category in your niche. For instance, a high-end t-shirt priced over $50 is acceptable but an everyday white T-shirt worn for lounging at home isn't. To find the most optimal price points, it takes some in-depth research.

Find Not-so-Popular Products within a Laser-Focused Niche

This type of product can be your cash cow. As long as you have access to the niche market, it might be the best type of product to sell. There are less-popular products out there and they're great products to sell because they're highly sought after by the consumers that want them. To find them, you'd need to observe and analyze niche markets on a deeper level. Some examples of not-so-popular dropshipping products that may sell well include: Bulletproof vests, paintball guns and diving equipment. These are highly-targeted products that some consumers want, but don't apply to all consumers.

Search Engines

The easiest way to find out what people are looking for is to use the keyword research tools that are available in the more popular search engines, usually for free if you register.

For example, Google has Keyword Planner, which is part of Google AdWords, and Yahoo has Bing Keyword Research. Some other free tools (usually requiring registration) that you may want to check out include:

- SEO Book
- Ubersuggest
- WordPot
- Wordtracker

You want keywords that get a lot of searches for obvious reasons, but these tools can also give you suggestions on related products that may also be getting a lot of hits.

For example, if you search for shoes, which is a very general keyword, keyword tools will suggest more specific items or a specific brand like "nyke". This can help you narrow your choices down.

Find A Supplier

It can be hard finding good dropship suppliers. In fact it is probably the first hard step in this business. There are many scams out there that will try and take money for outdated information and false information too.

Finding legitimate dropship suppliers can be a nightmare for new eBay sellers and site owners.It's hard to tell if a company is for real or just another fake. The good news is that it really pays to stick to it. Finding the right suppliers to work with , can be a lucrative part or full time business or add an additional revenue stream to your existing business.

Drop shipping as a way to make money on and off of eBay is not a new concept. People have been quietly using this strategy for years to build their own lucrative home based businesses. While drop shipping is still used today and continues to make money for people, the market is crowded. It means that now more than ever it is important to know if you are getting the best possible deal on the products you want to sell.

Outside of the condition of the products, there's still plenty of concerns about how your supplier conducts business.

Here's a quick-reference checklist of questions to ask yourself before signing on to do business with someone:

- How do they handle returns or damaged products?
- How long does it take them to fulfill an order, from sale to delivery?
- How is their customer support? (Feel free to test this yourself.)
- Do they insure orders?
- Do they offer fraud protection?
- Can you find reviews or references online?
- How long does it take them to ship after you've placed an order with them?
- What shipping methods do they offer? For example, ask if they ship overnight or internationally.
- Do they offer warranties on their products? If a product is defective, then you want them to replace it.

- What quality control systems do they use?
- Do they set minimum advertised prices? Ideally, they will. If not, then other drop shipping businesses could lower the prices too low for you to compete.
- Do they charge a monthly or annual fee? If so, then you might want to avoid them.
- Can you put their product photo on your website? Preferably, they will allow you to use their picture.

Note: Also don't forget the Dropshipping Agreement Contract

TIPS FOR FINDING SUPPLIER

Follow these tips so can avoid the back breaking work of find reputable dropship suppliers. It can and will make your life easier during this process of starting your business.

Test Customer Response Time

Before you settle on a drop shipper, you can test their response to make sure that they are available when you need them and answer emails in a timely manner. Find the contact information on their site and email or phone to ask a few questions.

Research The Company

Does the company appear credible? What do existing customers say? This doesn't mean that the company needs to have a sleek site, but they should have clearly visible contact information. A dropship supplier is someone you are considering a business relationship with so it's a good idea to do your due diligence. Another way to check out a potential supplier is to call or visit the BBB and you can check with them for any problems with the company.

Always Do A Test Sale

After you have signed up with a drop shipper, do a test sale to yourself before using their services . this way you will be able to see first hand how quickly the item arrives. You will also be able to make sure it was packed appropriately and arrived in good condition. Only after you are satisfied with what you find can you start using the supplier for auctions or your site.

Research Posted Prices

The first thing you should do when researching dropshippers is to have a look at their publicly posted price sheets to get a rough idea for your wholesale prices. Next, compare this with eBay sales and buy it now items. If these items are selling well at price that leaves room for a reasonable markup, you may have found a winner!

Products and Price

Just like any other business you need to check out their products they sell. Are they discontinued ones? Defect items? Used Items? Also see if their prices match other competitor prices and see if you can even make a profit on that item when you sell it on your dropshipping website or Ebay.

WHERE TO FIND RELIABLE SUPPLIERS

There are essentially two ways to find good dropship suppliers. You can either search online manually or use a wholesale directory like SaleHoo.

- Searching for suppliers online: You can simply type your product plus "supplier" into Google and see what comes up. Or you can search for your product on websites like Alibaba.com or Aliexpress.com. A lot of China-based suppliers use these websites to sell their items.
- Using a wholesale directory: This can save you plenty of time and help you avoid e-Commerce fraud. SaleHoo has more than 8000 suppliers that have been vetted and verified.

Chose the selling Platform

Nowadays except eBay there is a long list of other dropshipping website available on the internet where traffic of suppliers & buyers is increasing day by day. Some of these websites are even cheaper than eBay; you can select any preloaded website of your choice. The sites like Bonanzle.com, Ubid.com, Amazon.com and Wholesale2b.com also provide a large market with a wide range of different products.

Etsy

Etsy is said to have 54 million members, about 2 million active sellers, and about 32 million active buyers. It's extremely popular with women (84% of sellers are female).

Etsy has established itself as a more trendy online marketplace with a focus on arts, crafts, homeware but especially on handmade products.

Craigslist

You can sell almost anything on Craigslist (including yourself, in the "personals" section). There are no listing fees or selling fees, but it's super basic both in design and automation of the selling process.

It is, after all, just a forum.
Want to know exactly what you'll get with Craigslist that you haven't had with eBay? Here's the list:

- eBay charges to list and sell items; Craigslist only charges for a small post types, like job listings or vehicles. Products are free to list.
- eBay will get involved in disputes if necessary, while you're on your own with Craigslist.
- Craigslist requires you to sell locally, and often you arrange for pick-up or drop-off of items. This limits your market compared to eBay.
- Unlike eBay, Craigslist has a "free" section where people are trying to get rid os some items.
A lot of this will be junk, but you can keep an eye out for anything you could get and refurbish and sell .

Craigslist is best suited to sellers who are selling locally, and prefer to manage their transactions personally. It can be a good option for selling items also as furnitures that are too big to be shipped.

Some people may like as a sort of social element as they can actually meet the people they do transactions with. You can get cash-in-hand and you don't have to pay a network or shipping fees. If you instead are a little bit too careful and scared to be scammed it may not be suitable for you. Accepting cash in hands must done with care and be aware of potentially being given fake currency.

If you are good on fixing items or have a good eye for antique or can make up a lackluster then work your magic and sell your re-new items on Craiglist or other selling platform. This can be a hit-and-miss strategy, so be sure to only select items that you're confident you could sell for a profit. List items that will sell well locally, save on listing and shipping fees, and you could make a hefty profit margin without the effort

But If that's not your cup of tea consider only doing wholesale goods.

eBay

eBay is not technically includes in the platforms for drop shipping, since it's really an auction site. You can list fixed price products there, but you'll have to constantly monitor your pricing if you want to sell.

Getting started on eBay is pretty fast and straight forward. This is a definite help for anyone who wants to simply start selling. However,there are no customization options for eBay listings therefore you won't be able to do anything for your listings' visual appeal part. In terms of branding, your limited customer contact options will also limit you from building a loyal following, eBay is all about the products.

The fees on eBay can kill your business quickly if you're not careful. You may not have to pay for your listings, but you might be charged an insertion fee for each item, which depends on the category. Your insertion fee is based on either your minimum opening bid or your reserve price, whichever is higher. You will generally pay from 10¢ to $2 per listing with no reserve price for auctions and up to $2 for fixed-price listings. For each sale, you also pay a final value fee of at least 8.75% for items below $50 and an additional 4% on items up to $1,000. This fee is based on how much the item actually sold , plus the shipping cost and other charges that the buyer pays. The final value fee also applies if eBay catches you offering your contact information or trying to take customers out of eBay.

Similar to Amazon eBay has a good flow of online shoppers.

eCrater

eCrater: The "100% free" online marketplace

The main appeal of eCrater is that it's free to set up a store and it even has templates you can use to easily create an attractive store. It's known to be easy to import your listings from eBay, which is good if you're looking to transition entirely. There's not a lot of information on eCrater online, but there's said to be at least 65,000 active stores on the site.It's best used as complementary to your your business.

eCrater is a good option for someone who's totally over eBay, but it looking at using another marketplace, such as Amazon or Etsy, as their main platform. In our opinion, eCrater doesn't quite have the numbers to be viable as your sole marketplace despite being a excellent, low-risk and low-cost complementary option.

The key to making sales on eCrater is investing heavily in your store's SEO and marketing.

Amazon

Amazon is without a doubt the best online marketplace. It ranks only third, however, on the list of platforms for drop shipping. This is mostly because Amazon has very strict seller metrics and specific policies for drop shippers. This makes it harder to run a drop ship store there because of the lack of control you have. Particularly you can't control the quality of products that you can't personally inspect before the shipment. However it is very possible to succeed with a drop shipping business on Amazon.

Amazon subscriptions start at $39.99 monthly, or you can pay 99¢ for each item sold. Then there's an additional 3% to 45% for referral fees with a minimum of $1 or $2 depending on the item and category, plus variable closing fees for media items. You don't need a subscription if you sell fewer than 40 items per month, which can help if you just started your business. Plus, on the professional plan, you can offer gift wrapping. In relation to the costs but also know that drop shipping margins on Amazon will be lower because of higher shipping costs for single orders.

The great thing about Amazon is its reach. No other online marketplace has been able to truly compete with the online retail giant. Walmart has come close, but with Amazon's unending expansion plans and internal improvements, it is unlikely that the world will see a real competitor anytime soon. Amazon traffic is simply unbeatable, and its sales reports are incredible. As a seller on Amazon, you can take advantage of its brand reputation, which is primarily based on its customer satisfaction ratings.

The FBA program is not a huge attraction for drop shippers, who don't pack and ship their own products anyway. Amazon does insist, however, that drop shippers use FBA exclusively. This means more fees. With drop shipping, you will also have make sure that products can be shipped as fast as the Amazon standard.

One last thing to note is that your sales data is an open book an Amazon. If you want to keep these numbers to yourself, this is not the right platform for you.

Shopify

Drop shipping sellers will have the smoothest experience selling their products on this eCommerce-ready website builder.

It takes less than a day to set up shop, which is a lot faster than other platforms for drop shipping. Just choose one of the 10 free or 44 premium theme templates and pick a variation that suits your brand best. Each one is responsive and can be easily customized for color.

You'll need to find an available store name and purchase your own domain, but it's still an affordable option. This is a very important aspect since most drop shipping businesses don't start with large capital investments. Shopify can cost as little as $21.75 per month for hosting plus a 2% turnover fee and around 3% + 30¢ per transaction for the payment gateway. Shopify offers Paypal and other several other payment options. You can also get lower fees if you are based in the USA, UK or Canada and you opt for Shopify Payments.

One of the best things about Shopify is that it doesn't have any metrics that sellers have to maintain. This makes it a lot easier if you're just getting started. If you are, however, able to meet very high standards of product quality, shipping time and customer service, you can also sell on Amazon through your Shopify store.

WooCommerce on WordPress

WooCommerce also offers a fairly quick website setup with almost any WordPress theme. It's even easier if you choose a theme that was built specifically for WooCommerce integration and designed for eCommerce stores.

There are several WordPress themes to choose from, and about a thousand WooCommerce-specific ones. Around a hundred of the latter are free, and there is also a variety of child themes that you can purchase from Woo from $39 to add more customization options.

WooCommerce pricing looks a lot cheaper on the surface

compared to Shopify's, but the fees aren't that straightforward. Hosting your store can cost as little as $5 per month, but it is offered through third parties and therefore not guaranteed. The WooCommerce plugin itself is free, and so are many WordPress themes, but you have to consider what you will pay for any additional extensions that you'll need. You will also have to get your own SSL certificate to accept payments, probably from your hosting company along with your domain, which costs at least $100 per year. And at the end you will have to deal separately with all these third parties.

The great thing about WooCommerce is its connection with WordPress. WordPress has proved itself to be one of the best website platforms out there. It's a highly customizable platform, offering you almost no limit options to grow your store without having to upgrade a plan. WordPress was also built with online searchability in mind, and offers you the best chance for organic Google rankings.

PROS

- You have complete control over branding, design, layout etc.
- You're building a business independent of a third-party platform
- No fees and higher profit margins
- No direct competition from other sellers on the same platform

CONS

- It costs money to set-up and design your own store (web hosting etc)
- You miss out on the guaranteed traffic (customers) from established platforms
- It takes time to rank on Google and you'll have to invest in SEO and marketing

Bonanza

Bonanza is headquartered in Seattle and, though it's relatively new to the e-commerce scene, it's doing incredibly well. The Bonanza marketplace encompasses more than 22 million items ranging from Godzilla garden gnomes to taxidermy alligators.

A lot of sellers are making good money on Bonanza. The site has merchants and shoppers in nearly every country around the world. More than 40,000 sellers have already created businesses here.

Bonanza is one of the easiest selling platforms to use, and its popularity is on the rise amongst sellers. In the Sellers' Choice awards, Bonanza has taken out the top rating for communication and were voted the most recommended selling venue. They were also recognised in Entrepreneur's 360 best companies list.

Want to know exactly what you'll get with Bonanza that you haven't had with eBay? Here's the list:

- Bonanza is similar to eBay so the sky's the limit

for what you can sell.

- Unlike eBay, however, many items on Bonanza are quirky and unique - extraordinary items do well here.
- Because Bonanza doesn't make money until its sellers do, you'll see much higher profit margins. It is absolutely free to list an item on Bonanza, and the average fee per sale can be as little as 3.5%, which is considerably less than eBay.
- Bonanza is a fixed-price marketplace, meaning that buyers pay the listed price, not likely ebay.
- Bonanza sends every item listing to Google and Bing, and sellers have the option to get more exposure by advertising their listings in other channels and Bonanza's affiliate advertising program.
- Many online sellers like to list their items on multiple platforms, which is why Bonanza has easy-to-use import features for listings on eBay, Etsy, and Amazon.
- Although Bonanza's monthly traffic is lower than eBay's, the ratio of shoppers to sellers on Bonanza is much higher: 1,300 to 1 on Bonanza vs. less than 10 to 1 on eBay. That means far less competition between sellers, and far more chances for buyers to see your products.

Who is Bonanza Best Suited To?

Bonanza is best suited to any merchants who have something to sell online. Although Bonanza specializes in unique items and one-of-a-kind finds.

Getting a tax ID

Before starting the business some wholesale dropship suppliers need you to have a tax ID. US or Canada residents require a sales tax ID (also known as retail or resellers license, tax ID, resale number resale certificate or vendor's license). Thus you must mention your supplier about that and you have to fill a separate form also. Getting a tax ID is an easy process.

But in case of sales tax ID you must be a business organization as well as you must also have a Federal Tax ID number.

Local Business Licenses

Most cities and towns require businesses to get a business license that needs to be renewed on a regular basis. However, this requirement may differ for dropshipping businesses, many of which will likely be operated from home offices. You'll want to look into your local laws and regulations to see what, if anything, is required.

Setting your Strategy

Now that you have a selling platform for your dropshipping business, you need to attract customers to your store. This is where a customer acquisition strategy comes in.

Customer acquisition is the art of persuasion. You can think of it as advertising and marketing. Sounds expensive, right? But it doesn't have to be. You can take the fast (paid) path or the slow (free) path to gaining new customers. Let's take a look at both strategies in more depth.

Facebook Ads for Dropshipping

Facebook is the world's largest social media platform. It's a great place to advertise your products as you can tap into a huge audience. This is how Facebook makes its money, so every customer you acquire through this method comes at a cost. Facebook ads are a good option for the following reasons:

- It's easy to get started
- You control how much you spend a day
- You can target highly-specific demographics (location, interests, relationship status etc)
- It can yield fast results
- It helps to increase brand awareness
- A good ad or boosted post can go viral

Google Ads for eCommerce

Google is the world's most popular search engine by far. If you have an online store, you want it to rank on the first page of Google. You can achieve this organically, or you can buy ads for your store to appear at the top of the page for the keywords you want to rank for. Google ads are a good option for the following reasons:

- You can achieve great exposure in search results
- It's the largest advertising platform in the world

(Google search, Youtube, Gmail)
- You can target highly-specific demographics (location, language, device etc)
- Maximise exposure to your ads with high volume keywords related to your niche

Social Media Influencer Marketing

Influencer marketing has become a huge part of customer acquisition for retail brands in recent years. It could play an important role of any customer acquisition strategy in 2019. It can be particularly effective if you are in a trendy niche. One post can result in a bunch of new fans and customers. The cost of influencer marketing depends on how famous the influencer is.

Social Media Marketing

It's getting harder and harder to achieve organic reach on social media, but it is still possible. If you can consistently create and share great content on your social media channels you'll eventually build a following converting it later into customers.

Email Marketing

Building an email list is still one of the most effective ways of acquiring customers. You need a way of capturing email addresses, such as a request to sign-up at checkout, or an offer or competition that requires an email address. Once you have a good list of email addresses you have a way of reaching a large group of people regularly, for free.

Content Marketing

This most commonly takes the form of a blog on your store website, a Youtube channel, trendy Instagram posts, or witty posts on Twitter. Content marketing is meant to involve the creation of profitable content that helps to build an audience . It's not as explicit as advertising and should always be more about serving your audience than your brand.

Poll

As you can see there are several strategies to attract customers to your store. What is your preferred method of growing a new dropship business?

Blog or Forum Marketing

This involves finding blogs or forums that are related to your product/niche and actively participating in discussions. By positioning yourself as an authority in your niche and including a link to your website, you can increase traffic and acquire new customers.

Right Pricing

One of the more common questions asked by dropship resellers is "What price should I be setting my products at on my ecommerce website?". There are a ton of different dropship pricing strategies to choose from, and depending on your products, supplier(s) and business model, your approach can vary. There are some that argue that the only "right" strategy is that your pricing should always be changing as you test what works and what doesn't. Regardless if you buy into that notion or not, choosing a dropship pricing strategy is one of the first steps in launching a dropship ecommerce business and greatly impacts how your customers will perceive your brand.

It would serve most resellers well to take time to evaluate the different pricing strategies and how they affect both their profit margin and their buyer's perception of their business.

Here are a few of the more popular pricing strategies to consider:

Fixed Markup on Cost

This can be calculated by adding a pre-set profit margin to the cost of the merchandise. You can use a fixed dollar markup or a fixed percentage markup. When you are looking at using a percentage vs. fixed dollar markup, the first thing to look at is the average cost of your products. If most of your products are low cost cell phone accessories or a dollar store supplier, then a percentage markup might not be the best approach. For example, if most of your products are around $10, then using a 15% markup would mean you are only adding $1.50 to each product. However, if you choose a $3 or $5 fixed dollar markup, then your profit margin per item will be much higher.

Many pricing strategies exist and each one is based on a particular set of circumstances.

Tiered Markup on Cost

This is a solid price setting approach when your supplier has a varied type of products offered with many items of both low and high dollar values. If you are worried about pricing your expensive items too high while not making enough on your low cost items, then using a tiered structure might be your best option. You can set tiers or levels for your items so that items below $10 get a higher markup like 50% while your items between $200-500 might have a smaller markup of say 15%. You can set as many tiers as you like. Some users like to use very specific tiers for their settings having 10 or 20 different price levels, but in general, your goal is simple: use a higher markup on the lower dollar items while lowering the markup on your higher dollar items.

One reason this can be a good strategy is that many stores use a simple or single markup. It can be difficult for them to set a tiered setting if they are pricing products on their own. This means that if you have a 30% markup on all items and another store has a 25% markup, then it might be difficult to compete. However, if they are looking for a laptop and some accessories, even if your markup is slightly higher on a power charger or wireless mouse, the laptop on your site will be cheaper and can help you win the entire shopping cart sale for your site. Again, the option you select will depend on your prices. If you sell general merchandise from a supplier with a large product catalog for example, you will have great variety in the price levels of your products. But, if your supplier sells a more niche product type like silk flowers, the variety in your products might not be as great allowing you a simpler price setting.

Price vs. Shipping Markup

Some store owners are worried about having a price that is too high for their items, so they markup their products low, but add a small hidden fee to their shipping module or product weights to increase the cost charged for shipping. The goal is to have a product price show lower than other stores, while making up the needed margin with an increase to the amount charged for shipping. Other owners look to increase the cost of their item prices more significantly, while promoting free shipping on their site. These users recognize that many customers might be more focused on your unique deal or temporary free shipping promotion and will be less concerned about the product prices being shown.

Store owners can build their entire approach around one of these strategies while others might change between these approaches or change from a more traditional price strategy to one of these methods and back again multiple times over the course of the year. Regardless of the approach used, when implementing one of these more custom approaches, it is important to promote your significant price discounts or "free" shipping promotion to make sure it gets the attention needed from the traffic on your website. NOTE: Incorporating the amount charged for shipping into your overall pricing strategy is a more advanced approach and will require a more experienced store owner to make sure that the total amount charged is enough to cover both your needed product margin and shipping costs.

Manufacturer Suggested Retail Price (MSRP)

Setting your price right at the MSRP is also a common strategy used by the smaller retail shops to avoid price wars and still maintain a decent profit. By pricing products with the suggested retail prices supplied by the vendor, the retailer is out of the decision-making process. However, even with suppliers that might provide excellent MSRP levels for their products, if you do not select some discount below MSRP, it will be very difficult for you to have an advantage over the competition.

Psychological Pricing

This is used when prices are set to a certain level where the consumer perceives the price to be cheaper based on the price shown. The most common method is "odd-pricing" using cents ending values in 5, 7 or 9. It is believed that consumers tend to round down a price of $9.95 to $9, rather than $10. Along with the very common sense ending value approach like ending in 99 or 95 cents, some users try to use the cents ending value to price below the competition. As more users list with 95 cents as an ending value, you can lower yours to 85 or 45 cents or even 9 cents for all products to always try and achieve the lowest price. While the psychological pricing and the cents ending value is very common on ecommerce websites, using a much lower cents ending value might be a better approach when listing on a marketplace with multiple sellers like Amazon, eBay, Walmart and more.

MAP-Based Pricing

MAP is the "minimum advertised price" for a product listing that is typically set by the manufacturer. This means when listing the item for sale you are not allowed to price below MAP, or risk potentially losing your ability to resell products from that manufacturer or distributor.

When working with a large distributor that carries products across hundreds if not thousands of manufacturers, you will want to speak with them about their MAP policies and how it might vary across products. Some products may have a "hard MAP" in which it is strictly enforced and you can see this by quickly researching the product online to see all pricing meets this criteria. Other products may have a "soft MAP" where the MAP isn't really enforced and is a general guideline by the manufacturer. Determining which products have MAP and whether it is enforced or not factors depends in : a) whether you want to resell the item or not and b) how to price it. Ideally, your distributor provides the MAP price in the data feed and you are able to build rules around this pricing to easily list products that are competitive but do not put yourself at risk of losing your reseller privileges.

Mark-Down from MSRP

Setting your price as a mark down or "discount" from the Manufacturer's Suggested Retail Price (MSRP) is a very common approach. Many store owners think in terms of a discount being offered as the key reason why someone should shop on their ecommerce site. If the MSRP is $100 and you have a 20% discount, then that is a very clear savings offered by your store. Just like marking up your products, you need to evaluate your product types and competition before selecting your discount. Does your supplier have a variety of MSRP levels for your products? Also, does the MSRP for your items seem to represent what the market recognizes?

Just because the supplier says the MSRP for an item is $77, if many stores seem to sell that item for $50, then an MSRP based pricing might not make sense. In general, electronics tend to have very recognized MSRP levels. People have a general idea about what a flat screen TV, MP3 Player or laptop might sell for online, so the MSRP for these items might be close to what the market tends to use for its promotions. However, a smaller or niche supplier might not have an MSRP level with much significance. For example, if you are using an action figure or RC hobby, most customers might not know what the manufacturer recommends for that statue or remote control accessory, so it might be more common for these items to have a price that is more independent of the manufacturer's suggested price.

Fixed Dollar Addition

The use of a fixed dollar addition can be an important part of your price strategy for your wholesale dropship products. Let's say you are setting a profit margin for your products, but have you calculated in the amount to cover your marketplace or dropship fee? Are you making enough on some of your low dollar items to be profitable? The use of a fixed dollar addition can allow you to easily evaluate your potential profit. For example, let's say you have a 20% margin on your products. If an item costs $5.49 cents, a 20% margin would add $1.10. However, if you used an additional $3.50 fixed dollar addition, then you know you might cover a dropship or listing fee or have some additional margin built into your products. The markup is a larger percentage of your low dollar items while essentially being a "hidden" markup when applied to your much higher dollar items.

When you process an order, it does not take any longer to process an order for a $500 item vs. a $5 item, but when you have a fixed dollar addition added to your markups, then no matter your fixed dollar or percentage markup, you know you have a guaranteed fixed dollar amount added to every product sale to help compensate for any needed fees or processing times.

Featured Product or Product Specific Pricing

This is perhaps the most effective price strategy, but is the most time consuming and therefore the most overlooked option. Many resellers want to take the "set it and forget it" approach and apply a simple price setting, but what they forget is taking the time to price some individual products can maximize your website traffic and conversions. Many wholesale dropship resellers select 10-20 items or so to feature on their website, such as on the main page. All major ecommerce platforms have a "featured product" display option. Smart store owners use this section to promote their more popular items to their customers, but you are missing an opportunity to leverage your traffic if you do not utilize a product specific price setting for these or other items.

You do not need to price every product on your store with a 5% or 10% margin, but for those items displaying clearly on your main page, listing them at a much more competitive price is the best way to make a great first impression. A customer might add one of these easy-to-find products to their cart after recognizing the instant savings compared to other websites online, and then continue to add 2 or 3 more accessories or related items where you can make your additional margin. For the price conscious customer, they might do a lot of research for the "must-have" item that brought them to your cart, but they can be much less price sensitive once they see the huge savings on their favorite item while adding some additional items to their cart to spread out their shipping costs.

How to start Dropshipping with Shopify

So, you already have a product or niche in mind and you're ready to start building your Shopify store. To help you do this, here's a detailed review of the steps you should take to get your dropshipping website up and running.

Step 1: Create a Shopify account

First things first, register an account with Shopify. Head to their website, and click "Get Started" to begin the process. When doing this, it's best to have a store name in mind, because that's one of the first things required to set up an account.

Upon successfully signing up, Shopify will ask you questions of questions to aid in the setting up of your store

Regarding the first question, you have four choices to choose from:

- I'm not selling products just yet
- I sell with a different system
- I'm just playing around
- I'm selling just not online

Since you don't have a shop and want to create your Shopify dropshipping store, you can choose "I'm not selling products just yet" in the meantime.

For the question, "How much revenue does your business

currently make in a year," you can enter "$0 (I'm just getting started)."

Once you've chosen those answers, click "Next."

You will then need to complete your order details by filling out your personal information.

After submitting your details, you will be redirected to your dashboard.

Shopify Plans

Once you have created your account, you need to subscribe to a plan to unlock all of Shopify's premium features. While you still have a 30-day free trial, it's best to settle your plan from here on out, so you also don't have to worry about this later on. To do that, once you're in the dashboard, click on the "Select a Plan" button.

There are three plans to choose from – Basic Shopify, Shopify, and Advanced Shopify.

Since you're just starting out, it's best to choose the Basic Shopify plan. Later on, assuming that your shop takes off, you can change the plan to take advantage of more features.

Step 2: Set up and design your store

Once you've set up all your products, you can move on to designing your store. To get started, click "Online Store" on the left-hand sidebar of your Shopify backend. Depending on your budget, you can choose to opt for one of Shopify's free themes or explore their marketplace.

Once you've selected a theme, go back to your Shopify backend and click "Customize."

Step 3: Customize the look and feel of your site

You'll be taken to your theme designer, where you can edit the look and feel of your online store. To customize the elements of your site, click through the options on the left-hand toolbar of your theme builder and go from there.

The specifics of this stage will vary depending on your theme of choice. If your theme has a header (which it likely has) then you can upload a logo and customize its size and positioning on your site. If your theme has a slideshow, then you'll need to add images for each slide.

Speaking of which, images play a big role in the design of your site. And like most things on the Shopify platform, adding images to your store is super easy. You can either upload them from your computer or select pictures from Burst, Shopify's free stock photo tool. You can do everything — from searching for images to previewing how they appear on your site — right from your theme editor, so no need to navigate out of the page.

You can also customize more general theme settings, including the layout of your site, colors, typography, favicon, social media, and checkout page. Play around with different options and see what works best for you.

Once you're happy with the look and feel of your website, click Save.

Add pages

The next thing you need to do is to create pages for your site. These could include your:

- About page
- Contact page
- Shipping & Returns
- FAQ

To create a page, click the "Pages" link on the left-hand menu of your Shopify backend, then click "Add Page."

From there, enter the title of the page you want to create along, with the copy to go with it. If you're well-versed in SEO, you have the option to change the meta title, description, URL and handle, so you can specify exactly what you want search engines to see.

Once you're happy with the page, hit Save.

Repeat this process for every page that you want to create.

Set up your navigation

Once your pages and collections are set up, you can move on to your navigation settings. At this stage, you're going to specify which pages or collections would appear on your main menus.

Have a think about how you want people to navigate your website. What categories and information do you want them to find?
Take time to figure out which pages or links should appear on your menu, and which ones to place on your footer. Once you have this mapped out, follow these steps to set up your site navigation.

- Click "Navigation" on the left-hand menu of your backend.

- Select the menu to which you want to add an item (i.e., link, page, collection, etc.)

- On the menu page, Click "Add menu item."

- Enter a name for your item, then in the "Link" field, select the relevant item from the list of pages, collections, or products that you've already set up. (Note: this is the reason why you should set up all your products, collections, and pages prior to editing your navigation.)

So, if you want to add your About page to your menu, select "Pages," then click your About page. Or, if you want to add a particular category or collection, click "Collections" then select the collection that you want to add.

Edit your site's general preferences

Now let's talk about preferences. This is the section of your Shopify backend in which you can edit your site's title and meta description. This is also where you can add your Google Analytics code as well as Facebook pixel.

You can find it by clicking the "Preferences" link on your left-hand menu.

Step: 4 Add products to your Shopify dropshipping store

It's now time to add your niche products to your store. To add a product page, click "Add product"

Once you are on the Products page, you need to fill out the details of your product.

For the description, you may want to edit whatever that's given to you by the supplier. Make your descriptions more compelling to convince your target market to purchase it from you.

On the right sidebar, under the Organization section, you need to edit the product type and vendor to categorize your product for the benefit of your visitors. You can also include this product in a collection so you can lump together similar products and showcase them to your potential customers altogether. Lastly, you must enter keyword tags for your product so visitors can locate it on your search bar.

Product page title and description

Below the product title and description is the Images section. Upload all the images provided to you by the supplier. Make sure that the images are hi-res and of excellent quality to improve the chances of getting people to purchase your product.

Product pricing

For the pricing, enter the most appropriate price based on your research. Comparing the watch to the ones sold on Amazon.It is arguable that we can increase the price to boost our profits, but the pricing above is merely an example.

Adding product delivery details

Regarding shipping, you can also leave this blank since your supplier will manage it. However, you need to discuss the details with your suppliers on how to proceed with each order to ensure that the products get delivered on time.

Shipping

Below Shipping is the Variants page which lets you set the different variations of a product. If your products are available in different colors, sizes, and others, then you need to enter it here, so people have options to choose from and potentially increase conversions.

Finally, you can edit the product's search engine listing.

Click on the "Edit website SEO" link to input your meta title and description, as well as the URL.

For the page title, you may want to consider adding your dropshipping store's name at the end if there are enough characters. For the meta description, you need to be as detailed as possible about the product. Maximize the available 160 characters as efficiently as possible so you can convince users browsing search results to click on your link. Regarding the URL, you can also edit it to shorten it if possible.

You also need to consider a keyword to optimize for this product page. You can use SEMrush to find keywords that are not difficult to rank for so you can increase your chances of ranking higher on Google or Bing.

Once you're done, save the product. Apply the same process for all of the product you plan to sell on your Shopify dropshipping store.

Automatically adding products to your collection

The benefit of creating a collection of products is to compartmentalize products with the same brands, type, theme, or other factors that bind them together.

Using the product I entered above as an example, let's say we want to sell more genuine leather bracelet watches on our shop – we would use a collection.

Create collection page

On the first half of the Create collections page, enter the name and description of the collection. Apply the same principles used for creating your product here. Be as descriptive as possible so you can provide the necessary information to visitors to help them make an informed decision.

Collection image

For the Collection image, ideally, you want to upload an image that shows most of the products you're selling, so visitors will have an idea of what to see and purchase from your collection. If not, you can probably download the product with the best image regarding quality.

To make products much easier for you to add to your collection, you can automatically add newly created product pages based on certain conditions. You can choose from product type, price, vendor, tag, and others, so you don't have to enter them in your collections manually. You can also add multiple conditions to ensure that products that meet any one of the conditions you entered will be included in the list.

Finally, edit the page's SEO so you can compel more people to click on your link as it appears in search results.

Once finished, click on the "Save collections" button.

Step 5: Add A Domain

Got your store all set up? Great. At this point, you should consider adding a domain name. Without a proper domain set up, your store's default URL is https://YOUR-STORE-NAME.myshopify.com/.

And while it's technically possible to run your store without a custom URL, having your own domain name will help your store appear much more professional and appealing.

Fortunately, adding a domain is easy with Shopify. You can find your domain settings under "Online Store" on the left-hand menu of your Shopify backend. Once you're on that page, you're given three options on how to handle things:

1. Connect a third party domain to Shopify

If you already have an existing domain (i.e., through a provider like Bluehost, Hostgator, GoDaddy, etc.) you can connect it with Shopify so the system points your domain name to your Shopify store. This process will vary depending on your domain provider, so check with your vendor or visit Shopify's help page on the topic.

2. Transfer a domain to Shopify

You can also transfer a domain to Shopify, in which case you will be able to manage, pay for, and renew your domain directly from the Shopify backend. Do note that

Shopify and your domain provider may have guidelines on how to do this, so check with both platforms to ensure that you're able to transfer your domain.

3. Purchase a new domain

Don't have a domain yet? You can buy one through Shopify. Custom domain prices start at $11 USD per year.

Step 6: Add A Payment Gateway To Your Store

As an eCommerce site, you want to provide the shopper with different payment methods so they can use whichever method is most convenient for them. Normally, shoppers would use PayPal or credit cards for online transactions. Regarding the latter, you can use Shopify Payments so you can accept payment directly through Shopify – no setup required.

One of the best features of Shopify Payments is the ability to keep track of all transactions made via your Shopify dropshipping store. Also, if customers want a chargeback from their purchase, you can respond to them with a customized template to make your life easier as a shop owner.

Unfortunately, Shopify Payments is not available in all countries. If that's the case, thus the next best option is using PayPal for transactions.

Paypal at shopify

By default, all purchases will be made using PayPal Express Checkout. You can also accept credit cards through this payment gateways, and there are no transaction fees, so you get to keep all the profits.

Credit card payment at Shopify store

Regarding credit cards, if you want to accept payments using a third-party processor, you need to choose from the list available under the "Accept credit cards" section.

Shopify offers hundreds of payment options that will surely satisfy your target audience. With a list of options this huge, you can't make an excuse that people can't buy from you because you don't accommodate their preferred payment method.

All you need to do is choose the payment gateways that you want to set up from the list, assuming that you're already subscribed to the gateways you will be selecting. If not, you will need to sign up for them. Once you have chosen from the list, you need to fill out the necessary details to process your option so you can accept payments via credit card using your preferred gateway.

If you want to add more payment options, refer to other applicable methods under "Alternative payments" and "Manual payments."

How to start Dropshipping with Amazon

Step 1 Create an Amazon Seller Account

Have you considered drop shipping through Amazon.com, but are unsure of the best way to get started? In this section, I'm going to show you step-by-step how to successfully use amazon dropshipping and leverage its power to make over $10,000 per month.

Step 1: On Amazon landing official home page

Find the bottom of the page "sell on Amazon" - "Start Selling" click, and then you can process Amazon account registration and open your own amazon seller account.

Fill in the name

If you have another shop on the website, you can post the URL of the shop. If you don't have one, you don't need to fill in it. Finally, the certification is: 1. there are more or less three chances existing . If one does not reach the phone, change the SMS immediately; 2. Pay special attention to confirm whether the phone number you filled in has appeared before the Amazon seller system. If there was any, it was What kind of use, now do not use, it is easy to associate; 3, when you select Call, the page will pop up a page shows the PIN and four digits, the phone rings, enter it; you choose SMS, you will receive a Four-digit PIN code, enter the pop-up page.

Bind the credit card

Fill in identity verification

Preview W-8BEN Content

Provide Electronic Signature.

In order to save time, this place suggests that everyone choose to agree to provide electronic signature instead of sending the form via mail, which is simple and effective. After selecting the electronic signature, multiple options and input boxes will pop up. Select these check options, and then write down the company name or your name, email address and country, and click OK.

Confirm System Alert Message

If you select the second option in the previous step, the system will display a reminder in the following figure to inform you that if you agree to provide the electronic signature, your information will take effect immediately if you do not agree to provide Electronic signatures, then your information will only take effect 7-20 business days after you receive your mailed form. So once again remind everyone, if not necessary, it is not recommended to send the form by mail.

Generate W-8 Form

Fill in the product information.

Select Sales Category

Here are multiple options. If you sell multiple categories, you can check them all, and then click "Finish". Luckily, now you already appreciate how to dropship on amazon.

Step 2: Locate Low-Cost Drop Shippers

The secret tool that most successful amazon sellers use to make an excellent profit through amazon dropshipping is Salehoo—a drop shipping supplier. To get this.

First, get a Salehoo subscription in order to get the most out of its filters and tools. Try to find local drop shippers that will ship in less time and with less fees.

While you may find cheap suppliers using Google, the fact is that most successful sellers who do amazon dropshipping prefer to have a Salehoo subscription. This is because the cheaper suppliers don't have marketing budgets; instead they focus more to lower the cost of their items.

Step 3: Find Supplier Catalogs and Identify their Low-Cost Items

Look through supplier catalogs for high-selling, low-cost items that can be drop shipped. The difference between the supplier cost and Amazon cost should be enough for you to make a good profit.

How to start Dropshipping with Ebay

Create your seller account by choosing between these type of account: ebay icon

- Individual seller account: free account with a monthly limit of 50 listings.
- Basic Package: a € 19.95 monthly subscription with a limit of 250 listings.
- Premium Package: a € 39.50 monthly subscription with a limit of 1,000 listings.
- Anchor shop: a € 139.50 monthly subscription fee and with 10,000 listings per month.

Upload your products

Upload photos and product features that you create or from the supplier that you've chosen. Create a product page as professional as possible to gain your customer's trust. A good feature on eBay is that you can customize the photos and even make them unique with a watermark.

Good's Delivery

Every time a customer purchases your product, you need to contact your suppliers and give them the details of the delivery. Be careful: if your customer pays with PayPal, your payment can be blocked for 21 days, until the item is received by the end customer.

Payments from eBay

When the customer receives the goods, eBay will deposit in your bank account the product price after deducting eBay fees which are equal to 10% of the final value of the object. When you set the price for your products, remember that all prices on eBay taking into account VAT and, in the case of PayPal payment, will also include Paypal fee.

How to promote your Brand and your Products

So at this point, you've found your product and built your store, now's the time to market your dropshipping business like there's no tomorrow. This is a crucial step in your dropshipping business plan. So don't keep making tweaks to your store design and pretend like you're making improvements. You don't need to be scared of putting yourself out there. Getting your first sale is one of the best feelings!

If you're just starting out, you're probably on that super tight budget. Some of my best marketing ideas have come from those super frugal moments. Here's a few to get you started:

Influencer Marketing

Starting a dropshipping business will require you be a bit scrappy in the beginning. If you can't afford to pay influencers their rates, trust me this is a good thing, you can offer them an affiliate commission instead. Why is this a good thing? I learned the hard way that sometimes even a niche specific influencer doesn't actually convert. It's almost like a shot in the dark. If you pay an affiliate fee for every sale, you lower the risk for your dropshipping business and it's up to the influencer to convert the sale. Plus, you'll get some pictures which will help increase your social proof for your brand. If the influencer has real followers, they could potentially make a lot more money as an affiliate than they would've if they were paid a flat rate. Thus, giving them a chance to make even more money.

Get Free Media Coverage

Using the free HARO tool you can subscribe to a three time a day email list where reporters reach out to you to get stories for their article. Some may be looking for influencers in a specific niche others may be looking for product recommendations. Either way, if you've got that retargeting ad running, that free traffic back to your website could result in some sales. Instead of adding a link to your homepage send it to a product collection or a specific product to create a more targeted focus. You can still add your brand's name as the name for the hyperlink.

Facebook Advertising

You need to keep your budget low at the beginning to be able to afford experimentation. You don't even know what your best selling product will be at this point. Create several ads to figure out which product sells best. When it comes to targeting, create a World ad but remove Canada, Australia, United States and U.K. this will keep your ad cost lower. As your business grows, or if you have a bigger budget, you can create separate ads for those four countries. So United States will have its own ad, as will the remaining three.

Retargeting Ads

If you're really tight on budget, I really like retargeting ads because they keep the cost low. This ad works great if you have a store with tons of traffic. Maybe you're marketing for free on Pinterest and getting a lot of traffic from there. Maybe you wrote a blog post on your website, featured influencers and now influencers are sharing your blog for free. With a retargeting ad, you take that free traffic and it's a lot more likely to convert into a paying customer. Even better than a standard Facebook ad. Plus, it's a lot cheaper.

How to use SEO to skyrocket your business

What is SEO?

When we look up something on Google, we usually stick to the websites for answers that Google returns on the first result page, also known as Search Engine Result Page (SERP). Hence, most logically, if you want your online store to be noticed, you need to appear on the very first SERP on Google.

Simple reasons why you should improve SEO on your your Shopify dropshipping store

It doesn't really matter how big or small your eCommerce business is, SEO is extremely critical for each one of them for three simple reasons

If you improve SEO, it can grow your bottom line while being cost-effective

Paying for website traffic can at times cost you many dollars per click. With effective and well-implemented SEO, you are less dependent on such marketing costs for results. For start-ups, SEO can be a real life-saver which increases sales and keeps the profits flowing. Unlike paid search traffic, yourorganic search traffic comes "free" — with no cost per click, Impression or conversion. Hence, SEO has always been so popular. With SEO, you can attract quality organic traffic without paying for it directly.

The effects of SEO are long-lasting and far-fetched.

Unlike many other marketing channels, SEO doesn't have a shelf life. There is no "pulling the plug" on SEO. For instance, the moment you stop paying for your paid advertising, your traffic drops. SEO on the other hand, keeps going working for you.

SEO builds upon itself to grow stronger gradually and over time. Plus, there is this option of layering upon what you did last year and updating your SEO strategy according to what works till the time you dominate your market. Also, unlike paid advertising, the stream of your website visitors and sales won't stop the moment you put brakes on your SEO.

SEO helps customers find you

Google alone shares a major chunk of profit-producing traffic. Hence, this alone proves that search is the single decision-making criteria. Optimizing search process is what will get you your website traffic and ultimately conversions. By ignoring SEO you're taking a huge risk of not being visible to your customers when they look for your products. When you aren't found on search results, a less number of customers know about you and therefore, you sell less – which slows down your growth.

How to improve SEO on dropshipping store – in a nutshell

KEYWORDS

For better SEO rankings of your dropshipping business, you should pay special attention to the length of content on each page of your website. The number of words you include on your pages, the easier it will be for search engines to understand your page.

Few things to remember if you want to improve SEO via keywords:

- Maintain an optimal ratio of keywords in your web content.
- Include at least 350 to 500 words per page.
- The content needs to be useful and relevant to your target audience.
- The content must be natural
- Your content will be the platform from where you will have to optimize your keywords, links etc.
- Avoid stuffing content at the end of the page, under a menu or an expandable field.
- In your product page, add content which describes your product using keywords
- Avoid using duplicate content.

LINKS

Links, internal, external and backlinks are all very crucial aspect of understanding dropshipping SEO.

How to improve Google search results with internal links?

Internal links basically directs from one page on your site to another. By linking one page of your website to another, you are signaling search engine webpage crawlers to navigate to the page that it's linking to, which gives ranking power from that page to the next. In a nutshell, by using internal links, you are telling the search engines which pages to rank for specific keywords.

How to increase Google ranking with external links?

Quite contrary to what internal links do, external links take the user to other sites. If you own a dropshipping ecommerce store, incorporating external links into your blog posts may be a good idea because it will then navigate the visitor to another relevant site to help them understand your post better. However, external links can be a little tricky because it always has the risk of taking your prospective customers away from your site. So, use them prudently.

How to increase SEO ranking with backlinks?

Backlinks play an important part in driving traffic back to your eCommerce site. Backlinks are links that point from

239

another website back to yours. When this is coupled with the content on your website, these can be an important means to through which you can get a website to rank highly in search engines. However, avoid buying backlinks to increase your domain authority. You might be heavily penalized.

SITEMAP

Incorporate a site map on your website. A sitemap essentially lists all of the pages on your website that Google should know about. Starting from the high-level pages, they're broken down and goes on to include categories, subcategories, product pages etc. Sitemaps can be created in multiple ways with XML feeds and links. Avoid having a 404 or 301 redirect and pages on your sitemap.

TITLES AND TAGS

If we go by search engines, your H1 tag is one of the first things that describes what a visitor will find on your website. In case of your product page, your H1 tag will be the product title. If it's a category page, your category name will be your H1 tag.

In Dropshipping business, title tags are important. When someone searches for something, it is the title tag that shows up in search results.

Few things to remember if you want to improve SEO via titles and tags:

- Avoid overdoing it with the keywords in your H1 tags to prevent getting spammed by Google or face an over-optimization penalty.
- An ideal Title Tag should be below 55 characters.
- it should be relevant to search terms you want to rank.

META DESCRIPTIONS

Descriptions are crucial for dropshipping SEO rankings. Meta descriptions appear right below the title tag and should be between 120 and 155 characters. These should be relevant and describe precisely what a person will find on the page if they click on it. If you are able to nail this, you'll stand out from the crowd.

Few things to remember if you want to improve SEO via meta descriptions:

- Make sure your description tags encourage peoples to click.
- Include information such as a how-to guide, a great price or an attention-grabbing list.
- For inspiration, read the title tags and meta descriptions of some high-ranking pages.

Create your own website

Dropshipping is one of the most popular forms of practicing ecommerce today and the reasons are obvious. Dropshipping involves the retailer which is you selling products to your customers but your supplier or manufacturer handles the inventory, shipment and delivery of orders.

If you are planning to jump into dropshipping business and want to start a your own dropshipping website, but have no idea of how to set up a dropshipping website, then you are in the right place.

WHY CREATE A DROPSHIPPING WEBSITE?

Dropshipping can be very successful especially if you utilize a great strategy and select a good niche for your ecommerce business. Dropshipping only works if you have a great website which will serve as the link between you and your customers. The following are some of the reasons why you need a dropshipping website:

- Suppliers and manufacturers want to work with a reseller who can show they have an existing website and already have an existing customer base (however small). The website acts in your favor when looking for suppliers because they feel they can trust you will sell their products.

- All your competitors especially in dropshipping all have websites so why not you? Competitor analysis is a key component of ecommerce and therefore lacking a website could prove to be detrimental for your business.

- Most of your customers are online and having a website gives your business legitimacy.

- A website helps to showcase all the products and services that you offer in your niche.

HOW TO SET UP A DROPSHIPPING WEBSITE?

The popularity of dropshipping can be attributed to the low startup costs and the reduced risk that the whole business model poses.

The model consists of three main elements namely the website which serves as the home for your products, the suppliers who ensure you don't suffer stock deficiencies and handle all your shipping requirements and lastly the customers who place orders and keep your business alive.

Most newbies often fear setting up websites because they have no experience in programming and assume that the cost of hiring a developer might be too expensive especially if they have a very small budget. Web development and ecommerce has significantly changed over the last decade and setting up a website is now easier than ever. Even without any experience in programming, there are several platforms today that teach people how to build dropshipping websites easily and some even do it for you in less than a day.

Assuming that you have already selected a niche and carried out intensive competitor analysis, the following steps should be followed when building your dropship website plan.

Step 1. Identify an ecommerce website builder/platform

As mentioned before, building websites and ecommerce websites in particular has become extremely easy. Several companies offer website building services by either doing it for you or giving you templates/blueprints for you to edit and how to make a dropshipping website yourself. As with all softwares, different companies have better features than others and some are suited to different types of websites than others.

Depending on your budget, the type of platform you choose could easily determine how good your website is and how many functionalities you will have access to. Some of the most popular ecommerce platforms today include Shopify, BigCommerce, and WooCommerce by WordPress, Wix, Magento, Weebly, SquareSpace, 3dcart and Volusion. Each of these platforms has their own strengths and have different pricing models again based on the features and the target audience.

Step 2. Get a domain name and hosting

The domain name is the name of your website on the www. This will be the name that will appear on the address bar of people's browsers when they search for your business online. A good domain name is short, simple and relevant to the type of business that you are doing. Domain names aren't very expensive and you should include the cost in your budget. The second thing is hosting, basically means placing your website on the www.

It is what guarantees that your website actually exists on the internet. It also costs a certain amount based on the hosting provider that you choose and will have to be renewed after a certain period of time mostly a year. Some of the most popular hosting providers include BlueHost and GoDaddy. Always choose a hosting provider with fast servers and good reviews from existing customers.

Step 3. Building the website

Shopify for example will want you to open an account and choose a price plan. They will then build a store for you but customization will have to be done for you. WooCommerce will require that you install WordPress first before installing the WooCommerce plugin that is for ecommerce stores built using WordPress. For most platforms including Magento, Weebly, Wix and BigCommerce, they will only give you the layout of the site or give you a template to edit. Customization of the store is left up to you and will involve the following:

- Selecting a theme – most platforms have several themes that you can choose from and edit. Most of them are free but others will cost you some money depending on the features.

- Placing your logo on the site.

- Content – Ultimately what you place on the site will be left to you in terms of text and images or any other relevant content.

- General settings – Shopify for example wants users to setup their return and refund policies before they begin selling. Other settings include payment settings, shipping information.

- Structure – This is the dropship website design and while the platforms will provide the layout, you will have to consider the entire customer journey from the time of entering your site to placing an order and checkout. Most themes should give you builders that should make this easy. You should also research your competitors to see how they do it. Structure will make it easy for you to know which part of your website to place different types of content such as you're about page or FAQs section.

- Pages and categories – Most platforms will do this for you and you can add more pages if you need them. Most ecommerce sites have categories and sub categories for different product variations. Every category should have their own page.

- Additional widgets – These includes search, rss feeds, social media links, tags and several others.

- Plugins – Plugins are necessary if you want to have a robust website with advanced features and most of the good ones have a price but most of the essential ones are free.

- Security – This is a very important often overlooked. Most price plans for all platforms come with SSL certificates installed in your website.

- Blog – you may want to add a blog just so as to make your website more interesting. Most platforms can do this for you as well.

Step 4. Finding a reliable dropshipper with suppliers

your website is useless if you haven't identified a reliable dropshipper with suppliers that you will use to populate your store with products. There are many examples to look at such as Chinabrands, Aliexpress, Doba and others.

Step 5. Add products to your website

The products are the main attractions of your website and therefore once you find reliable dropshippers you can add their product items to your site. Most of the best marketplaces have automated solutions or plugins that will allow you to import products to your website directly.

Step 6. Edit product descriptions and images

For SEO purposes it may be wise to edit the product descriptions using your own words. Also if you have images you can use to depict the product well and good but using the supplier's images won't affect you as much because most product images often look the same.

Step 7. Order system

Work on your order system and this means discussing with your supplier how they will handle shipments and whether the customer's billing address will be sent to them automatically. Discuss the entire supply chain.

Step 8. Marketing

The website may be beautiful and dynamic but people will still need to find it. Marketing begins with competitor analysis and is a never ending process for ecommerce entrepreneurs. There are plugins that can help you for on-site marketing techniques but all the off-site techniques will be left to you. They include social media, blogging, email, events, flyers, word of mouth, referrals and many others.

Use social media marketing

Whether you're just getting started on your entrepreneurial journey or looking to branch out into new marketing channels, you may be wondering how you can create a social media marketing plan that will help your ecommerce store grow.

It's well known that social media is a marketing channel that many ecommerce brands have already used effectively to skyrocket their stores' growth, so I've created this book to provide you with some tips and tricks to help you find that same level of success.

WHY SOCIAL MEDIA IS ESSENTIAL FOR DROPSHIPPING SUCCESS

Are you one of the many entrepreneurs out there warming up to start a dropshipping business?

If so, there's something you need to know.

If you're desiring to succeed in a world where everything we do is tweeted, liked, and shared, The marketing in Social media can't be simply left as an after-thought.
The truth is that , many home base business makers are already following the trend creating Facebook pages or setting up a Pinterest board and then just diving into building a following to make social media really work for them.

Early Research and Identifying Your Niche

Of all the social media tools at a home-based business owner's disposal, the ones that are often overlooked the most are trending topics and search features.

Long before you even start a dropshipping business, these tools can prove extremely useful in helping you finding a niche in the market that will be productive.
Identify who your main customers are, and how you can best give them what they want.

- Twitter is the ideal platform for listening in to the conversations people are having about the niche you're planning to bring into the market.

249

If you're plannind to start an online business of clothes, Twitter's trending topics, moments, and search features can help you find the kind of styles and garments that are most trendy.

This information can prove helpful when it comes to make decisions about which dropship wholesalers to partner with, and which items to stock when you do eventually set up your online boutique.

You can also use these tools to discover what customers are saying about similar businesses.

When listening into Twitter conversations about your niche, be sure to ask critical questions such as:

- What customers like about the stores they currently shop at?
- How can I challenge those appealing factors in my own business to help me make money dropshipping?
- What customers don't like? What should I do to avoid it?

Of course, you're not just limited to Twitter. All social media as Facebook, Instagram, Pinterest, Tumblr, Youtube have their own unique marketing tool and all as well have search functions that can be used to help you create a winning strategy for your new store.

Enhanced Search Engine Optimisation

Social media ialso plays a major factor in your organic search engine rankings.

As any experienced home-based business owner will suggest, search Engine Optimisation (SEO) has an important role to play in ensuring that people searching for keywords related to your niche and your products can find your website on major search engines like Google and Bing.

Over the years, Google has modified the algorithm it uses to determine how sites should rank in organic search results multiple times over, each one adjusting to meet evolving ways that customers search the web.

Over time, that algorithm has been reshaped to use social media as one of the determining factors when deciding on a rank for a website. Meanwhile, Bing look at the 'social authority' of a website or article's author when deciding whether that page should be the very first search result shown, the very last, or somewhere in between.

For the most part, this 'authority' is made up of factors such as the number of followers though other factors, including number of likes, retweets, and shares of any content are also taken into consideration.

Social media marketing can make a big difference to SEO for your dropshipping business, perhaps improving your search engine rankings and therefore the number of people that visit your website, but what if I told you that you could use social media to develop instant sales without using your website at all?

Building a Brand and Driving Traffic Post-Launch

By all means it's all well and good talking about using social media to build an audience when you're first getting started, but what if you're already well past that stage?

Have you got your new drop shipping website off the ground? Or if you're planning to go down the route of supplying an online business for sale and starting there?

If that's the case, you're actually in a great position to start using social media to its full potential in driving traffic to your website and building up a loyal following of repeat customers.

There's literally number of ways to do this, but whichever one you choose, it pays to remember the one golden rule of social media:

Add Value

Think about all the ads you see on a daily basis.

From television adverts to billboards, flyers, leaflets, and yes, a over-abbundance of advertising on just about any website .
You care to mention, we're bombarded with advertising so much these days that most of us simply tune it out.

On social media, that 'tuning out' basically means unfollowing, muting, or completely blocking your account, ultimately leaving all your efforts useless.

You don't need me to tell you what a colossal waste of time and energy that can be.

So no, you're not going to get very far if you simply blast your social media follows with one ad after another. Even those ads are ultimately amazing, they're eventually going to become so repetitive that your audience just stops paying caring, especially when they've got so many other things competing for their attention.

If it's not cute cat pictures, the latest viral video, or meme competing for their likes and shares, it's news, posts from celebrities, and even competing for eCommerce businesses.

In order to make your drop shipping website stand out from the crowd, you're going to have to create content which is so irresistible that it stops users mid-scroll and makes them simply unable to resist interacting with you, be it via likes, shares, comments, retweets, or whatever the platform of your choice allows you to do.

Include pictures in your posts and Users are far more likely to interact with your social media channels,However this isn't a guaranteed method for success if those posts don't in some way add value to your readers.

As an Examples of starting an online clothing store you could ask customers to share selfies of them wearing new outfits they purchased from you that you can then include in a video or a pictures gallery. You could post a blog with advices about this season's fashion must-haves, or you could even use live streaming features on Facebook and Youtube to interact with your customers in real time.You could as well answering questions about your products, your business, or fashion in general.

Similarly if you're starting a dropshipping business selling gardening products for istance you could create graphics which provide tips ,How-Tos and tutorials, or even better testimonials from your customers about what a difference your products have made .

Social media can be the most powerful tool at your disposal for driving clientele to your website and building your brand. Again, the only limit is of your own creativity,as long as you stick to the golden rule and remember to sell less and engage more.

Start Building a Brand Before You Launch

With your planning and researching at hand you're now ready of actually starting your dropshipping business.

Unless you're purchasing an online business for sale and setting out your own journey, this usually means spending not a considerable amount of time building your online store and taking care of all the endless tasks that go into starting an online store.

Surely there are few things worse than investing all that

money ,time and hard work only to launch your new business in a world which honestly ,doesn't know or simply doesn't care that you exist.

Without at least some level of pre-launch marketing, that's essentially when you'll end up.

Social media may empower you with the tools you need to start building a brand long before you go-live with your dropshipping website so that when you do finally launch, your customer will be exited about it.
Again, let's use the example of starting an online clothing business.
The only limit to the possibilities is your own imagination, and the best part of all, is that most of them won't cost you anything.

You could start by building Pinterest boards to show off the kind of collections you'll be selling in your online boutique, using appropriate access word to make them noticable , and well-written accompanying text inviting potential customers to follow you for details about when their favourite items from your Pinterest boards are available for sale.

You could reveal 'exclusive' previews of new products on Instagram, again using relevant keywords to start building an audience. Using this type of approach to pre-launch marketing has another hidden benefit besides showcasing your upcoming lines.

It helps you measure reaction to your products and get

some idea as to which products are more likely to prove the most popular when you launch your new business.

If, for example, you have one outfit with 200 Instagram likes and a second with only half that amount, then that's a clear sign that the outfit with 200 likes should be promoted more largely than the other one in order to drive sales.

Another handy tip for Instagram followers is to include a link to a landing page from each of your posts. On this landing page, place a form so that visitors can subscribe to a newsletter and get alerted when you launch your store.

Social media marketing can also be used to establish a loyal following with Facebook and Twitter.

In the weeks leading up to your launch day, you may share 'countdown' posts with an attractive visual, and perhaps even offer people a 10% discount when they like and share your posts and/or subscribe to your newsletter.

That way, your existing audience do a lot of the hard work for you, sharing your content among their own social networks and reaching a far greater audience than you could on your own.

 Even if Losing 10% of every sale in the early days of your business might not seem appealing , compared to other marketing methods, its' a very low-cost way to build up an initial customer base who are likely to come back to you time and time again. Eventually you'll may recoup that small loss many times over.

Sell Your Products Directly via Facebook Stores

There's a useful tool called the "Facebook Store application" which allows you to import your store onto your Facebook page and sell your products directly via that platform. Whether you find an existing dropshipping website for sale and buy it or build your own from scratch using any number of popular eCommerce platforms,

Though there is a small charge to use the app ($19 USD per month), it may well be worth the investment to increase sales by enabling customers to buy directly from you on a website that they already use instead of than registering a new account and typing out their payment details again on your website.

Deliver Five-Star Customer Service

As the owner of an online store, it's tempting to fall into the trap of believing that the most important aspect of your entire business is your product.

After all, that's where the money comes from, right?

Certainly but the truth is, product itself is only one small part of a much bigger plan.

The other, even more important part of that equation?

A Good customer service.

Studies shows that the majority of customers value good service over the price of a product.

Why?

Because a good customer service provides trust and reassurance and customers know they are dealing with a reputable business, and they will certainly be helped if they have questions or if an order doesn't turn out quite as they expected it to.

Good customer service also helps to build reputation.

If you Take a look on any review website and you'll find tons of unhappy customers saying all kinds of negative things about companies they've had bad experiences with.

Those negative reviews do not go ignored by other potential customers. They're read, taken into account, and used to help make a decision about which company to buy from.

It might not seem like the biggest deal to respond to every question personally or to ensure a customer always find a way to get in touch if an order goes wrong but it's absolutely critical if you want to maintain the kind of solid reputation that keeps customers coming to you, rather than your competition.

The good news, is that social media helps providing customers easy and painless.

It enables customers instant access to someone who can help and when things go wrong, that instant access can make all the difference to an unhappy customer.

Using social media as a customer service tool is also a great way of personalising your service. You may skip the conventional automated email responses, skip the call-waiting messages, and get straight to making your customers feel valued and appreciated by presenting them with a real person they can interact with on a personal level.

INSTAGRAM

You can use Instagram marketing as a social media marketing strategy for your dropshipping business. Instagram has millions of users today. You may be one of them, certainly. Post photos and videos on Instagram, right? Did you ever think that it can be used as a perfect marketing strategy for your dropshipping business?

Millions of people viewing your products. Won't that enhance your sales volume? Making use of Instagram as a marketing strategy for enhancing your sales and profits is a pathway to successful dropshipping business as all you need is doing some research.

Why Should You Use Instagram Marketing For Your Dropshipping Business?

Wider User Base

Instagram has nearly 500+ million active users, millions of daily active users and around millions of images and videos shared on Instagram each day. You may guess it can grab so many views and likes in a single day.

Thus, it can be beneficial to use Instagram Marketing for your Dropshipping business as a social media marketing strategy. It would be really promotional for your business as you may get higher audience coverage and an increased conversion rate.

All Organic Traffic: Less Investment

If you are going really well, choosing the right niche, posting regularly on your Instagram account and answering the queries well; it could be the golden era of your business as there will be lots and lots of 'organic traffic' generated without paying a single penny.

Instagram has much more users than many other social media networks. Most of the potential buyers of US market are active users on Instagram so it can be a boost for your business.

Amazing right? There's a lot more for enhancing your dropshipping business.

No Advertisement Cost

Although you can carry on with the paid advertisement on Instagram, it's not an issue if you don't want to spend a single penny. The advertisement for your product line can be totally free with Instagram Marketing for your dropshipping business.

What else do you need?

Making so much of customers without spending something is good for anyone so don't you think that it would be perfect to use Instagram as a marketing strategy for dropshipping.

Simplicity

It is quite easy to set up an Instagram account and then add posts of your products to it. You only need to follow a simple procedure and its done. This is the best thing about Instagram. Moreover, you could also set up a different business account for yourself which can be done quite simply.

So, there are so many benefits of using Instagram as a marketing strategy for your business. Its usability may help you to upgrade the level of your business and enjoy massive profits as well.

Advantage Over The Competitors

A survey proves that though, Instagram has millions of users however when it comes to business marketing, entrepreneurs still rely on Facebook and Twitter for marketing their business.

Only 2-3% business units use Instagram. Thus, you may have the advantage of facing less competition as most of your competitors may be using other social networking sites for promoting their products. Therefore, it would be perfect to use Instagram as a marketing strategy for your business.

Visual Content Is More Effective

It is natural human behavior that visual images appeal to our mind more than the written words. The use of hashtags makes it easier to locate what the customer is actually looking for. Posting images and videos related to your product line along with your employees provides the users with a better insight and links your customers with your business in a better way.

How To Create Your Dropshipping Business Account On Instagram?

First of all, you need to sign up for an Instagram account.

- The next thing you need to do is choose a username for your account. It's better to use your brand name as the username when you are using the account for business marketing.
- You need to add a profile photo, a bio of nearly 150 characters and a link to your website. Remember, you can't hide your bio from anyone so if you don't want to show it, it is better to remove it.
- Link your account to third-party sites like Facebook. The benefit of this is that you will get an option to share a post with the third-party site you are linked to from the same screen where you add a caption.

Tips To Optimize Your Instagram Business Marketing Strategy

Starting Username With Brandname

Though it might not always be possible to do so, you should put in an extra effort to add your brand name in the very beginning as it would seem to be much more effective. Try avoiding the use of 'a', 'the', 'only' before your brand names and go straightaway for the name itself.

Take Action At The Perfect Time

Posting your content when the users are most active may prove to be a blessing for your business. Posting at that time would definitely generate more engagement and can even give you a shot at getting on the Instagram Explore Page.

MAKE THE BEST USE OF INSTAGRAM TOOLS

There are various Instagram tools that can be used to optimize your Instagram marketing technique like it allows users to e-mail, call or text the business. You just need to switch to a business account from your personal one as business profiles would unlock the access to insights and the ability to promote.

- 'INSIGHTS' would provide your business with information about who your followers are and which posts are being responded to .
- 'PROMOTE' allows you to change the most

popular posts into adverts. Through adverts, you will be able to initiate your targeted audience just at the click of a single button.

Tempting Visuals

If you want your brand to be recognized easily by the users, you need to work on the visuals you use. Just adding visuals would won't work. It is equally significant to make them noticeable.

This can be done by:

- Using Instagram filters to create better visuals.
- Try to be consistent with the color and the style of the visuals.
- The quality of your visuals matters more than the quantity.
- The captions around your visuals should not be too much to hide the influence of your visuals.

Involve Yourself

Getting involved with the users is the most important step, I would say.

Your followers would remember you if you are active on the social media. Engage yourself more and more with partners, bloggers and publishing networks you want to get featured into. If you want others to follow your content, you need to follow their content as well.

Using Right Hashtags

A research shows that, post with at least one Instagram hashtag gets more engagement than a post without Instagram hashtag. Thus, using hashtags and more importantly the right ones can make your products visible to the targeted audience.

Just add a small caption and some hashtags to all the posts you create. These hashtags categorize the photos and videos and make it easy to optimize them. Using the right hashtags can benefit you much. Throwing any random hashtag at the end of your post won't really do. So be careful with your hashtags.

You need to follow some guidelines for making the best use of hashtags like:

- The hashtags must be relevant to the content.
- Try to find out which hashtags have been used by your competitors.
- Use hashtags that fit your brand.
- Try to create your own branded Instagram hashtags.

FACEBOOK

Anyone with a home dropshipping business would benefit immensely from having a great Facebook page! Even if you don't know anything at all about social media marketing, it's quick and easy to create a killer Facebook page for your dropship business.

Here are some tips to creating a Facebook page that will greatly enhance your business:

- The first step is to establish a Facebook personal profile if you haven't already done so. The individual in that personal Facebook profile will be the one who is officially the creator of that particular fan page. Therefore, to streamline things, your Facebook fan page will use the same login as your personal page. Don't be uneasy about mixing your personal and business profiles on Facebook because nobody except the administrator or page owner can see both. In other words, people who visit your personal Facebook page cannot see your Facebook dropshipping business fan page and vice versa.

- Next, click on "Create a Page" on the Facebook profile page and choose the type of business you have. There are several choices plus a place to put your business name, address and category.

- Then, click "Get Started" and from that point on

Facebook guides you through the entire process. It's easy! If you want to skip a step, you can always go back and do it later. You will have a place for your business logo and other info about your dropship business, including the types of products you sell.

How to Handle Security Issues with your business

In today's scenario, no business can be counted safe from security breaches. Renowned companies are preferred targets for hackers but small businesses face security issues too. It is always suggested to be alert and keep yourself updated regarding business security methods.

Small businesses are more and more victims of data breaching. According to experts, these conditions arise as they are not updated regarding security controls. There are some precautionary measures you can take to protect your small business.

Here are some of steps you can take to protect your business.

Select The Right Platform That Is Secure

To begin your own Dropshipping Business, one of the most essential things you need to do is pick the right E-Commerce platform. It is surely hard to choose which internet ecommerce platform is best to outsourcing. It is evident that WooCommerce is the most utilized web based business platform on the planet, nearly followed by Magento and Shopify. Then again, BigCommerce has a little piece of the pie, and OpenCart isn't even in the rundown.

Set Higher Standars For Password

Usually, it is said that hackers attack passwords to get a hold on potential data. So to protect your devices like business computers, mobiles, networks and accounts, the employees should change the default password to a strong password. A complex password is where a variety of characters are used. The password should be changed once in every quarter at least.

Secure Your Physical Store.

Investing in first class security solutions for your storefront can help you rest easy about break-ins and theft. First and foremost, you need an alarm system. The best type of alarm system varies widely from business to business (Surely jewelry store probably needs a different kind of alarm than a coffee shop), so it's wise to do your research. Most reputable alarm system providers will come out to your site to do an assessment before recommending an option. So shop around — and make sure to get a solution you're comfortable with. Also to impede theft, security cameras are also a good idea.

Antivirus

Evidently, protecting your premises physically is a challenge in itself—but your online property is just as valuable. Consequently, given the growth of identity theft, it pays to invest in antivirus, antiphishing, antispyware and a firewall to ensure that your network and your employees' personal information are secure.

269

Access to business computers should only be for authorized employees.

You should create a particular user account for each employee. This will help restrict access to your business computer. It is also essential to limit the network access for computers in or around your location.

Maintain Security On Mobile Devices

If your employee uses mobile devices to access company information while being at work or after work then it is sure that your business confidentiality is more vulnerable. Most of the companies allow their employees to use their own device at work which increases the exposure to malware and many other issues related to security.

It is better not to access business data on a personal device and to only access it on the official device which is equipped with cyber security tools.

Prefer Encryption Of Data

When information is encoded it is known to be encrypted. No matter whether the information is stored on a device or cloud or being transferred through the internet, if encrypted, the information can only be decoded by a person or computer having the proper key.

Small business should go for systems having a built-in encryption option as you simply need to activate it and your data is secured.

DdoS Attacks

Hiding from the attacker won't stop the attack. Instead, develop a response plan towards the attack.

Depending on the size of businesses, teams need to be settled up to respond to the attack.

Understand the infrastructure and develop comprehensive defense strategies.

The way you start the battle fighting against the attack will decide how it will resolve in the end.

Ensure that your IT team and the data center are well prepared and aware in advance of the adversities of the attack and the roles each key member has to play to fight against it.

Further, there are the primary essential elements, those are same for implication for every company:

System and Infrastructure Checklist

List down all the assets you have which you can implement to identify the threat, assess it and the filtering tools.

Also, ensure the hardware and software level security.

How To Handle Your Customers And Provide Exemplary Customer Service

Focusing on customer service and becoming better at it helps your drop shipping business boost sales. It increases customer loyalty because you make them feel important thus they reciprocate the favor. One happy customer may multiply your clientele if they are pleased with your service. The word-of-mouth action becomes stronger reaching as many connections as it can.

Generally, being nice to your buyer is not difficult at all.

Still, from time to time, something might go wrong, and you might receive unpleasant emails from angry customers asking for a refund. How to deal with such emails and save your money?

Set customer expectations.

Let your customers know what you can do and what you cannot do. Setting customer expectations can also help you make exceed customer expectations upon delivery of service. Make sure your standards and policies are mentioned in the description of every item you sell.

Treat your customers with respect.

Customers are the heart of your business. Therefore, they deserve respect regardless of how irate they are about your product or service. Irate customers are frustrated, but when you treat them with calmness and show respect, they cool down eventually. Listen and empathize. Sometimes the most angry customers can become your most loyal ones.

Empathize with your customer.

Empathy is understanding what others feel – "putting yourself into the shoes of another". When you empathize with your customer, you create a connection and make your customer feel special.

Treat customer complaints in a positive view.

Complaints will always be part of any business. Deal with complaints effectively. Listen to the customer, understand the source of complaint, apologize, and come up with an appropriate solution. Don't blame them and view complaints as a chance for your business to become even better.

Listen to your customers first.

Customers are reaching out to you because they want to be heard. So listen first and understand their issue, then you can speak to empathize. This means you should read their messages all the way through, and carefully notice what they say.

Follow up on feedback.

As a business, feedbacks are super important. If you received a positive or a negative feedback, follow up with a thank you or if it is a complaint, follow up with a solution. Feedbacks are a great way to showcase your customer service skills, and to make more customers happy.

Follow up after sales. Following up after sales make your customer feel important and that you care. Thank them for doing business with you. Ask how well they are pleased with your product or service. Creating a touchpoint also allows you to present other products you offer.

Handle customer returns effectively.

Effectively create a standard on customer returns. If your customer received a defective product and would like to return it, you should be able to replace the product on time as stipulated by your terms and conditions.

Understanding your customers' needs and wants. Customers reach out to you because they have a specific need. Find out what they really want. Knowing what your customer needs are at the center of a successful business.

10,000/Month Strategies

There are many different ways to make money with your own online store. Here are strategies that will make you earn 10,000/Month.

Material

Difference of material could be affect product's durability, functionality and appearance. Let's take a stainless steel product as example.

What do you need to know? $304 stainless steel is much expensive than $430 due to it's better performance of rust-proof. When you get understood of this, you can mark the title or description like: "304 stainless steel made, won't be rusting".

And you can also use thicker material of stainless steel to claim "25%/35% thicker stainless steel won't warp".

All of these will become unique selling points for your amazon products. Surely, it will lightly increase your cost, you should pay attention to the cost and make sure your pricing if acceptable by your potential customer.

You have to be proactive about this, building good relationships with your supplier because they would not tell you anything before you do business with them.

Packaging Option

A good packaging design will help you stand out in similar products.

Do some research of your competitors packaging to see if you can beat them in this aspect.

If yes, go to Fiverr: The Marketplace for Creative & Professional Services or Elance to hire a good designer to improving it!

Just one thing need to keep in mind, DON'T go with oversized packaging. It will be costly on shipping and warehousing.

Get a good photographer and quality images. Looking cheap won't help you and may get you look suspicious.

List your items on Amazon. Sign up for Amazon advertising, it has low competition. You'll get a good price for your ads. ROI on average is about 80%.
Get a free 100$ Google Adwords voucher. Get traffic to your product for free. Google in my experience is slightly more expensive than Facebook—but hey, this is a free voucher.

Work on your SEO.

SEO (Search Engine Optimization) is a free way to get more traffic. Optimize your product titles for search engines and get higher in search results. Free traffic is your best investment. A good way to learn more about SEO is by taking SEO course.

Make your titles eye catching, create a clickbait.

Provide The Best Customer Service And Care About Your Customers.

Once the customer bought something from you and got its package delivered they will trust you. They will talk to their friends about your store—make sure they say good words about you. Include handwritten notes, send them thanking emails.

Create A Loyalty Program.

Reward your returning customers. People like getting discounts. It will also give them a reason to return to your store.

Do Keyword Research.

Create long tail keywords for the products you are selling. Make sure people are looking for a product you are selling. Check Google trends for more information on demographic data to better target your audience. If this sounds unfamiliar start by learning SEO.

How to scale your business

Scaling up a business horizontally means going wide instead of deep.

Let's say you're spending $5 per day on a Facebook and and your ad set is going well.

One way of scaling the ad set is to increase the daily budget in small increments. So rather than finding a new audience, you're just adding more money to a well performing ad set.

So let's talk about how to scale up a drop shipping business horizontally.

"Franchising" Method

A great way to scale up a drop shipping business is by something I call franchising.

I'm not talking about McDonalds and Starbucks here, but you can use a similar approach to scale an existing drop shipping business. Instead of expanding your customer base in a given country, you simply duplicate your entire store and target customers in the new country.

For example:

The first drop shipping store I even built targeted Germany.

Within a few days of running Facebook ads I was making $200-$300 per day of which a big part was profit. After this initial success I decided to duplicate my store in Spain.

My wife speaks Spanish, French, Portuguese and English which I took advantage of.

I asked her to translate my German store and all of my ads into Spanish. I let her do the customer support and shared 50% of the profits with her. Within a few days I had a duplicate of my store up and running and the store started generating around $200-$300 per day.

What I did here is go wide and scale horizontally.

I later on did the same with a store in Portuguese targeting Portugal and Brazil.

Now what if you don't have a multi-lingual wife like I do?

What if you only speak English?

Then simply team up with someone who speaks another language. Create a new online store with the exact same design, products and layout. Get the person to translate everything. And then share 50% of the profit with them. This is a win-win situation for both of you.

If you have no friends and don't know how to network then simply hire someone.

You can keep them for customer support.

Build Your eCommerce Website.

The fastest way to launch a website that supports a drop shipping business model is to use a simple ecommerce platform like Shopify. You don't need a tech background to get up and running, and it has plenty of apps to help increase sales.

Even if you have a small budget that would allow you to hire a web design and development company to create a custom solution. In the beginning it's a much wiser move to use one of the plug-and-play options. Once you are established and the revenue is coming in, then you can explore additional website customization.

Create A Customer Acquisition Plan.

Obviously having a great product and a website is great, but without customers looking to buy, you don't have a business. There are several ways to attract potential customers, but one of the most effective option is to start a Facebook ad campaign.

This allows you to generate sales and revenue right from the beginning which can contribute to quick scaling. Facebook allows you to place your offer directly in front of a highly targeted audience. This gives you the ability to compete with the largest brands and retailers immediately.

You also have to think long term, so search engine optimization and email marketing should also be taking into consideration. Collect emails from the start and set up automated email sequences that offer discounts and special offers. It's an easy way to leverage your existing customer base and generate revenue without additional advertising and marketing spend.

Shopify Inventory Management by Veeqo

Veeqo is an all-in-one ecommerce software that allows retailers to manage and automate their entire business. The software's multichannel inventory management allows retailers to sync inventory across multiple Shopify stores, channels, ecommerce marketplaces and warehouses in real-time ensuring that you never oversell again. View, edit and print orders taking complete control with Veeqo's order management software. With multichannel shipping and fulfilment capabilities you can ship customer orders from any sales channel directly in Veeqo with just a few clicks. By integrating with the world's leading couriers, it's easy to ship to customers anywhere in the world.

Perform Competition Research.

You may remember that you will be competing with other drop shipping operations as well as retail giants such as Walmart and Amazon. This is where a lot of potential drop shippers go wrong, because they look for a product that has little to no competition. That's a sign that there isn't demand for that particular product.

There are different reasons why a product might not have a lot of competition, including high shipping costs, supplier and manufacturing issues or poor profit margins. Look for products that have competitions as a sign of high demand.

Secure a Good supplier.

Don't rush to partner with a supplier as to partner with a wrong one can ruin your business, so it's important that you Conduct proper due diligence. Most drop shipping suppliers are located overseas, making communication extremely important, both in terms of response speed and the ability to understand each other. If you are not confident in the communication abilities of a potential supplier, move on and continue your search.

Alibaba has become one of the largest online resources to identify and communicate with potential manufacturers and suppliers. Always make sure to ask a lot of questions and learn what their production capabilities are in the event that your business grows exponentially. You want to be certain they have the ability to scale with you.

Try to learn from other entrepreneurs who have walked this path in the past. There are plenty of information sources available, from business and tech blogs about drop shipping. It's a popular topic that can help you avoid costly supplier mistakes.

Add More Product To Your Inventory

If you run a retail business, one of your major concerns should be how you control your inventory. If you're new in retail business, here is a little definition of what an Inventory control system means. According to Inc, an inventory control system is a system the encompasses all aspects of managing a company's inventories; purchasing, shipping, receiving, tracking, warehousing and storage, turnover, and reordering. It is important to have all these features in place will lead to a stress-free and management of a successful retail business.

Product Inventory Information

- Inventory Management: Select the Inventory Management type.

  o Managed - When a buyers places an order, the quantity they order will be deducted from your inventory.
  o Unlimited - If you choose this the product is treated as though it is always in stock on LeafLink. This can be used by brands who are forecasting production needs, and/or brands who are tracking inventory using another platform. If you select Unlimited Inventory, you cannot use the backorder functionality.
  o Inherited - This is a style of managed inventory used when a product's varieties "borrow" inventory from the parent product. For example, you might have 5 pounds of flower (the parent product) that you package into various sizes (the varieties).
- Inventory: This is the quantity of the product you have in your inventory. If you select Managed or Inherited inventory you must enter the starting amount of inventory before launching this product.
- Unit Denomination: Enter the amount of the product associated with the unit of measurement.

283

For example, flower may be sold in 1 ounce increments, so your unit of measure would be ounces and your unit of denomination would be 1.

- Enable Sample Requests: Select whether or not you will offer sample requests for this product by checking the affiliated box.

- Min Order: This is the minimum amount of a product a buyer must order in a single transaction for the order to be placed. If the minimum is not met, the order will not be processed and the buyer will be notified. If there is no minimum, leave this field blank.

- Unit of Measure: Select milligram, gram, kilogram, ounce, pound, unit, or case.

- Product Availability: Also known as "product drop", you can appoint a new product to be released on your menu as Available at a certain date and time.

- Max Order: This is the maximum amount a buyer can order in a single transaction. If the maximum is exceeded, the order will not process and the buyer will be notified. If there is no maximum, leave this field blank.

- Sell in Multiples: If selected, retailers will select the number of cases or packages to purchase, rather than individual units.

Dropshipping Tips

A dropshipping business gives you the flexibility to work from home, from your 9-5 job, or even while on vacation. It's a perfect opportunity to create a supplemental income, and can even give you the ability to choose when and where to work.

Dropshipping is a business model that gives you the flexibility to operate an online store, without ever having to carry the product. You process orders, and ship directly from the supplier to your customer.

In the beginning, some may find dropshipping a bit intimidating. Thankfully, it doesn't have to be. That's one reason I have designed these dropshipping tips and best practices tips to help you take your existing dropshipping store to the next level, maximize profits and increase conversions.

Sell What You Know

One of the best dropshipping tip is to sell what you know makes sense, especially if your expertise turn out to be in high demand, innovative products. Moreover, the beauty of having the right product knowledge means you are able to take most of the guess work out of your choice of products. It will show in the way you present the product on your website, the confidence in the deals you offer, up to the level of customer service you will be able to provide. And because seller ratings are a major driving force in ecommerce, knowing your product well will increase your customer's confidence in your business and ultimately attract more potential customers.

Try A Product Specific Pricing Strategy

A wholesale dropship reseller understands why strategic product placement on an online store is important to business. More often than not, customers decide in just a matter of minutes whether to stay on your website or to move on to the next one based on what they find on your main page. As a result, smart store owners have adopted a featured product display section on their main page where they show their most popular products. But why stop there?

Once you've caught the customer's attention with your featured products, the next thing they will do is to compare your price with other sellers. Most resellers opt for a simple pricing strategy, forgetting that offering a more competitive price for their featured products can potentially close them the deal. This pricing strategy, known as featured product pricing or product specific pricing, may initially sound like too much work, but it only takes a few minutes to apply while giving you a great opportunity to leverage your traffic.

Customers will add your featured product to their cart once they recognize instant savings, and will then proceed to add more accessories related to the product to spread out their shipping cost where you can make your additional margin.

Light & Durable Is Better than Heavy & Fragile

In terms of what products to sell via dropshipping, you might easily be tempted to offer just about anything that can generate a good profit as long as there are suppliers around. But before you post photos of those large vases or paintings or those home theater systems that you couldn't believe suppliers are selling at a really low cost, remember the risks involved in a dropshipping business. Logistics should be one of your top concerns when shipping an item, so it is better to consider light and durable products instead of heavy and fragile ones. It's also wise, especially if you're just starting out, to steer clear of products that require more than simple technical assistance to set up.

Don't Limit Your Suppliers

Limiting yourself to one supplier can lead to long term issues. That supplier may discontinue your best-selling product, or sell out unexpectedly. Using multiple product suppliers also means that when you order your samples, you choose the supplier that has the best product. Having many suppliers will also give you a wider selection of items to choose from, so research alternative dropshippers to source your products.

Know Your Niche

I've saved the best (and the most important of the dropshipping tips) for the last. Don't choose your niche based on what someone else says is going to sell. You need to select the best product for yourself. If you aren't interested in the product that you are shipping, that's going to come across to your target customers. They want to buy from someone who cares as much about their interest as they do. Otherwise, they'd order from Amazon.

Your interest, knowledge, and expertise are part of the package. Choose products that make sense for your niche. If you don't succeed at first, your shop can go in a different direction down the road. When your website is too general it won't make sense to your customers, and they won't want to shop from you.

Create Custom Content

Custom content is a fantastic way to generate traffic to your site. One of the best dropshipping tips is to do live product reviews on your social media pages. Start blogging to compare different types of products. Most importantly, make it about the products that you carry. If you carry women's fashion, write about fashion week. If you feature children's toys, share the top 10 toys for each of the last five decades, etc. Create content that people will want to share.

Attend Ecommerce Events

There is no better way to start your journey into ecommerce and dropshipping by attending events like the Internet Retailer Conference & Exhibition (IRCE). Attending means learning first hand from already established online businesses that have extensive knowledge in the dropshipping industry. It also won't hurt that you'll be able to network with trusted wholesalers and retailers who you may do business with someday..

Among the major reasons why you should attend IRCE:

- It caters to online businesses of all sizes
- It's not as expensive as it seems
- Highly educational
- Motivates your creativity
- Takes away a lot of the guesswork in setting up your own business

Marketing is Gold

Automation tools are great for advertising on the go. Pursue your life, go to your 9-5. But don't forget how valuable manually checking in each day can be. Check your social media business pages at all times and respond to customers. Answer questions, Today, nothing is more valuable than authenticity. Spending a little bit of time connecting with your customers leads to higher conversion.

Get a Shipping Partner

ShipBob does everything FBA (Fulfillment by Amazon) does, but better and cheaper. ShipBob doesn't charge for picking or packing or warehousing. If that sounds too good to be true, their business model is that they negotiate cheaper volume-based rates for shipping, they charge you only what the normal postage price would be, and they keep the difference. They have a great API and integration with everything.

Use Alternative Dropshipping Platforms

Aside from the usual dropshipping platforms, consider using alternative ones as well. I recommend trying AliExpress. It has the same vendors who also have eBay accounts in US locations. They are usually faster, as they do not want to get penalized by eBay. They normally have US partners and warehouses and they provide a USPS tracking number. This can be provided to your customer, and makes for better customer satisfaction than providing them with a Chinese international tracking number.

Establish a Good Retailer – Supplier Relationship

In every supplier-retailer dropship relationship, a myriad of details must be worked out in order for either party to see lucrative sales. Aspects that need to be considered include: How are product content and data managed, and how does it make its way onto the retailer's site? How is inventory updated and synced to the retailer's site? When orders are placed, how does the supplier receive that information? Who gets paid for what percentage of the sale, and when? How are items actually shipped—whose carrier account is used? How are returns dealt with?

Obviously, dropshipping is a complex, multifaceted practice that necessarily means that retailers and suppliers are constantly exchanging data back and forth. To succeed then, the key is to always remember that dropshipping is a relationship between retailer and supplier, and it requires efficient communication, transparency, collaboration, and organization on the part of both parties.

Ship via Epacket

It's a fact that shipping from overseas can take forever, which isn't the best way to keep your customers happy. By selecting vendors that use Epacket you'll be able to get your product to your customers and without exorbitant shipping prices. Your customers will be happy, and your reviews will reflect that.

Plan for Returns and Other Issues

As in any other business, dropshipping also poses a number of potential problems. Issues like back orders, lost shipment, and returns can be a little more complicated when dropshipping is involved. For one, you don't have direct control over what the merchandise will look like when it reaches your customer. However, planning for these contingencies is possible too. Discuss policies and obligations and come to an agreement with your dropshipper from the start to make sure both sides will put in the maximum effort to avoid these kinds of scenarios.

Test Your Product

As a drop shipper, it's important that you take the opportunity to get to know your product. Have you ever ordered an item online, and what you received wasn't what you expected? You have a responsibility to your customers to know what your product looks like. As a bonus, when you order product samples you'll be able to take better photos of the product, have products available for SEO generating content creation (blogs, how to videos, etc.), and be able to answer customers' questions.

Automate Your Website

Website automation is one of the fastest ways to ensure that you are able to generate a passive income. When you use automation tools, life opens back up to you. Automation tools automate social media postings, targeting emails, and so much more. Automating your website will make your life easier and give you free time.

Make Quality Presentation of Your Merchandise a Priority

One of the key dropshipping tips to remember is to not just rely on the XML feeds that are provided by wholesale suppliers, manufacturers, and other stores. The descriptions are typically generic, which not only can decrease your conversion rate, but it's also bad for SEO as you're competing with all the other dropshippers that are using the same material for their stores.

While it may be a pain and time consuming, it's well worth creating unique product descriptions that are optimized for the keywords that you're looking to rank for. Your product descriptions should mention features and benefits while connecting with shoppers on an emotional level. Remember, on the whole, people are irrational – making that emotional connection through a unique product description can help a dropshipper take advantage of a person's natural cognitive biases.

Additional tips: When dropshipping from AliExpress, always make sure to select ePacket shipping, and ensure that it is sent via ePacket and not China Post. This is because ePacket can easily be tracked, and China Post is a much difficult platform to navigate as it is mainly in Chinese.

Dropshipping Mistake to avoid

It may sound easy, but there are lots of things to understand before proceeding to drop shipping business model. Now we want to share the top mistakes that all the beginners make. Understand and try to avoid this mistakes from the start of the drop shipping business, and you would reach the top soon.

Paying For Access To A Dropship Supplier

When you're looking for suppliers and you use Google, most of the results are likely middlemen suppliers.

They aren't the kind of companies that you wish to dropship with. That's because they make most of their money by charging fees.

These fees will come in two ways. The first will be an application fee to be approved by them. The second way will be dropshipping fees for every order you place with them.

If a dropship supplier wants you to pay upfront, it's most likely because that's how they make their money.

They aren't interested in a long-term business relationship with you. You want suppliers that will take you on because you're going to work together for years to come. You're both going to make money with each other – it's a beneficial business relationship.

Not Picking Reliable Suppliers

Your choice of suppliers will make or break your drop shipping business. At the end your suppliers control your inventory and handle fulfillment for your customer's orders.

If you get a supplier that delivers packages late or consistently sends defective products, your business will have close to zero chances of surviving past its first year. Don't even get us started on suppliers who engage in fraud or sell counterfeit products.

Don't spring for bare-minimum service either, though. Sure, your supplier might have decent products, but can you work with them? Do they answer your inquiries promptly? Do their sales reps know what they're talking about?

Finding a supplier that works is only the first step; it's very important and crucial that you find one that you can work with.

Check inspected directories — big platforms like SaleHoo, WorldWide Brands, and Oberlo maintain lists of trustworthy suppliers. If you're seeking out suppliers directly on sites like AliExpress, take the time to check their ratings (aim for at least 95% for each seller) and reviews. If you can afford it, place test orders so you can check a potential supplier's delivery and customer support processes yourself.

Picking a Wrong Niche

That's where all the beginners fail. Selecting a proper niche is very important. If you don't have a passion for the industry you want to drop ship, then you are throwing money away.

Drop shipping is possible in any industry you can think of. So, first, you have to understand the basics of that niche. Don't go into the niche which is very overrated and has no value. To be successful at drop shipping, you've to deliver value. It means that niche/industry you want o to operate in has to provide value to people.

Drop shipping professionals always use free tools to understand whether the niche is a winner or not. Just think of various things, go out and look at the banners on buildings. Go out and listen to people in the metro, bus or taxi. You'll find lots of niches and industries you did not know about before. You can track down those industries on your notebook or notes. Go to "Google Trends" and check each niche (probably keyword or idea). There you'll find whether those niches are worth investing or not.

Spend Way too Much Time on Niche Selection

Pick a niche and go with it. Commit yourself to 90 days in ONE niche and you will succeed. I have yet to see anyone not succeed when COMMITTING to it for 90 days. Consistency is the key to your success .

General Store

Most marketers recommend picking a general store to sell anything and everything. Great in theory, but it makes it so hard to target. It also leaves you an "out" where you can jump from niche product to niche product and never really knowing your market.

Not Developing Your Brand

You're not manufacturing your own products, but you're still running a well established business. Your name and your services are the only things making a difference from other drop shippers sourcing from the same suppliers. If others out there can sell your target customers the same thing, you better give those customers a good reason to pick you over the rest.

A strong brand identity and a unified offering of value-added services will help you leave a mark on your customers. These pave the way to recurring transactions and, hopefully, lasting loyalty from your market.

Figure Out Your Branding And The Services You'll Offer.

Craft a nice logo and place this prominently on your website, all communication Deliver to customers, and even the shipping labels used for customer's order when possible. You want to be sure you are known as the best option for buying certain products, and strong branding will help you fulfill that.

Selling Trademarked Goods

This is by far the biggest mistake people make. Shopify stores are being shut down everyday because of this. I know of a well known marketers that got sued for $2.1M because of this. If you do not have a license to sell movie, music & sports items — DO NOT SELL THEM

Customers Service: Huge Advantage

As a newbie in the dropshipping industry, what's your offer to the world? What will be a something unique that people will love and won't go to another store?

If you offer a low price, then soon you may end up without a budget for investment. You may provide fast delivery and shipping but believe me; there will be others who will deliver products faster than you. So, what's your best bet? It's customer service. You could be better than your competitors if you created and established strong customer service.

Your buyers need information and updates about product shipment on a weekly or even daily basis. That's where the customer service team comes into the game. You've found and recruited very passionate and hard working persons for your customer service team. You need to be ready for customer's questions on 24/7. There won't be any rest, and you should be prepared for this.

Never underrate"word of mouth marketing." All your happy customers with customer service will go and tell their friends about your store and compelling customer service. That's the cheapest and easiest way to market and grow your brand.

Ridiculous Expectations

Most expect instant success. Like any business this takes time. This takes work. This takes failing a lot with Facebook ads. For every 10 products you run ads to, you should find one winner and one that does alright.

Not Planning a Proper Strategy for Promotion

Don't listen to those gurus who say that you can start earning money from drop shipping store with just 100 or 200 dollars.

IT's IMPOSSIBLE!

Just understand one thing – Drop shipping is a business model, and you've to act like a business owner. None of the business owners can earn money with just a few dollars investment.

Before you proceed to Drop shipping business model, first you have to create a smart and proper plan for promotion. You can't wait for huge ROI (Return on Investment) from the first promotion, but the stats and data you'll get from the first campaign would be priceless.

There are a few ways of promotion. You can either pay money to someone authoritative in that industry/niche or go for paid ads.

- Create a simple plan to test five influencers (reliable) and have a specific budget for it.
- Create a simple plan for paid ads (Facebook and Google Ads) and have a particular budget for it.

Don't wait for magical numbers in first few weeks. Test waters and get the data which is very valuable for every store owner.

CONCLUSION

Going back a couple of years, most people looking to set up a dropship business would choose, what was at the time, the simplest business model for success. You would see what products were selling, find a supplier for your drop ship products, and then simply list them on one of the biggest marketplaces in the world, eBay, and wait for them to sell. With the millions of people who were looking to buy items on eBay everyday, as long as you had the drop ship products they wanted to buy, at the right price, it was one of the easiest and fastest ways to start making money with dropshipping.

So is this the end for dropship opportunities? Hardly. What is does mean is that those who have the right approach, and see it as a business rather than some kind of get rich quick scheme, have adapted to maintain the kind of profits that will sustain their dropshipping business. They now look at other ways of marketing their drop ship products; Amazon, their own websites, Search Engine Optimization and Social Media.

Has it become more challenging to develop a profitable dropship business? Possibly. But running any business is a challenge, which is why it's worth it when you get it right. If anything, the changes in the dropshipping market will mean that it becomes less attractive for those looking for a quick buck, and who generally give the industry a bad name. Which means that the professional dropship businesses will continue to grow - great for them, and for the customers. Also, more and more people will start to see dropshipping as a way to get started, before developing their enterprise using other business models. With its low cost of entry and sustainability, dropshipping is a way for ecommerce businesses to establish themselves, so they can gain the investment capital and experience needed to move on and start using traditional wholesale suppliers, who offer greater profit potential.

While the concept of dropshipping hasn't really changed, how you need to approach it in order to be successful certainly has. Those who still see selling drop shipping products as an easy way to make some quick money, will not doubt end up being the ones that say a dropship business can't succeed. While those who approach it as they would any other new business startup, investing time and effort, and looking to grow their business with a view to the long term, will be the ones that prove a dropship business can still be a great opportunity.

SOCIAL MEDIA MARKETING 2019

Use the newest successful strategies to mastery the best channels including Youtube, Instagram, SEO, Facebook and LinkedIn - Rapidly Skyrocket your Personal Brand

Blake Davis

Table of Contents

Introduction

Social media, which relates to the sharing of information, experiences, and viewpoint throughout community-oriented websites, is becoming increasingly symbolic in our online world. Thanks to social media, the geographic walls that divide individuals are crumbling, and new online communities are developing and growing. Some examples of social media include blogs and vlogs forums, message boards, picture- and video-sharing sites, user-generated websites, wikis, and podcasts. Each of these tools aid communication about ideas that users are ardent about, and connects like-minded individuals throughout the world.

According to Universal McCann's Wave 3 report, released in mid-2018, social media is rising and it seems unstoppable. Amid all Internet users between the ages of 16 and 54 globally, the Wave 3 report suggests the following:

- 794 million users watch video clips online

- 746 million users read blogs

- 721 million users read personal blogs

- 707 million users visit friends' social network profile pages

- 703 million users share video clips

- 602 million users manage profiles on social networks

- 648 million users upload photos

- 616 million users download video podcasts

- 615 million users download audio podcasts

- 584 million users start their own blogs

- 683 million users upload video clips

- 560 million users subscribe to Rss feeds

Social media insertion seems to be a continuing trend. Social media marketing (sometimes referred to by its acronym, SMM) helps service providers connecting , companies, and corporations with a broad audience of influencers and consumers. Using social media marketing, companies can gain traffic, followers, and brand awareness - and that's just the beginning .

History of Social Media Marketing

Social Media seems to be a new trend, but its birth stretch to the beginning of computer era. What we actually see today is the result of centuries-old social media development. Usernets, which was launched in 1979, was the first ancestor of social media, and the journey from Usernets to Facebook is a long one. Usernets helped users to post on newsgroups. It was followed by bulletin board systems (BBS) which allowed users to login and collaborate. Online platforms like progidy were the precursors to BBS. After online services, internet relay chat came into light which gave way to instant messaging.

In the 90s, dating sites and seminars were on peak, which led to the augmentation of social networks. But they did not let users make friend lists. Six degrees launched to overcome this feature. It allowed profile creation and listing pears. It was aquired and shut down after playing for a decagon. Blogging emerged in this phase, creating a passion in social media. It is very popular even today. Other sites like BlackPlanet (African-American Social Website) and MiGente (Latino) trimmed off having provision to create profiles and add friends.

State of the art social networks came into picture post 2000. Apple launched its Friendster in 2002. It has lots of users. Hi5 and Linkedin were launched in 2003. Linkedin is a place for professionals to reach out to one another. MySpace also originated in 2003 and became well known by 2006. Similarly Facebook was commenced in 2004 and surpassed MySpace, Orkut, Multiply, etc., and is still expanding. These years also conceived media sharing platforms like photobucket, flickr, youtube, instagram, etc., along with news and bookmarking platforms like Digg and Delicious.

Since 2000, Social Media has prospered to horizon and is still prospering limitlessly. Along with media sharing, many other portals that provide real-time updates were suggested for example, Twitter, Tumblr, etc. In 2007,

Facebook launched its advertising system. The gravity of social media is undebatable. It is a potent channel of marketing – a game changer for any business. It provides us the resilience to impart at both personal as well as business levels.

Field owners can improve search rankings, leads, sales, and traffic using search media. This can be done at reduced marketing costs. Besides business, it is a cool platform to associate with friends and dear ones.

Where We Are Now

Until recently, the Internet was predominantly an explanatory medium. Notwithstanding, in the last couple of years, the Internet has become progressively social. We are now looking at websites, obsessions, and demeanors of our peers in order to make well-informed and well-read findings about our next move, be it a buying decision or another sanctioned article to read late at night. Websites such as MySpace and Facebook have turned up to make communication between peers fast and easy. Social websites have been created to unify individuals with similar interests: social news sites that are governed by the "wisdom of crowds," social bookmarking sites that allow individuals to identify websites that a large number of people have already discovered, and alcove social networks that consolidate individuals under a common interest. As such, a new discipline, social media upturn, also called social media marketing, has developed.

What Is Social Media Marketing?

Social media marketing is a process that legitamize individuals to endorse their websites, products, or services through online social channels and to communicate with and tap into a much larger neighbourhood that may not have been available via long-established advertising channels. Social media, most first-foremost, accentuate the unified rather than the individual. Associations exist in peculiar architecture and amount throughout the Internet, and people are talking among themselves. It's the job of social media marketers to advantage these communities properly in order to adequately communicate with the community shareholders about relevant product and service contributions. Social media marketing also requires listening to the communities and establishing relationships with them as a representative of your company. As we will discuss later in this book, this is not often the easiest feat.

In essence, social media marketing is about listening to the community and responding promptly but for many social media business makers it also refers to reviewing content or finding a notably useful piece of content and promoting it within the vast social sphere of the Internet.

Social media marketing is a newer peripheral of search engine marketing, but it is really in a class of its own. It doesn't mean only searching; it relates to a broad class of word-of-mouth marketing that has taken the Internet by its horns. Fortunately, the anomaly is only growing at this point. At last social media marketing can achieve one or many of the goals listed in the following sections.

This book will help you not only understand the culture-shifting philosophies that make up marketing in the social media world, but also the strategic reasons social media marketing is used for business. It will;

- Help you grasp what social media can do for your business

- Help you determine what you want it to do for your business

- Show you how to calibrate what it can do for your business

It is not an establishment to social media, but to social media marketing blueprint. It peels away the touchy-feely advancement of early evangelists and gets down to business, because you are a businessperson. You don't have time for levity, games, and all that gibberish. You need to know the time and money you spend on social media is performing something for you. You need the nonesense take on social media marketing.

Why Social Media Are So Important Today

For years running a business was not so simple - you had a store or office, went to work each day, kept everything running, printed flyers or brochures to promote your business and used your profits to pay your employees and bills.

To do business in the 90' you probably needed a Fax machine and a newspaper ad, to do business in the 2000's you needed a website and a mobile phone. All you need to do business in this decade you need a Blog and Social Media. With the arrival of computers and the internet things have changed dramatically and if you want to be a presence online then social media really is that important.

These days it's very easy to start a business. In some cases depending on the type of business it is, you can be up and running on the net in a couple of hours and many of today's businesses are run solely online. For many small business owners, an online business is a fantastic way to build their business, while keeping overheads low. E-stores for example, allow people to store all their stock at home and employ maybe one or two people to arrange packaging and postage - far cheaper than renting a warehouse and an office for admin staff.

In today's tech-savvy world it pays to use as many outlets as you can to build an online presence. Whether you want to believe it or not, the majority of your customers, clients and competitors are online and unless you're there too, you're losing money.

Social media networking sites such as Facebook, Twitter, LinkedIn and YouTube give you the opportunity to reach a greater audience and to connect with your customers and clients in ways that simply weren't possible ten years ago.

We all know that creating and maintain relationships with customers is the key to a successful business but prior to now we had only distant tools to maintain and build these relationships. In the past we've had the phone, recently email and text messaging but these are one-to-one communication mediums. With Social Media we can still have this one-to-one conversations but now we involve others in the same conversation. This is very powerful from a marketing perspective.

I know that I are more likely to purchase something if it's recommended by a friend rather than if I simply saw an ad on TV or in the newspaper. Now, you have reviews in so many different ways. By combining your website with a Facebook page, Twitter account, YouTube Channel, Blog and information-rich articles, you can not only increase the number of people who know about your business but provide them with information, discounts and promotions that you can't do with print media. And with Social Media the cost is simply your time, unless you'd like to run Pay Per Click marketing campaigns which you should.

You will find over millions of users on social media sites today, sites like Facebook, Twitter, Instagram, Facebook Messanger, WeChat, and WhatsApp have made a big impact on people's life. Not only sharing photo's and information, but trades and business have also flourished. The numbers are ever rising on the social media sites, the mass number of users on each social platform clearly indicates how important is social media in today's world, it has changed the entire concept in the field of Information and Communication.

There are several reasons why you need to be on a Social Media platform today.

Communication: Social media platforms such as Facebook, Twitter, Google and more have made it easy to contact and get in touch anyone just by searching for their names online. Smartphones and tablets have also played a very big role, previously you needed to have a PC or a laptop, but now you can be in touch with all your friends and relatives on the move, even managing the business it's simple and fast.

You can connect with customers and clients all over the world from promoting your business and selling products to finding new clients, new media can put the world in your hands with the click of a button. And sites such as Facebook allow your customers and clients an opportunity to communicate with you, no matter where you are.

Photo sharing: With the advent of Facebook, Instagram, and Snapchat, one can now share photos about exciting moments of our lives with friends and family members miles away from us. People were deprived of such things in the past and now they are just a click away from sharing the loving moments with their loved ones sitting miles away.

Awareness Campaign: When we speak about raising funds or helping poor, social media network is always seen as a big podium to raise millions of dollars for charity or different awareness campaign such as the Boston bombing victims, where nearly about 200,000 dollars was raised.

Don't let your competition take away your business. Use social media to its fullest to create an impact online and increase your presence to customers old and new. If you want your business to survive in today's technological world you need to be where your customers are - online and on social media networking sites. Increase your presence and your business, and start your social media marketing campaign today.

Promotion: Promotion on Social Media sites has gained a lot of determination in the world of business and entertainment, people can advocate their work and increase the fan base by sharing information about their events and themselves. Through this platform, they can raise funds and transform their business in money Also, business makers can get information about what the people feel about their products through reviews.

If you've been put off using Facebook, Twitter, LinkedIn, YouTube or a Blog, you are reducing the opportunities you have to reach your customers and clients. There are still many businesses without websites, which not only makes it difficult for people to find them, but drives people to their competitors. By creating an online presence you will increase your availability to your customers and be a greater competitor to your competition.

Differences Between Social Media Marketing And Social Media Advertising

Social media marketing is the qualification to create specific plans or techniques that target social networks and applications to spread brand awareness or encourage particular products. Social media marketing barnstorm usually center around: Establishing a social media existence on major platforms. This is how you present yourself or your business to the world.

You apply social media marketing in your everyday social media posting and everything that implicates your account. This is the most important part of your journey. A successful social media marketing strategy brandish every single attitude of its profile to give users a better piece of information about your business.

First, identify who is your client . If your buyer is female, from 25 to 54 years old, based in Central London, you should put your attention on talking to this audience. What are those customers interested discover more? In this case, your market should be more abroad than when doing advertising.

- New product lines
- The benefits of using moisturizers
- New applying tecniques
- Best colors for different skin tones

- Cosmetics around the world
- Organic or cruelty free beauty products
- Interesting stories
- Makeup tutorial videos
- Cohesions with customers

A social media specialist does not need to be an expert on every topic or trend . To come up with a few of suggestions it only took me a few seconds and my experience with cosmetics goes as far as daily moisturizing. The ability or skills to understand what a costumer might desire comes from within your own company and specialists will help you to better tailor your content to fit into your business approach.

Note that the main goal with all the suggested topics is to educate and entertain. That's the fascination of social media. It allows brands to present themselves as authority in a given subject. Once your audience follows you and applauds and respects the content you put out you are likely to have earned a new patron.

Before we get into advertising let's evaluate a proper study case. You are holder of a travel agency. You have an imminent offer for three different countries: Brazil, Greece, and Japan.

- Brazil – Summer destination, the carnival is the principal attraction. Perfect for people looking for crowded parties, beach holidays and sunny weather with hot temperatures.

- Greece – It is low season in Greece and your company wants to push packages for couples that want to enjoy quiet time in Greek heaven.

- Japan – It is winter time. Best known for its rich art, Japan is the perfect destination for a food experience , cultural shock and city holidays.

You have three very different destinations and each one of them targets a completely different type of customer. How to advertise each one of those destinations on social media? Should advertising that destination be part of your online marketing?

This is a grey area for most of the artists out there. Advertising should be developed differently from your marketing but linked to each other somehow at the end. When users follow your brand on social media they are interested in what you have to say, your approach and what your brand stands for. They are all tied to one topic and one very idea. They are all tied by the ambition to know more about your company.

If you absorb hard sell posts into your social media calendar that endorse just one of your products you will generate the consideration of only a very small percentage of your audience. Remember, your audience on social media relates to each other by a subject activity and not by a specific product. Hence among your audience, you have a very different type of people, with different interests when it comes to traveling.

When you create a post exclusively to promote one of

those stations, you're subversing all the rest of your audience which is not so interested in that particular offer. The result could be repetitive and not engaging timeline of posting. When you users realize your brand has nothing else to say than advertise its own product on social media, your brand may start losing followers and your commitment levels will drop down. And the reason is simple, your brand isn't fulfilling a need, neither is providing information and answering questions.

Your brand is only interested in selling products, making it futile for it to develop an online charisma. Users are people and they tend to connect better with other users than brands. For that reason, developing a brand personality will help your brand to bring the warmth and responsive approach it will need to allow people to connect. Once this connection is established and working you more likely have earned a new client.

Social media advertising on the other hand, is an extension of social media marketing. It works as an extra tool to help marketers to better reach their customers, spread brand alertness and promote their products. Social media advertising (SMA) cannot (or should not) exist without SMM. Although SMA is born within SMM's strategy, it has to be handled with different criterion to measure its success and return on asset. The best ways to assimilate advertising into your marketing strategy is to use your creativity in creating content at full influence.

Creativity works well within social media. It will allow your brand to talk about your products and start new conversations with your audience in an organic and alluring way. Instead of you creating a twitter post saying "Winter in Japan for "this price" you can create a blog post with the title "Japanese winter wonders". Write an article about how preposterous Japan is in the winter, what are the main appeals and why this is a great choice for your customer's next trip. By particularly writing a very explanatory article describing all the benefits of going to Japan, you are basically doing a form of advertising, totally embedded in your marketing strategy and integrated into your social media planner.

When you develop content that solves the need for a customer you are providing fair information. And, by doing that, you are automatically advertising your own product without mentioning the parts about the sales at all.

Small parts of advertising should be incorporated into your social media marketing and still provide an important source of content for your social media planners. Returning to the travel agency example, the Japan blog post will add extra value to the travel agency company, showing up on online searches as results for "travel in Japan". It will naturally reach many other users that after reading your article might have their curiosity trigged to see the offers the travel agency has to offer. This piece of content will be forever introduced on the main webpage and it's now an extra source of information about your own services.

Although it is emmensely important for your organic

social media marketing/advertising, it does not represent a powerful way to increase sales and convert new clients . However, the return on investment is very positive. The organic reach of users does not require investment, leaving the only investment in this case to the creation of a content. And it will also improve your SEO rank, leading new search to the content your brand is developing . If you have a solid team that produces quality content frequently, integrating advertising in creative and sophisticated ways into your social media calendar will ignite your business online presence.

In denouement, every social media achievement should start with a well thought-out social media marketing strategy. But simply looking at a social media profile you should know exactly what that person/company is talking about . This is how you will set the tone of your online presence and tell the world what are yours abjectives. Social media marketing is the online "humanization"of your brand. This is the only way your brand carries an actual voice and participates in the public opinion. This is what brings the spice, your public is looking for to feel nothing more than entertained. The main contrast between SMM and SMA is that marketing will win new customers/followers with personality and knowledge; while advertising will fulfill a need and provide a service. Understanding the difference between those two approaches is the first step to a incredibly successful journey on social media.

Social Media Marketing Strategy

In my opinion, almost all strategic planning try on acquiring new customers. When you take a hard look at your collective objectives, don't they always boil down to getting more people to say "yes" and buying products and services from you so your business will rise ? Internet marketing serves the same purposes and objectives . When it comes to marketing, there are three channels or lanes people will use to connect with your business.

1. **Direct or Return Traffic**. This is when an individual has bookmarked your website or has received marketing collateral (business card from a salesperson, brochure, newspaper ad, etc.), or heard about your business in some way and they visit your website. Direct or return traffic to your site should increase over time. People may become aware of your business through the other channels (i.e.: social sites or search) but when they return, they will most likely just type your website or blog address into their browser.

2. **Search Engines.** One of the most important channels to leverage for growing sales is search. In North America alone there are over 25 billon searches conducted within search engines every single month. This offers huge potential for companies who know how to become visible in this channel. That's why I dedicated a whole chapter on

how to make your content as search engine friendly as possible. The visitors you receive from search should also grow over time. You'll also want the phrases that are being used to find your business align with the targeted key phrases you've used when optimizing your web content.

3. **Social Media Sites.** Social media sites such as Twitter, Facebook, LinkedIn, and YouTube also help customers find you and drive traffic to your business website. You'll develop strategies to grow followers and entice them to visit you. This traffic should also grow over time.

When your potential customers land on your page, four things could happen.

Leave instantly. Visitors can land on your blog or website, gather the information they need and exit, or they could decide that you're not relevant to what they were hoping to find and quickly leave. Think of your site as a leaky bucket. Part of developing a solid Internet marketing strategy will be to identify and monitor where the holes are within your site and plug them up with better content and calls to action. Website abandonment is when visitors land somewhere within your environment and hit the back button before clicking to a deeper page. This is also known as bounce rate. You'll want your bounce rate decrease over time.

Decide to follow you. Regardless of how and where someone finds you it's critical to make it easy for them to follow you. Make sure you have links to Twitter,

Facebook, LinkedIn, YouTube and RSS feeds easily reachable on all of your Internet platforms.

Opt-in. A visitor can decide to request further information from you by filling out a form, registering for an event, or downloading value-based content. A well optimized climate should expect 2% - 10% of visitors to opt-in. There are two types of potential customers who will connect with you this way, which I discuss later in the book. For now it's important to understand that once someone has opted in, you'll need to provide them over time with useful information and multiple touches to turn these potential buyers into new customers.

Reach out to Sales. Some visitors will decide to pick up the phone and reach out to your sales department, ask a question or make a purchase. Make it easy for them by putting your phone number in a highly visible place on every page of your site, blog, and social media platform. This will prevent them from having to dig for the information and cause you to potentially lose sales. This is another area where you should see an increase over time.

When developing a social media business plan it's important to be mindful of this process and all the different ways to target and engage your audience. The best way to do this is to identify, define and document what winning looks like for your business.

Your Three-Legged Stool for Success

Any strong strategy starts with laying a solid authority and your social media marketing plan is no different. Just like with SEO 2.0, there is a three legged stool and each leg is a critical component to establish a successful strategy for your business. These three legs include characterizing your goals and objectives, measuring your performance against those goals and objectives, and then refining those goals. Let's look at each of these in parts. Just like any three-legged stool, these three elements bind together to achieve a common purpose. Remove one of these legs and the whole strategy will fall apart. You actually can't refine your strategy without measuring and you can't measure without defining what to measure.

First Leg: Define

The first step in developing a successful social media marketing strategy for your business is to identify, define, and document your goals and objectives. Over the next few pages, I outline a process and point you to resources that will help you think through this critical step in strategic planning. Begin by considering your corporate objectives. Social Media must tie into these objectives to lay a proper foundation for success. Corporate objectives represent the highest priority for your company during the next 12 months.

Business owners often struggle with differentiating a corporate objective from a marketing objective. Recently, I was training a group of business owners and I asked everyone to share with the group their corporate objectives. One member said, "To hear my phone ringing "When I asked her why did she wanted her phone to ring, she said, "Because when my phone rings I make more sales." Then I asked her why she wanted to make more sales and her answer was to be richer and I followed up with one last question, "Why do you want to increase your marketing?" Her response was perfect, "Because businesses must grow or get smaller and I want my business to rise ." I said, "Perfect! You now have your associates bjective, to grow your business. All we need to do now is figure out by how much you want to increase your business." Her answer was 50% then explained to the class that this owner had just worked out a lot of her objectives:

- Grow revenue by 50%. This is a sort of a corporate objective

- Increase sales by receiving more calls from eventual customers. This is a marketing objective.

When you can answer the question "why?" to an objective, then you really have a lower-level objective or tactic. It turns out that "making my phone ring" was really a marketing objective, not a corporate objective. Once you can't answer why anymore, you are more than likely at your corporate objective. Push yourself to ask why until you can't anymore and this will lead to your true corporate objectives. After you've done this, we can move on to connecting these objectives to social media.

Creating Your Purpose Statement for Social Media

A key step in this first leg of the stool is to determine your purpose statement for social media. In essence, what is it you are hoping social media will do for your business? To do this effectively you'll need to connect the dots between your purpose statement for social media and your mission and value statement for your business, as well as your current overall corporate objectives. Here is a simple template to use for your social media purpose statement:

XYZ will leverage social media to [corporate objective, or element of value statement, or mission statement] in [year]. This will be accomplished by [list high level actions-these will typically center around building community, leading with value, delivering quality content, and include your high level way to convert your audience.]

Once you've written a purpose statement for social media in general, I recommend you actually write a purpose statement for each of your social media channels. For instance, how will Facebook help you accomplish that purpose statement? How will LinkedIn do that? What will YouTube do to help your business?

Here is an example of a purpose statement for Twitter;

To increase sales by:

- Analyzing and connecting with influencers and customers

- Providing practical information to nurture relationships

- Drawing the community to our website and blog for additional information and/or special offers

This will be measured by:

- Increasing our community on Twitter

- The number of visitors that come from Twitter

- The number of Twitter visitors that respond

It will be difficult for you to accomplish if you cannot connect these dots because at some point if you can't answer the question "why am I writing this blog again?" or "why am I spending time following people on Twitter?" you'll someday give up. But if you can focus on how these actions are helping you achieve your corporate objectives, mission, and values then you'll have the perfect power needed to succeed.

Making a Comparative Analysis

As a business owner you know how much any new venture will cost you before you start to lay the foundation for a well-structured plan. The same is true for social media marketing. How would you like to put social media marketing on a quota and know exactly how many new customers you will need to produce from your efforts for social media marketing to make sense? The easiest way to accomplish this is with a provisional analysis. To come up with your social media quota, take your social media expenses, for example the dollars you're paying individuals within your organization or outside advisors, as well as, any advertising dollars you're planning to spend within the assorted social channels, and divide them by your ongoing cost per lead or procurement. For example, if you are planning on spending $3,000 per month on social media marketing and your current expense per lead is $100, you would divide $3,000/$100. Social media marketing will need to achieve 30 leads per month to be equivalent to what you've done in the world of conventional marketing. You wouldn't be reading this book if you didn't already know traditional advertising is eroding and therefore comparing social media marketing to your previous advertising expenditures is an early stage benchmark to get a good overall picture of your future outcomes.

Who is Your Target Market?

Another key step in the Define leg is to determine your target market. When it comes to social media, your target market has a much further reach than traditional marketing, as well as different visible players. Just like in the past, your present customers are the low-hanging fruit of your marketing efforts. In addition, people who because of what they do or their interests are also potential customers for you. What makes social media marketing unique is your target market also includes influencers. These are the people who are online talking about your industry in social media and whose followers are your current and potential customers. These influencers may be partners or vendors you are currently working with who are stakeholders in the success of your business. They could also be competitors. Yes, I just said that one of your targets in social media could be your competitors. I told you early on that social media marketing is the upside-down and inside-out world of marketing.

Each of these groups is valuable to your success and it is important that you identify them in your social media business plan, understand where and how they are using social media so you can engage with them. Where are they spending time? What sites are they visiting and commenting on? This knowledge will help you manage your time as well as the content you need to create and share. For instance, if your industry and your customers are engaging on LinkedIn more so than Facebook, you'll spend more of your time in LinkedIn.

You might acknowledge breaking your target audience into primary and secondary audiences. For example, customers and prospective customers might be your primary spectators and influencers like partners, vendors, and competitors would be a secondary audience. Once you have cut them into groups, you should consider what your desired actions would be, by target audience. Actions by audience could be things like:

- Following you in your Social Media

- Visiting your websites vlogs or blog

- Appreciate and therefore likeing or sharing your content

- Opting-in for an event or for a specific premium.

- Requesting a quote for something or ordering a product

Identifying Social Media Profiles

There are different types of users within social media. Your target audience, regardless of whether they are customers, potential customers or influencers will utilize social media differently. Let me define the different ways people engage social media to help you understand the varying behaviors. This will help you determine desired actions by audience. Forrester Research has defined the different profiles as Creator, Critic, Joiner, Spectator, and Inactive. Let's take a look at each.

Creator: At the top of the social media food chain is the creator, which is someone who creates social media content. Creators write blogs that typically exist inside of an environment they own or control. They can also create videos or video blogs they share within their blog site, on YouTube, and as podcasts through iTunes, etc. By following the approach outlined in this book, becoming a creator is in your future.

Critic: The critic is a person who creates social media content but they publish it in someone else's environment, typically as comments to blogs or other social media content. This is a person who may not have a blog themselves but is active in others' blogs or they are commenting on seminars or even going to sites such as Trip Advisor and talking about vacation destinations, accommodations, and restaurants they enjoyed or didn't like. Critics don't just "criticize " they are primarily expressing their opinion. Think of it like a movie to be judged . You will also need to become a judge. This will be important to your success.

Joiner: The joiner is a person who has a social media profile, like a Facebook profile or a LinkedIn profile, and they update their profile periodically. These are individuals who will follow you and read your social media content. You will also be able to gain a lot of insight about what people are interested in by watching what they post.

Spectator: Spectators are people who are unquestionably involved in social media today but they don't yet have a profile and they may never have one. They're may be watching YouTube videos or they're reading blogs. They may never create social media content as a creator or a critic, but they're definitely part of your target public.. I embolden you to not forget about bystanders. Just because they don't have profiles doesn't mean you won't be able to get to them through social media.

Inactive person: This is a person who you won't be able to reach through social media because they're not involved online. A very small percentage of your target audience would hit this category so you'll have to reach them some other way.

Conducting Competitive Analysis

Another thing you need to do in defining your goals and objectives is a competitive analysis. You need to understand what your competitors are doing. Are they on Twitter, Facebook, LinkedIn, etc.? What are they saying to their target audience? What type of content are they creating? How many fans and followers, etc. do they have? A terrific benefit of social media is that it is truly open. You can easily learn from your competitors by watching and measuring them. You can find your target audience by looking at their followers. At this stage of the process, check out your active competitors and note the following:

- What social media platforms are they utilizing?

- How many fans/followers do they have?

- How much content are they producing (i.e.: number of blogs per month and/or videos per month)?

Who Are Your Contributors?

Contributors are the subject matter experts within your organization who help you create social media content. It may be you, but I hope it's not just you. I hope you have product managers, technicians, customer service people, and other key contributors who can help engage in the conversation and create social media content for your company.

Second Leg: Measure

Within your social media business plan you also want to determine how and what to measure. The easiest and most obvious would be to determine and measure activity. How many blogs per month do you want to publish? How many Facebook status updates? How many Twitter posts are you going to do on a monthly basis? When we look at each of the major social media platforms, I'll give you suggestions on the appropriate amount of activity to consider. Document these in advance so you can see if you are getting off track once you begin the process. You'll also want to have results. Here are a few general social media cadences that you might consider measuring against.

1. The growth in exclusive visitors to website and blog.

2. How many contest sceptics entries you have.

3. The number of people who download or reclaim coupons.

4. The number of views of your YouTube video and total views in your YouTube channel.

5. How many times your company or products are being cited through social media.

6. The number of comments posted from the audience , either in your social media channels or on your blog.

7. How many friends, fans or followers you have.

8. How many times your post content reposted, liked or re-tweeted.

9. The number of inbound links your website or social media environment is generating.

10. The amount of inbound traffic you're receiving from social media.

All of these items can be easily measured and documented. Set goals for where you expect to be each month and compare your results with those goals. Also take a baseline of the things you can find out about your competitors. This will help you continue down the path of doing social media marketing. You'll be able to measure against where you started, where your competitors started, and how you're stacking up against their growth.

Third Leg: Refine

The refinement leg is a critical element of your strategy that will propel your social media campaign in the intended direction. By following the steps outlined in this chapter, you will develop a sound social media business plan that will serve as a road map you can measure against. This leg of the process will need to be reviewed monthly. First, you'll want to set new goals in the areas where you are exceeding initial expectations. It's important to raise the bar and push yourself further when you are achieving certain measurable targets such as cost per lead, cost per acquisition, and number of fans/followers per month, etc.

337

Next, take a look at those areas where you're not achieving set goals and where you're missing the mark because that will enable you to manage by exception and really hone in on certain areas of your marketing efforts. This process will force you to ask the difficult questions of why it is not working the way you had hoped, and how do I fix this. By asking yourself these questions, you'll come up with solutions and changes you can implement that will likely improve your situation.

Understand Your Audience Better Than They Do

With the great diversity of marketing styles and strategies out there, it's easy to lose sight of some of the fundamentals inherent to every strategy. Realistically, only a handful of principles are necessary for success in literally every marketing strategy out there. One of the most important is this: You have to know your audience, inside and out.

If you don't know your audience, you won't even know what strategies or media to choose, let alone what messages to give them or how to treat them once they become full-fledged customers. So let's take a look at some of the actionable, practical ways you can better understand your audience.

Do your research in advance - First, do your market research, and make sure the demographics you've selected are the right ones for your brand and product. A number of modern tools are available to help you here, some of which are free - like American FactFinder, which uses United States census information to help you find out key pieces of information about specific demographics. Don't just look at the one demographic you've assumed from the beginning; branch out to learn about related niches, and gauge interest in your product from other areas. Walk away with enough information to make at least a handful of conclusive statements about your target audience.

Look at your competitors - In some ways, this is an alternative form of market research. Here, you'll be looking at your competitors at least the ones who share the same target audience as you. Evaluate their brand, their brand voice, the types of marketing strategies they use and the messaging they bring out in their advertising. What techniques are they using? Why did they use this specific phrasing, rather than some other phrasing? This image rather than that one? There's a chance your competitors don't know what they're doing, either, but even then, you can start picking out what doesn't work, or what seems wrong and why.

Create a customer persona - The customer persona is a tried-and-true tactic used by businesses everywhere to better conceptualize their target demographics. Here, you'll work to create an outline of your ideal "target customer." In most cases, this takes the form of a fictional character, whom you shape with bits of information like education level, family life, career and income, and maybe even details like a name and personality traits. This helps you conceptualize and "talk to" your average target customer, and it serves as an ideal tool to get your other team members up to speed.

Get to know your clients personally - This is a big step, but you can only start taking it once you have some actual customers. When working with your clients one-on-one, take some extra time to get to know them on a personal level. How do they talk that's different from other demographics? What are they usually concerned about when they talk to you? What appeals to them, or scares them, or excites them? You can't always apply these insights to a general audience, but as you get to know more clients individually, you'll start to see overlap here, and then you can start making useful generalizations.

Monitor reader comments and engagements - Comments and engagements are particularly important if you're running a content marketing or social media strategy as you should be. Your goal here is to pay close attention to how many people are responding to your work, how they're responding, and how often they're responding. Generally, the more "engagements" you receive (things like comments, likes and shares), the better your campaign is faring. You can use this information to discover what content topics your audience values or what types of messages don't appeal to them. Gauge these metrics over time to establish patterns and learn more about your public .

Witness external social habits - Of course, you can also engage the tactic of social listening to see what other topics and engagements your audience members are competing in. The idea here is to "plug in" to the social conversations and engagements your target audience has

340

with other brands and other people, giving you the convenience to divulge new trending topics, new angles for your messaging or new approaches you may not have otherwise considered.

Conduct surveys – At last we have the most straightforward way to learn more about your audience: asking them questions. It doesn't take much to create and launch a survey, especially with a stylish tool like SurveyMonkey. Everything you want to know about your target audience, you can put in a question arrangement and submit to your social followers and email subscribers. From there, you can apparise the results (or read them manually) and walk away with all the insights you ever wanted. The only caveat is that you may have to motivate participation with a prize or reward.

All of these strategies will help you better understand your target demographics, but remember that this is still only one side of the equation. Once you know the habits, lifestyles, behaviors and preferences of your key demographics, you'll still need to mold and improve your strategy accordingly. All your insights need to have some measurable influence - otherwise, they'll stay confined to the realm of the conceptual. You need a bottom-line impact.

Repetition Is Key

Repetition is used in advertising as a way to keep a brand or product in the forefront of consumer's minds. Repetition can build brand familiarity, but it can also lead to consumer fatigue, where consumers become so tired of an ad that they tune out or actively avoid the product. Therefore, to be effective, repetition must occur in the right proportion, as too much repetition may be counter-productive as an advertising strategy.

How many times should a message be repeated for maximum effect before it goes the other way and breeds contempt? According to some studies, the answer is between three and five times

How to tap into the power of repetition to engage your audience:

Limit your messages - For the strongest impact, select a small number of messages and focus on repeating these through more frequent campaigns.

Create a plan of regular communication - Targeting your audience with one message will not yield results. Research shows consumers need to be exposed to your message at least three times before they will take action. Remember, frequency breeds familiarity, and familiarity breeds trust.

Use multiple channels - The best results come from targeting your customer across multiple channels: letterbox advertising, print, packaging, outdoor, in-store, email, social media, radio, PR and so on. Use subtle variations in your ads to recapture your audiences' attention.

Strike the right balance - What is the correct frequency for your campaigns? Take time to test and measure results so you can find the right balance.

Personal Branding

Personal Branding is a marketing strategy to make your skills stand out from other professionals in your industry. It is a system which differentiates you from the crowd and positions your work skills as superior to others.

The keyword here is standing out. When you stand out in your industry, people take note of you. They see you as a thought leader. You create a position where you can get more work and charge higher prices. Also, your network starts becoming richer.

So how do you stand out in your industry?

You do so by having a deep understanding of your target audience's needs and then solving those needs exceptionally well and in a medium they understand best. When you highlight their pain points in their own language and then deliver them an exceptional solution, you stand out. You become insanely more favorable than someone who is not establishing this empathy.

Everyone has a favourite brand - you just may not realize it. Wherever you've entered personal data, you've created a persona that makes up part of your personal brand. Add to these personas amass data like browsing history, shopping habits, and social media, and that's your online persona. Now, while you can't do much to change the data companies can gather regarding your online spending habits or the information deduced from your browsing history, you can absolutely control how you present yourself to the digital world via social media branding. By controlling your personal brand, you ensure that people see what you want them to when they Google you.

The right personal branding can help your career by helping you to establish yourself as an expert in your field, a thought leader, or an influencer. When there's a promotion on the cards or when you're actively seeking a new role, employers are likely to Google you, and if you've taken control of your personal brand, you'll dazzle them with your professionalism and your position as an authority in your niche.

What do you want to be known for? What is your ideal career, and are you hoping to move toward it? These are important questions, as without clear goals, you'll never achieve branding success, as your posts will be too scattered to be useful or influential. For example, if your long-term goal is to work as a senior digital marketer at a big brand, it's important that you join and participate in industry-related conversations and network with other influencers in this space.

Your target market feels - "Hey! This guy really gets me". From there on, they look at you as a solution to their problems. Of course, there are many strategies and tools which greatly amplify your personal brand. But at its core, it's all about understanding your audience and addressing their needs in a way no one else can.

The Importance Of Personal Branding

Personal branding has always been important. But in the age of short attention span coupled with the biggest opportunity since the dot-com boom, it is one of the most important disciplines to master for any entrepreneur or executive.

Here are some of the biggest benefits of building your personal brand in 2019:

Money - When you build your Personal Brand, your voice becomes synonymous with the voice of your industry. You are perceived as the symbol of trust, authority, authenticity, and quality in your industry. This can lead to high paying work opportunities and higher prices for your product.

Recognition - It gives you an instant recognition tool which opens a lot of closed doors and opportunities. This, in turn, gives you an instant head start over the competition.

Networking opportunities - You get to network with A-list influencers and CEOs of top companies. This allows you to make a quantum jump in your career. You are in a position to form relationships with these influential people and exponentially grow your business in a very short time.

Position - You achieve a position of power as a thought leader in your industry. Your words carry more weight. This aspect is more vanity based but great towards reaching your self-actualization goals. After all, who doesn't want to be famous and get respect from their peers?

A career full of perks - You get to speak and get invited to conferences and summits in your industry. This comes with perks like higher pay, less strenuous work, more visibility and traveling to amazing places.

Higher productivity - You become more productive and responsible. When you see the results of your hard work with people starting to notice you, you feel a sense of pride and power. These results make you more attracted to your work.

Confidence - You become more confident and it adds a positive touch to your personality. When your words and actions matter, you shed doubts about yourself very fast. You tend to become more confident and vocal. Overall you move towards becoming a wholesome personality.

Dream job - Getting your dream job becomes much easier with you being a known name in the game.

The Psychology Science Behind It

Most businesses starting out don't recognize the significance of branding in regard to marketing. Branding, to put it simply, is to give your service or product an identity; something that is recognizable to consumers and competitors. When you brand you are creating a symbol, name or design that differentiates you from the others in your industry.

This is best done through subliminal messages while still

using features of marketing that subconsciously impact consumers and potential customers. Most of the prominent and successful brands you see today use psychology to impact their consumers with effective marketing material. This is achieved through using specific colors and images to distinguish their brand, promoting their services or products through promotional values, give-aways, and sales. This also heavily achieved through the use of a fabricated lifestyle framed around what they offer.

Knowing your target audience is essential to this aspect of marketing a lifestyle. The demographic plays a big role in how well your audience will respond to what you are promoting. There should be consistency within the message being sent to the target audience to plant a seed in their minds as well as create something that is memorable within their subconscious. The personal perception of the brand is the most integral part of a brand's selling power.

When you are able to create demand for a supply that isn't necessarily essential, but deemed as desired or attractive, this is the driving force behind brands that have become household names. This is also what drives the bulk of their sales. That's when you know you have reached industry leadership. When the message of a brand is perceived as something that is easily assimilated into a consumer's lifestyle, they begin to identify with the brand and become a repeat customer as a result. It is important that when showcasing a lifestyle, you fully grasp what is so appealing about it and get that across to your target audience.

Customer satisfaction can be defined as a consumer purchasing a product that fulfills his needs and the certain amount of expectation he has for the brand he is buying. When those needs and expectations are met, this in turn creates a demand for that brand as a result and the retention of a customer for that brand. If the business is perceived as having the ability to give something to the consumer then in turn the customer gives back by purchasing. This can transform into a term called brand loyalty. Brand loyalty exists only when a consumer has a high opinion towards a certain brand exhibited through the action of repurchasing.

This translates into a cycle of repeat consumption. By appealing to potential customers psychologically, you are giving your brand the power to impact the lives and actions of those interested in what you are offering. When you foster a good relationship with customers you are feeding the process of transformation and in turn gaining more customers as a result.

There are other qualities that help shape the big players you see today, one being good quality customer service. If a business has poor customer service, 89% of people have said they would not return no matter the quality of the product. Giving consumers the ability to feel important is significant to the buying process, you must cater to their needs as they will give you what you need in return.

There is also truth to consumers associating a certain

brand with a particular service based on the persona or message that brand conveys. If a brand is depicted as luxurious or elite, the highest customer service and care is anticipated to match this image. If that is not the case, this can deeply influence a consumer's perception of how legitimate or desirable this brand is to them and the general public. The opposite applies, if a brand has a customer service policy that matches the brand in question's reputation, this can do a lot for the way the brand is received by those interested in purchasing products or services from the place of business.

Another outstanding approach is using attractive ad imagery and ad copy to appeal to the target audience. The three key aspects in marketing imagery are icons, type face (font), and a color palette. People accomplice a brand and their products or services on these features. Depending on the industry your business is in, it is important to abduct the principle of what your ideal consumer would want through these factors and the image the product gives them. A study called Exciting "Red and "Competent Blue" supports the idea that acquiring patterns are undoubtly indicated by colors due to their impact on brand impression. This means colors having a role in the way consumers define a brand's persona. Based on their opinion of the brand and what it offers in terms of a persona to those wearing or using their products/services, they will assume it worthy of their purchase or not. In plain English, to articulate that they must possess this product or use this service and if they don't they are truly missing out on something that can really change. Sounds dramatic, but that is the involvement most people have with their favorite retail items and repeat services that have become habitual after a certain point of consumption.

By giving off the deception of high-demand, you are not only filtering the interest of a potential consumer, but also a sense of urgency that develops once they know they don't have that item and seemingly so many others do. Prominent demand is a great tool to use for purchasing growth. By having an aspect product and understanding the mind of the ideal customer and your wider target audience, you are able to not only attract new buyers, but keep them coming back to your place of business and make a customer for ever.

Personal Branding Strategies

We are living in the golden age of internet. Building a personal brand has never been as easy as it is now. Yet so few people are taking advantage of this brilliant opportunity which marketers of the past would have killed to get a shot at. Let's not let this opportunity slip away. Here are step by step personal branding strategies which leverage the internet to make you stand out from the crowd.

Define your target audience - First and foremost, have a clear idea about who your target audience is. What do they want in life? What are their biggest aspirations? What are their biggest fears? What are their main problems and roadblocks in overcoming those fears? Where do they hang out the most? Conduct a thorough research on all these questions and then base your message on how best you can meet their needs and expectations.

Identify and narrow down your niche - It's nice if you are a Jack of all trades, but when branding, the key is to focus on one special superpower of yours. Think of what you are most passionate about and what comes naturally to you. Once you identify that superpower, make it your niche. For example, If you have a lot of passions but overall you are most passionate about improving lifestyle, select lifestyle design as your niche. Next, you should narrow down your niche to address a specific demography. For example, after you select lifestyle design as your initial niche, you can narrow it down to address a specific community and make your brand message custom tailored for them. So instead of lifestyle design, it can now become lifestyle design for entrepreneurs or lifestyle design for single dads. This way your message comes across as tailor-made for a particular set of demography and hence more appealing to them. If you have more special qualities, you can connect them under the umbrella of your main superpower. For example, if apart from lifestyle design, you are also good in personal finance, then after creating a string of lifestyle design related content, you can connect your insights and tips on personal finance as an actionable strategy to achieve a perfect lifestyle.

Stand for something - The key to building a brand is to stand for something. Create a movement by representing something which is unique to your personality and instantly identifiable to you. Remember to always be original even if at times your opinion does not have the popular vote. Have a set of values and own them by structuring your personal brand around it. Help people self-identify with your movement by giving them a title by which they can identify themselves and other members of the community with. A great example of this is Russell Brunson and his Funnel Hacker Movement. Russell Brunson is the Founder of ClickFunnels, a sales funnel software company. He created a movement around his brand by addressing his community members as Funnel Hackers. This gave the members something to identify with and added a sense of purpose to what they were doing. It made them loyal to the brand as they felt part of a community of entrepreneurs with similar values, ethos, and goals.

Create a Mini-Manifesto around your brand - Establish a culture around your brand by creating a mini-manifesto. This manifesto will list down all the values, mission and vision of your community in a mini-document. It will act as a rallying cry for the community and reinforce the values whenever the community is in doubt. It will show your industry what you stand for and against. This will help fellow members of the industry self-identify with your values and be magnetically pulled towards your brand.

Create a personal branding statement - A personal branding creation is your main value proposal presented in the form of a unique catchphrase. It tells your target audience (your prospective customer) what they can wish to get from your professional skills in the form of results and ultimate benefits. For example: "I help B2B companies (target market) double their leads (result) with LinkedIn ads (skill)." You can use your personal branding proclamation as part of your social media bio and as an introductory line while networking in meetups and conferences.

Create a strategic bio - How dire will it be if you win the leads with an awesome piece of content only to put them off with a crudely done bio? Your public impressed by your content will look into your bio to know more about you. Take levarage of it by crafting your strategic bio beforehand which highlights the single biggest benefit your audiences can get from you. Then engage this benefit with your superpower or special skill. The bio should contain not more than 50-60 words. Additionally, mention all your media features and showcase your worthy achievements. Influence it to the hilt by making it a common bio for your own blog and all your media columns/features. Remember that the bio should reflect your values,culture or opinions and what you stand for.

Have a brand logo - Personal branding is a process which involves both textual and visual content. Have a brand logo which assimilate the ideology and values you stand for. Create something which stands out and communicates your message visually in the best possible way.Treat the logo as more than a piece of design and more as your brand existence. Your customers will treat this image as compatible with you. So make something which represents your focus message.

Start creating content - Start a blog or a vlog based on your product and niche. Select the best keywords in your industry and start creating consistent content around it. What are the main pain points of the target audience? What are the strategies that work well in your industry? What are the latest trends in the industry? What are the popular tools to grow a business in your field? Write and make videos about all this. Put the articles in a blog and videos on YouTube and other social media channels. Above all, focus on being an evangelist of your niche to the outside world. Think what kind of information an outsider would need to get into your industry and create content around that. The more consistent you are with your content, the faster your brand will grow. The goal is to make yourself synonymous with your industry.

Share Content On a Regular Basis - In the early days of social media, the more you posted, the more engagement you could build up. Today, however, over-posting leads to boredome and annoyance. You want to keep the lines of communication open with your audience, but you also don't want to overshare so much that you look bold. A good amount of posts is around 3-4 times per week for individuals. As Michael Noice, founder of Entrepreneur Coach, explains, "A once-weekly Twitter post or monthly Instagram photo are not going to attain much, if anything. For this reason, its best to focus on two or three carefully chosen social networks and try to be active on them, rather than posting occasionally to a half-dozen." There will be days when you don't want post, and that's perfectly fine. Study the data associated with your posts and identify a pattern that works for you. If you're having trouble finding content to share and want more insight into what's popular among users, try searching via hashtag on Twitter, using news aggregator sites like Feedly, or signing up for Google Alerts.

Give high-value assets for free - See the demand in your industry and create assets to address those demands. It can be a piece of software or a free report solving some specific need or query in your industry.   After creating it, give it away for free on your blog in exchange for the prospect's email. This way you will be seen as an expert who does not hold back on giving value first. Doing this pulls all the critical levers in building an epic personal brand.

Focus on SEO - SEO is a great way to get qualified organic traffic to your blog. This traffic will consist of people actively looking to get information in your industry and thus qualify as high-value leads. If you can be the person who addresses their needs, they will start seeking you or your content for further advice. This will build your personal brand effectively for that niche. To execute this perfectly, you need to rank on the first page of Google (or any other search engine) and typically for the top 3-5 keywords in your niche. Doing this is a bit hard and can take a bit of time. Having said that there are a few growth hacks to rank faster for your content. Firstly, create epic content. By this I mean 10x the no.1 ranked article in your niche by adding more points, insights, creating relevant infographics and more. Aim for a minimum of 1900 words. Secondly, do not go for heavily competitive keywords in your niche. Instead, use long tail keywords. For example, if the main keyword in your industry is "Internet Marketing", then focus on a long tail keyword like "Internet Marketing for Freelancers" or "Internet Marketing for Home Based Entrepreneurs". The goal is to find keywords with high traffic volume but low competition.

Build a list - Build an email list. Give consistent value to your email list members. Nothing is more personal than being inside someone's inbox. Take advantage of it and make them into your brand evangelists. First, drive traffic to your site. Then once the traffic is on your site, ask them to submit their email IDs in exchange for some awesome content (lead magnet or content upgrade). Once they sign up, win their hearts by delivering exclusive top quality content not available anywhere else. Consistently giving value at a place where you are seen almost every day is a great way to engineer an awesome personal brand.

Import Your Contacts - You might be amazed to see how many people you already know on the social media networks you're using. There may be tens, or even hundreds, of people with whom you haven't yet connected with. Import your email contacts from Gmail or Outlook, or contacts from your phonebook, into your social networks to find out how many connections you're missing. Linkedin, Instagram, Facebook and Twitter all allow for a free import of a certain number of contacts.

Keep it Positive - You now know some of the things you should be doing on social media to build the best social impression for yourself, but do you know what not to do to keep that impression a positive one? Think of your social media interactions and content creation as part of a resume of your work and a reflection of your professional attitude and overall personality. Avoid inflammatory religious or racial comments, and be careful when making political commentary that others may consider offensive. If you have concerns about not being able to voice your opinions to the extent you wish, consider creating two sets of social media accounts: one for private use (say whatever you want), and one for personal use (in which your responses and shares are heavily calculated). Keep your personal pages private to just close friends and family, and use your professional accounts to build new connections and career opportunities.

Grow your social media audience (organic) - Start putting dedicated efforts every day to grow your social media audience. Focus on channels where your target audience hangs out the most and start putting high-quality content which helps them. Here are the exact steps to follow.

- Start by joining Facebook and LinkedIn groups related to your industry.

- Post exceptional quality content which helps the members of the group. Be consistent in your posting. Do not pitch anything. Once the members of the group notice your content, they will visit your profile.

- Put a link to your own group and other social media profiles on your bio or cover image.

- Take connections to the next level by connecting with other members through your personal FB/LinkedIn profile.

Over time you will build up an audience that will start associating you with your niche, thus forming stepping stones towards a robust personal brand.

Be omnipresent online - Be visible everywhere, be it your blog, admissible social media channels and other primary platforms in your corporation - both online and offline. The more present you are, the more sticky your message will become. Also, this is a good way to take advantage of the mere exposure effect which is a psychological circumstance where people prefer things familiar to them.. You will start building up a niche follower based on experienced people ambitious about your industry. You will become their favourite source for all things related to your field.

Get into new social media channels fast - Get into new and uncharted social media channels fast. You will have a higher chance of becoming an influencer there as there will be very less competition.

Repurpose your content like a pro - Remodel your existing content across different content channels like

Medium and LinkedIn. Use your existing article and record a video of you speaking about it, upload the video to Youtube and audio as a podcast. Also, ONE interesting way of standing out with your content in 2019 is by making infographics. Make an infographic out of your article using a clean design tool like Visme.co. Search Engines love Infographics because they simplify big intricated ideas into visually compelling and easy to understand images. It increases a visitor's time on your site and also rises chances of your content being shared in the community. All this adds great karma points to your brand reputation. So take your present content and add more modes of delivery to it.

Get a vanity URL - Get vanity URLs for all social media channels. The URL should either be your name/ your name + your niche / reflective of your niche. Do not play around much with it. Don't go artsy with fancy names that have nothing to do with your industry. Stick to basics and connect the name to an industry keyword. This will be great for making the audience see a connection between you and your industry. Also, this will be great for Social Media organic search optimization.

Find & Join Groups - Facebook and LinkedIn both offer thousands of opportunities to join groups focused on specific industries or topics. Use the search bar on each network to find groups that are linked to your specific area of expertise, then you'll be able to share your insights and build authority around your personal brand. Keep in mind that industry groups may be overcrowded with your competitors, so smaller, topic-based groups may be more fruitful in terms of reaching your audience. Once you're a member of your preferred social media groups, don't be afraid to jump into discussions and add your unique insights. It can be difficult to remember sometimes that that's what social media is all about. So don't be afraid to have conversations. If you simply join a group and don't participate, you won't gain any of the benefits listed above. On the other hand, showing that you're responsive will help you build your personal brand in larger communities beyond your own.

Build a Facebook Group to propel your personal branding - Apart from building a list, FB groups are another way to build a constant relationship with your target audience. Simply start an FB group in your niche, and provide consistent value to your group members through high-quality content. Solve their problems, talk about the latest trends, share the latest hacks and tools, do everything to win their confidence. The more value you provide, the more your target audience will see you as a leader in your industry. Building your personal brand on Facebook goes a long way as this is where people spend most of their time. The key is to focus on groups, not on business pages.

Ask questions - Humans are social animals. We love to share and tell stories. Hence everyone loves a good listener. A primary way to build a relationship with your email list and FB group is by asking questions. This will help you get critical insights and also build a rapport with strangers.

Keep Your Brand Voice, Image & Tone Consistent - You've probably already figured out that sticking to your defined persona is important. If a popular political commentator suddenly and radically switched parties, no doubt he or she would lose a lot of fans overnight. You must also remain consistent with your ideas and the ways you present them so that you're memorable and trustworthy. Dining the tone of voice that works best for your brand may entail some trial and error, but there are personal branding guides you can use to determine the best fit for you. It's not as easy as saying "I want to be funny," you need to further develop your ideas to support your approach. Following your brand guidelines helps to control people's perceptions. You can damage an otherwise flawless reputation if one of your profiles shows up with content or images that don't match up with your brand's voice.

Network with influencers - Start expanding your network by connecting with other members of the industry on Social Media. Type your industry keywords on Facebook and LinkedIn and join all the top groups which come up as results. Once there, start giving real value without an intention to sell. This way you will be seen as a valuable member of the community and not an annoying salesperson. Your ultimate aim should be to give so much value that your name becomes synonymous with everything good about your industry. Reach out to them with a "value-first" mindset. Provide them value upfront by giving your core service for free. Now I know the word "free" can make some of us frown. But when you do it to build relationships with people who are the stalwarts of your industry, then this free work will pay itself off in no time and skyrocket your growth. Just imagine a great video testimonial about your work from the biggest influencer in your industry Or an influencer blasting a mail to his 100k strong list recommending your work. You see the value now? Connect with influencers using networking tools like Meet Leonard or Duxsoup. These tools will help you send automatic connection requests to industry filtered members on LinkedIn. For finding email IDs of influencers, you can use a tool like FindThatLead. Another way to connect with influencers is by joining their courses/paid mastermind groups. Once a part of the group, provide upfront value to all the members to get on the radar of the influencer.

Get on major media platforms - List the top magazines, podcasts, TV shows, YouTube channels in your niche and approach them to feature you. You can pitch them to have you as a guest panelist, contributor, columnist or them doing a story on you. To do this right, you need to first build relationships with these platforms. Use the same value-first mindset and offer your help or something of high value for free. Once you get their attention, pitch them to feature you on their platform. Show them the value you can offer to their audiences with proven results of your work. Once accepted, give actionable value and do not hold back. The goal is to win the hearts of the platform's audiences. In the end, offer the audience a free cheatsheet or strategy call in exchange for them signing up for your newsletter. Add brand logos of all your media features on your website and social media profiles. Put pictures of your speaking gigs and TV appearances. This will build a lot of authority for your personal brand.

Document and showcase results - Results. They are by far the no.1 buying emotion, and hence the no.1 brand builder. Whenever you work for yourself or your clients, focus on documenting results. For example, if you are in the field of SEO, make it a point to screenshot your rankings for the targeted keyword. This will come as handy proof that you deliver on what you do. Likewise, if you work for your clients, make it a point in your contract that you are allowed to showcase the results you bring for them. Also, a very effective hack is getting video testimonials. When a number of your clients come on camera and share their success stories from working with you, your Personal Branding will skyrocket immediately. One of the world's leading consultants, Sam Ovens has more than 1000s of video testimonials on his site – consulting.com. Run paid ads on your video testimonials targeting potential clients.

Invest in paid ads - For all the amazing long-term benefits of organic traffic, we cannot deny that paid ads are the fastest way to reach your target audience. Use smart targeting hacks. Target people with an interest list of brand names only hardcore fans in the industry know about. The ad should offer something of value to your target audience and show your knowledge on the subject. Retarget the visitors of your site with a lucrative offer. Creating a personal brand on social media isn't easy. It requires a lot of thought and research to do successfully.

It is not about what you look like or where you live, it's about what you stand for and what people should expect when they see you've posted a new piece of content. Think long-term and remember to take note of what's working and not working and adjust as necessary.

Why They Should Want You And Not Another Brand?

The world is full of brands. There are more than 200 million small businesses in the World, and even more mid- to large-size businesses that boost that number further. Even if only a fraction of those businesses challenge with yours, that's a great number to deal with in an age where information is plentiful and digital exchanges are commonplace.

To make matters even more arduous, all those brands are competing with one other for visibility by using marketing and advertising campaigns to clamor for their target audience's attention. If you want any hope of your own audience noticing your brand among this mass of competition, you need to make something to stant out from others . But how can you do that? By making sure your brand has, and shows these seven important qualities:

Originality - First, your brand needs to be original. If you attempt to mimic a competitor's brand, people won't have a compelling reason to choose you instead of that other brand. If your messaging relies on clichés and sales talk, it's not going to resonate with any of your customers. Instead, find an angle that nobody has taken before, and develop an image and voice that are wholly your own. This is easier said than done, of course, but it's a necessary step if you don't want to blend in with the competition.

Sincerity - Next, your brand needs to demonstrate a degree of sincerity. If you respond to all your customers on social media with the same copied and pasted corporate response, people are going to see you as a soulless machine that cares only about turning a profit. Instead, show your human side. Invest in the "personality" of your brand, and speak to customers the way you would speak to a friend. You might make some mistakes along the way, but your customers will be able to forge much better relationships with you in the long run.

Understanding - The best and most popular brands are the ones that understand their target audiences. They demonstrate this by creating messaging that is relevant for only one target niche; for example, if you're targeting parents, you might mention a common parenting problem, like having difficulty with a morning routine. This will demonstrate a degree of sympathy and instantly make it easier for that audience to connect with you. In time, this will lead to increased interactions with your brand, which in turn will lead to more traffic and conversions. Make sure you research your target demographics thoroughly and on an ongoing basis, and adjust your wording and targeting as needed.

Boldness - In branding, risk often leads to reward. The boldest brands aren't afraid to experiment with new techniques, or take a stance on controversial issues within the industry. They're somewhat polarizing, which means they could alienate a portion of their audience, but they also encourage more loyalty and respect from the people who stick around, and they never run the risk of being seen as "boring" or "just another brand."

Consistency - It's easy to blend in as white noise if your messaging isn't consistent. If your brand standards aren't clearly defined, or you have multiple people executing those standards to varying degrees of effectiveness, you might end up alienating your audience. The goal is to get your followers and readers to stick around as long as possible; but to do that, you need to give them a sense of familiarity and predictability. The best way to secure those qualities is to lock down your brand standards early on, and ensure that all team members working on your campaigns are skilled at their execution.

Visibility - Obviously, if people aren't seeing your brand, they won't be able to respond to it in any way. Though some potential customers will undoubtedly trickle in through organic searches and other inbound routes, the only way to build your reputation from scratch is to make your brand as visible as possible. Leverage different opportunities to diversify your strategy; for example, you might post content on external publications to build your reputation, launch a social media strategy or invest heavily in advertising and promoted materials. The bottom line is that you need some medium to promote your messaging -- otherwise, it won't matter how appealing that messaging is. For help getting visibility for your brand, see How to Get Media Exposure for Your Startup: The

Value - Brands can also stand out by offering more value than their competitors; that can be done in a number of different ways. First, you could simply offer better products and services; if you offer a similarly valuable product for half the price, it will be only a matter of time before people start flocking to you. Unfortunately, most brands don't have the flexibility to get this competitive (without eating into profits). Instead, you might offer value in terms of better, more informative content, or a stronger dedication to personalized customer service. Originality plays a role here, too, so think carefully about how best to appeal to your customers. If you're just starting to build a brand, these factors should guide you in its development. If you have a brand already, and it seems lacking, consider implementing a rebranding campaign, or at least adjusting your execution of your brand standards to reflect these values. At the very least, take the time to audit your current brand strategy and evaluate your adherence to the standards you originally set.

Without a strong brand at the foundation of your campaigns, you'll just be more white noise to the average consumer.

Content Marketing

Content marketing is the contrary of advertising. It's about captivating consumers with the stuff they really want, in a way that serves your brand's purposes and ideals, rather than just trying to jam your logo into their periphery. It's reaching the exact consumers you desire instead of a vaguely defined demo. It's to provide an experience they want, instead of trying to distract them from the one they came for. In short, it is the very evolution of advertising itself into something more effective, more capabale, and much less abhorrent.

Content Marketing isn't also a ploy that you can just turn on and off and hope that it will be fortunate. It has to be a mentality that is embraced and encouraged. Content Marketing embodies an organization's core brand components. It uses a collection of media formats such as text, video, photographs, audio, presentations, e-books and infographics to tell your brand or company's story. It can be read and checked on a variety of devices including computers, tablets, smartphones and others. It's distributed via owned, third party and social media platforms and it provides measurable results through the use of convenient calls-to-action and advertising codes.

A winning strategy succeeds when technology and people work together. Automation and semantics can help to filter, facilitate and uncover hidden treasures, but it is the human touch – thoughtful selection and consideration of content – that will create a truly new and engaging brand experience for audiences to discover, enjoy and share. In this sense Content Marketing is a winning strategy.

Content Marketing isn't push marketing, in which messages are sprayed out at groups of consumers. Rather, it's a pull strategy – it's the marketing of attraction. It's being there when consumers need you and seek you out with relevant, educational, helpful, compelling, engaging, and sometimes entertaining information.

The definition of content marketing further depends on the author's viewpoint and background, but the rules of good content marketing and essential strategies and principles are very much alike in most cases. One of the key similarities in all the different ways of looking at content marketing is that the customer experience and the needs, preferences and questions of people and the so-called target audiences are at the center.

A consistent use of relevant content runs like a thread through all marketing activities. Good content is essential everywhere so using it in a smart way is key too. Content marketing is a narrative form of marketing that provides customers with useful information, at moments when they are interested in receiving it, in an engaging, not "salesey" way. This enables it to break through the advertising clutter that consumers ignore or view skeptically, while it gently persuades prospects and helps buyers and the public.

Even if Content Marketing may appear to be a recent

innovation in marketing practice, really it's simply a new technique to convey the same information that consumers have always wanted about products and services. Its power has been exponentially improved with today's social media platforms and other devices.

Business Objectives Of Content Marketing

There are numerous reasons why companies apply content marketing solutions. Basically, these reasons are the same as in the case of any other marketing practice. It does not come as a surprise that practically every company aims at winning customers (or maintaining the existing ones) and, as a result, at increasing the sales of its products and services. All actions within marketing are focused on this very objective. Content marketing is no exception.

However, if we assume that generating income is the objective, we will easily come to the conclusion that this objective is too obvious and too general. In particular in the context of the budget of the marketing actions, you must be perfectly aware of what the money is spent on and what effect you can expect. Precisely defined objectives will come in handy.

The major objectives of the marketers who decide to fire content marketing are as follows:

- Increasing brand information

- Lead a generation

- Converting force   into customers

370

- Building relation

- Customer confinement

- Website service

- Marketing

Depending on the approach, the objectives can be designated more or less accurately. Some marketers agree that generating leads and converting them into customers are completely different things. However there is more truth in the opinions of those who simply reduce the objectives to three categories:

- Rising sales

- Customer faithfulness

- Brand appreciation

This list seems familiar, does it not? After all, everybody wants to sell a lot and be identified within the industry. Here the key question arises – if the objectives and leads are the same as the ones of the traditional marketing, then why content marketing?

No need to look for the answer. Traditional methods do not always correspond to the real needs of the businesses. If you carried out a survey checking which of the above marketing objectives are not important for the company, you would learn that, regardless of the industry, company and market size or the turnover, everybody wants to sell and be recognized. This is what we know. We also know that if several companies try to win the customer, this is quite a challenge.

Bombarding customers with advertising content is becoming less and less effective. The human brain becomes resilient not only to the number of outdoor messages, but also the more or less classic forms of display. There are more and more advertisements, but the number of them noticed by us is dropping.

As customers, we also rebel against spamming (as we see it) in spaces, whether public (a lot of cities introduce restrains on outdoor advertising, especially in the tourist-attractive district) or private (filters blocking the ads in the internet browsers is a standard) with such messages. Yet after all, the marketer wants the best for all of us. They just want to let us know about a new chance which we could possibly miss . Like a hundred other marketers in a hundred other corporations.

As a result, the classic marketing often turns out to be ineffective, or at least inadequate. In principle, it focuses on the direct message put in front of the customer, which is in the way . It aims at stopping them in their tracks even for a moment and forcing them to react to the offer. While reading e-mails from our colleagues, we need to filter the promotions, and while visiting our favorite websites, we must look for the content among the threatening banners. Can it work correctly?

Inbound marketing is an alternative – it is based on the assumption that the customers will come to me themselves and get interested in what I offer, if I provide them with an interesting content. Instead of irritating them and often misleading by manipulation with the ad, I make them find me themselves. And it works best if I am able to offer them the access to what they are currently interested in and what they need.

It is difficult not to deem this approach ambitious, as effective implementation of content marketing is truly an art. However, the market enforces such actions and for some time they have already been a standard for many companies.

Extra Benefits Of Using Content Marketing

More inbound approach - Content marketing is one of the tools of inbound marketing. As we mentioned above, it is a situation where a company strives to draw the attention of potential customers by providing them with quality content. These actions are effective only after some time, as it is not easy to build one loyal group of recipients who we can expect to buy our product. Nevertheless, the companies applying the inbound solutions are considered as places where the real experts of the industry work. What comes with it is that the customers are more willing to spend their money on organization which they perceive as professional. For the customer, the very moment of "getting to know" the company and its offer is much more pleasant, as it comes without the hard sell. Building the company image based on inbound marketing is surely an action worth dedicating some time.

Customer engagement and innovation - A customer interested in the given subject is an engaged customer. Logically, any person reached by content marketing must be interested in the subject which the content relates to. Interest does not mean already a potential purchase, but one person who voluntarily sub-scribes to the company blog is a more valuable lead than a hundred recipients of e-mailing. If our recipients regularly read the contents which we provide, then in their eyes we are the experts and innovators of the industry. This is often decisive when it comes to a purchasing decision. The reach achieved by whisper marketing is an extra gain. People who frequently take part in webinars that we organize, will sooner or later tell their friends about it. Meanwhile, it is hard to count on the recipient of our e-mailing or brochures to become our ambassador.

Development of knowledge culture - Despite many critical voices referring to what can be found on the Internet, there is no doubt that if it had not been for the global network, we would have not become a learning society. The demand for constant development of our skills is enshrined in our times more than ever before. As it is often informal (school, university or trainings are not enough), the global network is an obvious medium. You can find knowledge in any field here. While applying the content marketing strategies, we become a part of this culture of knowledge as its very important elements – the creators. It is difficult to measure how much this contribution is reflected in the business, but it is equally difficult to underestimate the chance that we get this way in the business of the 21st century.

Better use of company resources - In many organizations, knowledge about tools as well as resources are wasted. Companies often prepare data for industry reports, but do not always have an idea of how this data can be used beyond the in-company circulation. Meanwhile, if it is properly processed and described, it can constitute a perfect and – most importantly – required white paper. Others willingly apply the tools in video conferences and they do not realize that often a tool used for the purposes of in-company meetings can be useful also as an online seminar tool.

The conclusion is that we can make a better use of our knowledge and other resources which we already possess and which in big part have not been used so far. The argument for this kind of use will convince everyone – lower operating costs and a better marketing effect. It cannot be assumed straight away that content marketing allows creating "something" out of "nothing", but the preparation and launch of a campaign in a way forces us to analyze the resources and think about what we can get out of them and what extra costs we will need to incur. This way quite a few managers who were convinced that they perfectly knew their company discovered completely new areas.

Content Marketing Tools and Tactics

As you already know, Content Marketing is a marketing tactic using knowledge and experience of the company to advertise its products or services. After the lecture of chapter three you already know what the goals of content marketing are and what purpose it is for. In this chapter you will see what tools may be used to accomplish these goals.

Generally, each content marketing tactic has different objectives to achieve but basically we can indicate the following factors:

- To connect on the social web and company's website;

- To ensure quality and endurance;

- To have a past view of the marketing strategy you should apply;

- To answer the question how your content fills the expectations of your customer;

- To lead and manage online content;

- To create, unite and distribute content.

Those tactics help to provide better content, and you must remember that the better content the more visible your product/service is. The importance of Content Marketing and its tools is acknowledged by many researches. According to Content Marketing Institute, 91% of marketers use content marketing. Content Marketing tools are a real heart of this new marketing technique, and it is really critical to know exactly the function of each tool and what you can gain using each ones.

Audio Content

Audio is the Achilles heel of webinars, as well as other forms of content - like podcasts, teleseminars, and videos - that rely on clear sound. When you think of content, a majority of marketers think visually-based products, like blog posts, whitepapers, infographics, videos, and other interactive content. However, audio-based content is seeing a rise in popularity, specifically with the resurgence of the podcast. For those who aren't hip with the latest millennial trends, podcasts are digital audio files that discuss a predetermined topic and are usually available as a series, which are released to subscribers in installments online.

How popular are podcasts? Over 57 million Americans listened to podcasts in the past month, and that number continues to grow. It's clear that the resurgence of podcasts is not a passing fad, but rather a unique way to approach and deliver content to an ever-growing audience of highly educated and affluent users. Innovative marketers are beginning to tap into this demographic by creating podcasts of their own. To help you decide if podcasts should become a component of your content marketing strategy, here's a look at the benefits they can offer your business, as well as a few examples of successful business podcasts.

Here are a few of the advantages that developing a company podcast can offer your business:

Help Develop the Authoritative Presence of Your Brand. One of the top benefits a business podcast provides is the further development of the authoritative presence of your brand. The same way whitepapers and blog posts work to establish your brand as a thought leader and authoritative source in your industry, podcasts do as well. Creating a podcast that touches on the topics and trends that are important and relevant to your consumers builds trust, from the consumer's perspective, that you are an expert on the topic. This leads consumers to trust the opinion, advice, and content provided by your business, which can be used to boost conversions and improve customer retention.

Expand Your Audience Reach. Creating a podcast for your business greatly expands your current audience reach. This is because audio-based content in the form of a podcast introduces your business to an entirely new kind of audience. Podcast subscribers tend to be highly educated and affluent, according to The Podcast Consumer 2019 study by Edison Research. These are consumers that other means of content typically can't reach, meaning there is greater potential for leads and conversions from new consumers through a podcast than through a blog post. The market for podcasts is also less saturated with competitors, which means the consumers you're targeting have a better chance of discovering your podcast content organically.

Boost Brand Awareness and Loyalty. By implementing podcasts into your content marketing strategy and regularly posting them, your business also boosts brand awareness and loyalty among consumers. Your business podcast serves as an advertisement of your expertise and in-depth knowledge on various subjects related to your industry and can highlight various products or services you offer. By consuming this content, listeners become more familiar with your business and more loyal since you provide them with something they need. This helps to improve customer retention rates and boost conversions driven by customer referrals to your business.

Affordability and Simplicity. As with any other digital marketing strategy, ROI is an important aspect to consider before pursuing new types of content marketing. Podcasts are not only simple and easy to create, but they are also affordable. All you need is a computer, microphone, and an interesting topic in order to create a podcast. Minimal investment needed for the creation of your company podcast means more net revenue, which is always good for business.

In addition to that, podcasts are simple and easy to create, which means you can pump out more quality content in less time. Rather than having gaps throughout the week while your content writers are writing the next blog post or whitepaper, you can easily supplement this with a podcast. This allows your business to have constant content creation, which means higher search engine rankings and better odds your target audience will find your content organically.

Struggling to determine what a successful podcast entails? Here are a few widely successful podcasts from businesses and brands to give you some inspiration for your own version:

Hubspot's The Growth Show: HubSpot, the well-known inbound marketing and sales software company, launched their own podcast called "The Growth Show." This podcast's target audience is business leaders looking to grow their companies. The weekly show covers everything the audience wants to hear, from topics on growing a company to growing a team. Tuning in to a few shows is a great way to learn how an effective podcast is made, a few best practices concerning podcasts, and how to effectively cover topics for a niche market.

TEDTalks Audio Podcasts: Almost everyone knows and loves TEDTalks. The insightful and impactful video lectures created by TED, whose motto is "Ideas worth spreading," have gone viral and educated the public on topics ranging from the future of money to the importance of strangeness. Rather that having these lectures solely available in a visual format, the forward-thinking business has also made them available in audio podcasts. This has expanded the reach of their content and allowed them to connect with listeners who prefer the audio format, furthering the awareness of their brand and authoritative reputation.

VaynerMedia's #AskGaryVee: Another great example of taking visual content and repurposing it for audio-only consumption is the CEO of VaynerMedia's podcast, entitled #AskGaryVee. This is an excellent example of an interactive podcast that engages the audience by taking questions from listeners on marketing, entrepreneurship, and social media and having Gary

Vaynerchuk, the CEO of VaynerMedia, answer them. Originally made for YouTube, the content has now been repurposed and reformatted for audio-only consumption which has helped expand the audience reach and boost attraction. If your business is already developing video-based content, repurposing it for audio-only consumption in the form of a podcast is an excellent way to expand the reach of that content.

As podcasts continuously grows in popularity, more and more businesses will begin to offer their own branded podcast in an attempt to tap into the enviable demographic that primarily consumes this content. Incorporating a podcast into your content marketing strategy is a cost-effective way to help expand the authoritative presence of your business, expand your current audience reach, and boost brand awareness and loyalty.

Video Content
Content marketing in its truest form is nothing but the production and online distribution of content that is educational slash informative in nature. The purpose of this content is to convert online content consumers into prospects/customers. And also to provide the current costumers with enough information and convince them to become repeat buyers.

Content marketing is used across many channels, with the help of different types of content. Which means it is not restricted only   to text and video, it's a big part of it. Since video is a strong and effective way to spread your marketing message, it can take your content marketing efforts to another level. But once again, this depends on how well you develop your video content marketing campaign. And what you want to get from it.

Reasons Why You Need Video Content Marketing

By now you should know what video content marketing exactly is and how it's growing extremely fast. It's a stratagem that your business needs to incorporate in order to get a higher return from your online marketing efforts. Let's now look into a few good reasons as to why you should invest in video content marketing and make it a part of your core business strategy.

More Conversions - When it comes to running an online marketing campaign, the ultimate metric that matters is the conversion rate. Because if you're not converting your prospects into leads or customers, your business isn't growing, it's as simple as that. By leveraging video content marketing, you'll be able to get more people to sign up for your newsletter or buy your latest product. When compared to other types of content, video content can give your prospects the needed clarity to make the final decision. It gives you a certain edge over the competition and since quality video isn't as easy to produce, it can take a while before others catch up with you. A recent research conducted shows that 71% of marketers have found video content more conversion-friendly. When done right, it can easily help you get better results with minimal efforts.

Better Emotional Connection - If you look around the social media landscape, you'll find that videos are being shared the most in comparison to other content types. While there are many reasons as to why people like sharing videos, one of the strongest "why" is that people connect to the right video content on an emotional level. By creating videos that appeal to the emotions of your target audience, you not only give them a reason to consume your content but also spread it across their own network. For example, if you look at a traditional blog post, you won't find the emotional cues that come with video content. Right from the tone of voice to the sound effects/music being used, everything can have a positive impact on the viewer. Which ultimately makes your content stand out from the rest and also memorable. When interested people watch your video that evokes their strongest emotions (happiness, awe, anger, etc.), it may not push them towards taking action immediately. However, it will help them make a buying decision later on when they see more such content from you. So whether you are in the B2B or the B2C market, impressing the emotions of your audience with video marketing, can and will help you bring in more business.

Higher Accessibility - Let's face it, video production is no longer the difficult task it used to be a few years ago. You no longer need to spend a ton of time on creating a video or have a huge budget to achieve studio level quality. Yes, we're talking about video content that only the big guys were able to produce before. Thanks to the advancement in technology and with new/innovative tools available, creating and launching your own video has become much more affordable. In fact, it will keep getting easier in the coming years as more and more businesses jump into producing their own videos and starting their own channels.

Stronger Engagement Levels - Many studies have proven that visual content works great when it comes to engaging your target audience. People today like to consume to content that is visually appealing and engrossing. Now, this isn't limited to pictures or photographs. Video content is proven to be a big part of the "visual content" movement. With more and more people watching video content on social media sites such as YouTube, Facebook and Twitter, you can see firsthand how video is helping generate strong engagement from target users. When you create and share video content with your social followers, you have a 10X chance of them engaging with your video, which often translates to more shares and comments. However, do keep in mind that the quality of video content marketing matters to a huge extent and has a direct impact on the kind of results you are able to generate.

Easier SEO Results - Does video content marketing have an impact on SEO? Can videos actually help you rank higher in the search engines for keywords that are hard to rank for? The answer is yes, given that you're doing it right. There is little doubt that Google and other major search engines like Bing love video content and won't hesitate to rank it higher than traditional articles. According to a study done by Comscore, by adding video content to your site, you have a 53% higher chance to end up on the first page of the SERPS. This just goes on to show that quality video content can make a big difference to not only your conversion rate, but also the organic search traffic you generate.

If you want your video content marketing to deliver results, then you need to take a calculated approach to it. You can't just blindly play the video marketing game and expect to see returns. Here are seven important tips to help you make the most out of your video content marketing efforts.

1: Grab their Attention fast

Internet users are not as collected as they used to be. Today, it's all about finding the good piece of content. So don't be surprised if people jump your video to look for another one if they don't find it exiting enough. The solution is to attract your viewers without wasting their time and delivering on your promise. You only have a few moments to entice them less than 10 to be precise. So have an interesting, relevant start to the video and don't wait too long to reach the purpose. Whether your video is long or short, give your viewers a motive to watch it without skipping it.

2: Deliver Real Value

Creative video content marketing is all about giving immense value to the viewer in whatever form you choose. Your content strategy should focus on adding value to the lives of your target Public . How you add this value is subjective. Because what's valuable for your audience may not be that valuable for a different type of public. So for example, if you find that you can give profit by creating and publishing entertaining yet informative video content, do that. Or if you want to choose an even simpler path by creating videos offering specific (niche or industry related) knowledge, even that's fine. Keep in mind that any video that you develop must be watchable and enjoyable. Because if it is a drag, then it's not valuable.

3: Go Beyond YouTube

While there is no doubt that your video content marketing plan cannot be complete without YouTube and it's vital it is not enough. Basically there are many other valuable video sharing channels/platforms that you can tap into besides YouTube. Your goal is to reach out to your target audience in the best possible way, and that can't happen if you only focus on YouTube. The most obvious reason as to why you need to consider other platforms is because of the potential to connect with a different audience. For instance, the kind of people you can reach with your videos on Facebook is not surely the same as YouTube. Because Facebook users discover video content in a different way using different tools in between. Also, different platforms developed have people from various age groups using them. This is why it makes sense to leverage as many video platforms as you can. However, designate the majority of your time to a platform where your target audience is most likely to be found.

4: Stay Consistent in Your Approach

Consistency plays a big role in making your video stand out from the competition. Why? Because videos are visual, which means you're not limited in how you present the content. With every video you create, you can help your viewers resonate with your message by being consistent. Your brand's personality, look and design matters to a great extent in keeping consistency high. For example, if you are creating videos with people in them, then keep using the same cast so that your viewers see faces they're already familiar with. Similarly, if your videos only have a voice-over, see to it that the colors and the design in the video you use stay consistent. You may also want to plan your video content well in advance (create a video content calendar) to make sure your consistent with timing as well. However, when it comes to video platforms, your videos need to be customized for each. The one size/look fits all approach doesn't work here. If you're posting a video on Instagram, then it helps to create videos that look more natural, unedited or spontaneous. But on YouTube and Facebook, people expect a professional feel, so that's what you give them.

5: Don't Ignore the quality Aspect

Just because you are creating and uploading videos on YouTube or Facebook doesn't mean that you should forget about quality. In fact, keeping up with quality is extremely important on these social media sites because they're moderated by real communities. Users won't think twice before giving your videos a thumbs down if they don't see quality. So say no to low-definition video and hello to HD video content that people like to view and share with others. As video platforms improve in quality and service, they expect to give their users a better experience. Which will only happen if you stop testing the patience of your viewers with bad videos. Remember, quality over quantity is the number one rule of creating amazing video content.

6: Optimize for Silence

Besides YouTube, other social media platforms such as Facebook, Twitter and Instagram tend to auto-play videos without sound. The user may or may not choose to watch the video with sound. But stats show that up to 85% of videos viewed on Facebook are watched with volume down to zero. The simple reason for the "silence revolution" in the online video world (especially on social media) is that people are increasingly watching videos on their mobile devices. Since the social experience is largely silent, especially with people around, it's no wonder that many users prefer to viewing videos with sound turned off. So how do you impress users when they are only watching and not listening? By creating attractive yet relevant visuals that make the video feel engrossing. If there's dialogue in your video, then add English subtitles. In short, have sound in your video but also optimize for silence.

7: Add a Call to Action

What's the use of video content marketing if there's no actual call to action in place? Businesswise, if you're investing in video content marketing, then you need appropriate results. Having a clear CTA makes real business sense and it should not be put aside. Call to actions in videos need to be convoluted . Simply encouraging viewers to visite your website or subscribing to your newsletter at the end of the video is usually enough. But if you want to go a step higher you may have a call to action come up right in the middle of the video when the viewer is deeply engrossed in the video.

Writing Content

When you look for content marketing, you probably think of blog posts. But they're just one of the many types of content that can help you establish your brand as a thought leader in your industry and attract new forces. By diversifying the types of content that you share, you attract virtual people with different needs. Let us consider the types you absolutely need in your content marketing strategy.

Blog Posts - Blogging may seem like an outdated practice – but that couldn't be further from the truth. Blogs are not only a powerful tool for creating trust with potential customers, but there's another important group that reads blogs: search engines. Your ideal customer will find your blog when they research content that relates to you and your business, and Google will read your blog to get a true sense of what your website is all about so that it can recommend your business in its rankings to those same researching customers. Blogs need to be updated constantly, they cannot remain a static portion of your website, like say, the 'About' page.

Further, they need to be about a specific topic to direct those leads to your brand. Riverbed Marketing is an inbound marketing agency, so I don't write blogs about Star Wars, or how well the Blue Jays did in the playoffs. Those topics would bring me plenty of Jedi and bat-flip fans, but the keyword ranking that helps search engines link customers to applicable content wouldn't allow me to educate prospective clients and share information about my products and services. So not only does blogging increase your site traffic – but it gets you better traffic. How? It custom tailors the audience you bring to your site so you attract the one's who are justifiably more inclined to do business with you. They're also a forever tool, meaning that once you click publish, that blog post is out there for good. It does not expire, or reduce in value over time – like PPC for example; turn off the money tap and the leads stop coming, too. Need to hear all of this in another way to convince you to hit the keyboard more often? 80% of daily blog visits are new, and receive 5X more traffic than blogs that post weekly. And, more blogs spell more traffic. You can generate 54% more traffic to your site once you've accumulated as little as 50 blog posts, according to Social Marketing Writing. Blogs should be at least 1500 words in length, according to quicksprout. Longer blog posts amounting to over 1500 words receive 63% more tweets and 27% more Facebook likes than shorter ones. 1500+ word blogs also achieve more SEO backlinks.

White papers - Case studies are designed to illustrate positive affirmations related to the inclusion or adoption of your business' offerings. They are compelling before-

and-after overviews of your customer's interactions with your products or service. They provide confirmation that an investment – of either time or money – is a good call. We're naturally drawn to stories as a species, and case studies satisfy our basic need for a happy ending. They're also integral to speeding up the decision to buy. Case studies help cater consumer behavior into smaller, quicker modes of thinking – because there's a lot of information out there already and customers are happy to cut through the pages and pages of copy to find out if the decision to purchase has been a good one for people like them. The case study is a great way to quickly show how your company was able to solve a problem facing your targeted market. Good experiences read well to buyers seeking similar results.

Guides - Writing guides is a great way to build authority as an expert firm on a chosen field in such a way that stimulates both education and rationality. When you're able to help your market learn, they'll continually have faith in you.   For example, maybe you're a catering company – why not write a few guides for readers about the different culinary neighborhoods in your city? Provide tips for getting a table at the new local hotspot; offer ordering tips, introduce the chef as a budding entrepreneur your company has respect for, and offer insight on the up-and-coming trends in the next big emerging food district. This gives your business the credibility to be trusted as savvy professionals and a strong presence in the arena. Guides allow your readers to understand you're in the know – further, they can outline multiple segments within a large topic. If you're writing about how great the foodie scene is in your city, you can touch on seafood, late-night, brunch, and mixology – all in one read. Writing guides can boost your company as a laid-back expert, inspiring this expectation from your readers; the next time they have a question, they'll be back for more info time and time again.

eBooks - If you have a need to communicate complex information in an intellectually stimulating way – ebooks are probably going to be a big part of your content marketing strategy. They're proficient in combining both rationality and practicality in a package that is geared at convincing your prospective customer you're the answer for their brand issues. Compared to other forms of content marketing, eBooks are extremely research heavy, relying on third-party statistics, and illustrations or visuals to help differentiate from whitepapers. Ebooks are also great ways to assist your SEO efforts, as their content is searchable and lends well to keyword research. In the scope of the inbound methodology, eBooks are great at seizing the customers attention during the convert stage. Hubspot tells us that eBooks are not only critical tools for nurturing your existing leads into more sales-ready positions, but they help feed your list of new contacts. In order to write a compelling eBook, you've got to bring a few different skillsets to the table. Journalism, design know-how, strategy, and project management all play a part in writing a good eBook - but don't fret - you can do it.

Infographics - Content marketing isn't just the written word. Infographics, which visually interpret data, appeal to visual learners. Not everyone loves reading content, and many people prefer to digest it in another format. If you've got rather dry data, turning it into an infographic is a great strategy for getting people to give a crap.

Guest Blog Posts - While these can cover the same topics and styles you used in number one, you'll be writing them for other blogs. By publishing content on other established blogs, you can expand your brand's reach. Just keep in mind: guest blogging works better if you establish long-term relationships and contribute regularly on the sites that are sending you traffic. Implement one or more of these content marketing strategies into your existing efforts and see if you can't expand your reach.

How To Choose The Right Platform

Many of the best social media platforms for business, like Facebook and Instagram, have become essential tools in the modernized marketer's toolbox. More and more public is using these channels to find new companies and engage with their favorite brands. However, most companies can't be everywhere at once, especially small businesses with stricht marketing budgets. That's why it's vital for businesses to be strategic about which social media platforms they work to build a character on. The key to successful social media marketing will be choosing the best social media platform for your career. This is based on a number of reasons including the type of business you have, what audience you are trying to reach, your specific goals, and much more.

Below, I've developed a quick and simple guide to choosing the best social media for business.

Instagram
Instagram is a staple of many small businesses' marketing campaigns. And for good reason. It has a large and diverse audience that is happy to engage with brands, resulting in high engagement overall. Research and case studies have demonstrated these benefits clearly, finding that they can translate directly into sales and leads.

Consider that:

- 80% of users follow at least one brand on Instagram, with 60% of these users saying they've discovered new products or services through this unique platform.

- At least 30% of Instagram users have purchased products they seen advertised on Instagram.

- 65% of top-performing Instagram posts clearly shows products.

People are happy to follow brands on Instagram, and they're actively discovering and purchasing products on the platform. That's a big win. Also worth noting is Instagram's continued efforts to embrace commerce. Instagram ads see excellent results and offer high engagement. Shopping on Instagram streamlines the Instagram sales process. And business profiles with over 10,000 Instagram followers gain "Swipe Up" links they can add to Instagram Stories to drive traffic directly to the site, something that was otherwise difficult to do on the platform. The platform keeps expanding, making it more valuable to merchants and ecommerce businesses, especially if they have products with a strong visual appeal.

Optimizing Your Instagram Profile

Most merchants know the basics about setting up an online profile; you need to fill out your contact information, have a keyword-optimized description, and choose a profile picture that's easily identifiable, like a logo. This is a great start.

But Instagram has rolled out several changes that affect business accounts. To get the most out of your limited Instagram profile space, you should include the following:

Clickable hashtags. These can now be added to your profile description just by entering # and then the desired phrase, just as you would on a post. Focusing on your branded hashtag is a good choice for most businesses.

Clickable profile links. There's several options for how to use this, but you can now also add clickable links to other user profiles in your own Instagram bio. If you have two different profiles for a sister company, you can use this to direct traffic there. If you're hosting a contest with another merchant, link to them when discussing the contest in your bio. You can also use this feature to send people to your personal profile if that fits with your branding.

Story Highlights. We'll talk more about Story Highlights a few sections down, but this feature lets you add "expired" Stories to different featured categories, which will be listed above your Instagram feed on your profile. This helps your profile to look fleshed out and allows you to showcase certain key Instagram content like UGC or posts that highlight your brand's story.

The Different Types Of Hashtags You Should Be Using

In order to fully expand your reach and get the most results from your Instagram marketing, you need to be using the right types of hashtags. There are six key types of hashtags that are crucial for ecommerce businesses to incorporate into their marketing strategy.

Branded hashtags: More and more brands will and should have a unique branded hashtag. They'll attach this to each post, place it in their profile, and persuade users to attach it to any posts in which they're sharing user-generated content. It may include your brand name, but it doesn't have to.

Contest hashtags: These hashtags are a type of branded hashtag created for a singular contest. These are often used to identify contest entries for photo submission contests, and to generate contest awareness overall. Furthermore, to the main branded hashtag contest, you should also incorporate general contest hashtags.

General appeal hashtags: There are certain hashtags that are popular among large, diverse audiences. These can help you get significant reach on your posts, because they're more likely to be sought out.

Niche-specific hashtags: Each industry will have phrases and keywords that are relevant only to their target audience. These hashtags won't get you the same reach as the general-appeal hashtags, but they'll get you more relevant traffic, such as #harrypotter (if you're selling jewelry inspired by the Harry Potter series).

Timely hashtags: Ongoing events and seasonal holidays can make great hashtags, especially when you factor in selling-focused holidays like Valentine's Day or Christmas. People are likely to be searching for content that's relevant at the moment, so take advantage of a few hashtags.

Entertaining hashtags: These will not help you with reach, but they will serve to entertain your audience and help you to establish your brand. They're meant purely to be funny or clever, and that is it. In many cases, entertaining hashtags might be grouped together, one after another, to tell a story.

For best results, do research on each of these hashtags, and use a variety of combinations of different hashtags in each category for your posts. This will strengthen your branding while helping you to reach the largest and most relevant audience possible.

Hashtag Best Practices

Hashtag usage is one of the most significant factors that will determine your success on Instagram, and they're unsurprisingly a little difficult to crack. Fortunately, the following best practices will help you maximize your reach and your results:

- Include your branded hashtag on your profile.

- List any entertaining hashtags at the very beginning of your hashtag list, where they're most likely to be read.

- Use a considerable number of hashtags. The limit is max 30 hashtags per post. However, numerous case studies have found that somewhere between 9 to 11 hashtags for each post will be the sweet spot, especially if you classify the types of hashtags.

- Switch up your hashtags. Don't use the same hashtags on every post. Create groups of hashtags that you can cycle through for different posts. Not only will this increase your visibility to different audiences, it can also keep your account from being flagged as spammy by Instagram.

- Take time to explore each hashtag. This can help you discover new hashtags to target, and ensure that you don't accidentally use a banned hashtag or jump in on a topic without knowing what it means.

Instagram Stories

Instagram Stories started out as an add-on feature borrowed from Snapchat: a way to share short-lived photos and videos that disappear in 24 hours with your followers. But it's developed into an essential part of the platform. Stories led to Story ads, and now Instagram has given us Highlights so that our Stories can live on forever. Let's take a look at how to use them.

There are a variety of strategies that you can use to get results from Instagram Stories, each of which will benefit your business in different ways.

Share content created by your audience. You can use Stories to showcase user-generated content, which is always a crowd-pleaser. Your followers love to see that you care enough about them and their content to feature it on your site. It also saves you from having to create the content yourself, and acts as powerful social proof.

Acquire content from your audience. Stories can also help you obtain UGC, which can happen in several different ways. You can place calls to action for users to share pictures of their latest purchase. You can also use poll stickers to get feedback and generate immediate social proof.

Share moments from events. Your Stories are also a great place to cover and promote events, whether they're several weeks away, happening right now, or from the past. This is a great way to provoke FOMO and show everyone what they're missing out on, which can build brand awareness and increase attendance.

Be authentic. Instagram Stories are quirkier than feed content, so it's a great place to showcase your fun side. Use images and videos to tell your brand's story, throwing in some behind-the-scenes content when possible.

Go live. Instagram Stories allows you to broadcast live right from your mobile phone, and your followers can engage in real time. You can host q&As, talk about a specific topic, or interview a featured guest or influencer.

Once the live is over, you can have it set to be played with the rest of your Stories.

Extending The Lifespan Of Stories With Highlights

Realistically , stories would disappear after 24 hours just like the Snapchat feature they were emulating. Instagram recognized that this was resulting in lost ROI on that content, and gave us the opportunity to create highlights. Highlights exist on our profile page, and we can add stories to them after their 24 hours have passed. You can create multiple highlights for the best effect, using one for user-generated content, one for brand storytelling, and one for your events. This helps users to find content they're looking for when they first come to your profile, which can help them get to know you and trust you a little faster. To insert highlights to your profile, click on the icon with the black + above your gallery. You'll need to give a name your highlight and select the stories you want to add to it. You can play around them at any time.

Instagram TV

All marketers know that developing a strong presence on social media is crutial for their business, so using Instagram TV to further promote your brand sounds like a no-brainer. With IGTV, you also get to jump on board sooner and get a head start on your competitors. Unlike most other new platforms, your reach won't be limited to just a few thousand early adopters. As explained above, all Instagram users can install and use Instagram TV with their known accounts. This surely means that your videos could potentially reach more than a billion users from the get-go.

What's more, if a user starts following your channel, your videos will play automatically as soon as they launch the app. That way, your message could reach millions of users without a single dollar invested in Instagram advertising. Instead, you can use some of the marketing money you save to produce high-quality content for the platform and reach an even wider audience.

Although IGTV is still in its early stages, there are already plenty of great ways you can use it to bring your brand closer to audiences, improve its reputation, and attract new clients as a result. Here are five ideas that could help you get your Instagram TV channel up and running.

Broadcast Live Videos. Until now, the only way to broadcast live videos on Instagram was to use the Instagram Live feature. However, those videos would only be available to your followers and would expire after 24 hours. With Instagram TV, your live videos will remain available on your channel indefinitely. You can use this format to broadcast live q'n'A sessions or transmit interesting live events. What's more, IGTV allows you to upload your videos to Facebook Watch, so your content will be available on both platforms at once.

Repurpose Your Content. With IGTV and the new audience it allows you to reach, all your old content can become new again. Take your old horizontal videos, edit them to fit the new vertical format, and post them on your IGTV channel. If you run a podcast, rather than sharing teasers and asking followers to visit your website to listen to the latest episode, you can post full episodes to your IGTV channel and accompany them with interesting visuals. This is much more convenient as it allows users to listen to your podcast without leaving the app.

Make Your Videos Instructional. Instructional content is always popular and doesn't have an expiration date. With IGTV, you can take your "how-to" videos to a whole new level by allowing followers to replicate what you're doing in real time. Whether you're focusing on cooking, do-it-yourself home repairs, beauty and makeup, or fitness, the 60-minute format gives you plenty of opportunities to create captivating evergreen content.

Rerun Your Best Instagram Stories. If you're investing a lot of time and effort into creating engaging Instagram stories, you probably want to preserve them and give them time to reach new audiences. With Instagram TV, you can now compile all your favorite stories into short videos broadcast on your channel. If you use Stories a lot, you can do periodic digest-style videos where you would include all your stories posted within a certain timeframe.

Create Your Own IGTV Original Series. In many ways, IGTV works like actual television, so you can also use it as such. We already mentioned sharing your audio-only podcasts on your Instagram TV channel. If this proves a hit with your followers, you could use a camera to simultaneously record a video version of the podcast and post it exclusively to your channel. Similarly, you can create your own weekly or biweekly IGTV show where you would introduce your products and services, answer your followers' questions, and chat with interesting guests.

Although Instagram TV doesn't yet allow advertising, there are many ways you can use it to bring your brand, products, or services closer to audiences worldwide. With more than a billion users and less competition than other, more established social media apps, IGTV is an excellent platform for marketers looking to attract new customers with engaging, creative content.

How Instagram Advertising Works

Since 2015 anyone can now learn how to create Instagram ads through Facebook's self-serve advertising platform. With it, you have total power over your ads, how they appear, and who sees them. And not likely sponsored posts and paid partnerships, your ads get posted directly from your own account. The advantages to this method of Instagram advertising include:

- Ascendable pricing.

- Self-serve and quick

- STRONG reporting so you're in control.

- Highly refined public targeting.

What's more, with Instagram's move away from a chronological feed in favor of a well curated feed, you never know how many of your followers will see your posts.

Types of Instagram Ads

Photo Ads - A Photo Ad is one simple photo in landscape or square format. These are the simplest in terms of visual asset needs, since you just need a single image. Here's an example of a Photo Ad from outdoor ecommerce brand Fimbulvetr Snowshoes, which takes users to the product page of the snowshoe featured in the ad creative.

Video Ads - Instagram used to have a 15-second limit for videos, but it has since lifted that rule. Now, videos can be up to 60 seconds long and shot in landscape or square format. Dollar Shave Club uses the Video Ad format in its Instagram advertising to promote a new membership deal, highlighting the various products included in the deal.

Carousel Ads - An Instagram Carousel Ad can have anywhere from two to ten images and/or videos that users can view by swiping through. West Elm uses Carousel Ads to highlight their range of products for their Instagram advertising campaigns.

Slideshow Ads - Slideshow Ads are similar to video ads in that they appear as a video in users' feeds. These ads, however, are made up of a series of still images which play as a video, much like a slideshow. You can add text and audio to your Slideshow Ads.

Stories Ads - Instagram Stories Ads is one of the newest kinds of ads available to businesses on the platform. Instagram Stories is similar to Snapchat in that it allows users, and brands, to share self-destructing photos and videos. Brands can also advertise on Instagram Stories with photo or video content. Online fashion brand ASOS has used Instagram Stories Ads with much success to build brand awareness and ad recall.

Facebook

If you would like your business to have a presence on social media, Facebook is probably one of the first social media platform you think of. More than 1.4 billion people use Facebook every single day, and multiple times a day. It is almost certain that your potential customers are on Facebook and using it actively to engage with their family, their friends, and their favorite brands.

Whether you're running a brick and a mortar store, an ecommerce site, an agency, or a software company, you can use Facebook for adverstise your business. In this guide, I hope to cover everything you should know to put your business on Facebook, to market your business, and to gather your results. The good news is you don't need a budget of Super Bowl proportions to get into this type of game. Sharing valuable content that help you connecting with fans and potential customers is your most reliabale play. For example, 93% of social media advertisers use Facebook ads, which clearly suggests that it's surely worth the while.And if you find that statistic motivating, I've compiled nine more helpful data points below to help inform your strategy and take your Facebook business to the next level.

1. 37% of Facebook users say that they follow Facebook Business Pages because they want to receive special offers. Offering those who follow your Facebook Page estimated offers will help motivate your target audience to smash that "Like" button. This tactic works for businesses both large and small.

2. A post's average organic reach is only around 6.6% of the Page's total likes. There was a marketing-world rumor that this reach only extended to an average of 2% of the page's total likes, but in actuality it's more like 6.6%. While having a high number of likes on your Page is important, the Facebook users who like your Page won't do the work for you - you need to produce engaging posts, no matter how many likes you have. The more you understand about how to generate engagement through your posts, the better.

3. 49% of Facebook users only access the site through the mobile app. That means that almost half of all Facebook users see your ads on their phones. Additionally, mobile app fans are arguably the more frequent users, as they have Facebook right in their pocket 24/7 rather than just when they can access a desktop computer. You know what that means? Your content needs to be mobile-optimized. In addition to making sure any landing pages your ads point to are mobile-ready, consider posting more vertical photo and video content, and keep long-form posts easy to read, limiting the use of the "read more" button.

4. One study says that the most effective length for Facebook ad titles is four words, with 15-word link descriptions. While there's definitely a time and place for long-form content, your Facebook ads and link descriptions apparently aren't it. If those four words in the title, plus a bit more info in the link description, can elicit FOMO (fear of missing out) and draw the reader in, even better. Don't overshare here, you want a high CTR after all.

5. Videos with auto-playing sound annoy 80% of users. Most of us scroll through our Facebook feed in public - on the subway, in class, or waiting in line at the grocery store. Ironically, these places each include about a dozen people who will definitely give you a dirty look when an ad pops up and starts sounding off immediately. Because of this, you need to consider that the majority of your ad viewers are going to be consuming with sound off, so ensure that you include relevant subtitles and visual queues to lessen the need for audio.

6. Videos with closed captions increase viewing time by about 15%. Reiterating the point above - closed captions will prompt viewers to stick around longer. This way, Facebook users can still watch and understand your videos, no matter where they might be.

7. Your video ad has about three seconds to capture viewer attention. Three seconds sounds like nothing, but your video has a ton of opportunity to pack a punch in that small amount of time. Similar to post titles, ensure the first three seconds of your video are informative, but mostly full of FOMO. A bit of suspense, or the idea that your video isn't revealing everything right away will give your viewers incentive to keep watching.

8. Shorter posts get about 23% more interaction than long Facebook posts. Keep it short and simple. Again, your audience is likely consuming on the go, so you need to get their attention fast and smoothly and trust that your subsequent landing page will hold their interest beyond that.

9. Video posts get more attention therefore shares than any other post type. This is another exceptional reason to incorporate video content into your Facebook marketing strategy - the average video share count is about 89.5 shares.

Facebook offers convincing opportunities for businesses, but also significant challenges. Hopefully these clues will point you in the right direction to help you drive better results from your Facebook marketing efforts in 2019.

Facebook Organic Reach

Before we move any further, let's take a step back and give a definition, in case you are not familiar with the meaning . In general, natural reach is the number of users who will see on their screens what you posted, with

$0 spent on your side. On the other hand, paid reach includes the users who see your content as a result of paid promotions and advertisement . In our case, the number of users that your content from your profile gets is the number of your Facebook organic reach.

Tip 1: Publish more content that your fans actually want to see. Many public pages just publish once a week but I recommend posting a variety of content styles over the week. Optimal post reach can be received just once or twice a day. You can line up the posts for the week in facebook scheduler to see what kind of content people react to. Check your insights to see what people most engage with and start forming a list to keep you on track for 2019.

Tip 2: Create a dialogue with people who may see your content by including a more enticing comment on your post. This is done by asking questions or telling a story. You can even say something observed about the image or video you're posting about. I'm giving you a ton of awesome examples and specific instructions for you to get that engagement popping today on the podcast.

Tip 3: Do you know who you're speaking to? Look at the people who follow your page and engage with your posts by going to their page and reading what they post about. You can also learn alot about your fans in comments. If you spend the majority of your time speaking with people on each post, then the post does much better and you can utilize your time more wisely by commenting and sharing additional things right on comments. Insights is also a great place to see how your posts performed. Listen to today's podcast episode to find out how to use this information to start posting smarter content.

Tip 4: Post Micro content that doesn't link off the site. This is anything that condenses your content and keeps people in the feed. Think of how you scroll though the newsfeed and think about what you engage with. People don't trust links as much as they used to and often they don't want to leave a social media page to consume it so try to design the majority of your content be consumed right on the social media page. For instance: publish a video trailer that promotes your youtube videos rather than always just sharing your YouTube videos on the page. You can still share a youtube video so it plays on the page but publishing directly to Facebook will definitely give your music a boost into the newsfeed.

Tip 5: There are so many mistakes that people make on facebook but here are some of the worst page killers. Posting the same link and photo's over again. Not answering comments at all of fast enough. Always be social and active. Never let a comment go unanswered for more than a few hours. I like to stay on a social media page for 30 minutes after posting so I can give attention to my first responders. Those first responders are your super fans so don't leave them hanging. Make sure you answer those comments. Ignoring messanger. Don't let that be your dead zone. That's where you can capture your audience onto email lists, nurture more supportive relationships and make sales. Stop linking off of facebook.

Tip 6: Be consistent: Many people give up way too quickly. They post a few time and then stop. Facebook knows how much time you spend on the app so when you post and leave, they are actually least likely to show your content to the majority of your followers. Posting regularly and staying on the app to engage with people in the newsfeed, answer comments on previous posts, and being present on messenger tells the app that you're an active user. All this activity boosts your posts and helps to qualify your account. Facebook also gives more credibility to the next post you publish after a successful post so try not maintain consistency and don't stop posting once you have achieved some reach and activity.

Tip 7: The best posts to try on facebook: live stream on facebook, post video directly to facebook, images without links, selfies, statements and quotes, funny memes, questions, polls, and trending or popular videos shared on facebook. Look at trending posts on facebook for possible topics of conversation that could improve your engagement. This does require some trial and errors and make sure that your choice of topic aligns with your brand and page content.

Facebook Ads

There are lots of good reasons to invest both time and money into Facebook Ads. All those options they offer, while seemed to be overwhelming, also offer immense customization and creative control over your ads. For example Want to target vegan parents of young children near Soho? Want to target these individuals, but only if they're already connected to your Page or business? You can actually do both simultanously . The targeting and retargeting options available through Facebook Ads are incredibly developed .

Facebook Ads are also connected to Instagram Adverts. You can work both in a single campaign, connecting you to audiences on both platforms. Since the largest goal of Facebook Ads is to put your content in front of users - without waiting for them to come find you, this is a great advantage. And while some people don't trust the cost of Facebook Ads, it's still pretty affordable compared to some alternatives, including Google AdWords. This is particularly true when your ad campaigns are given a high importance/value score, which means Facebook believes your ad is a good fit for your target audience, and they'll lower your CPC.

To fully harness the power Facebook has to offer, it is important to take into consideration the different ways that you can advertise on Facebook and when each approach is appropriate.

Boosted Posts: These engagement-boosting ads can be your daily go-to for any scenario. Did you know that the average percentage of your Facebook community that organically sees your daily content is 6.5% or even less? Facebook's algorithms cater content to show audiences what they prefer to see at first, but your content can get on that list. Belt this algorithm by putting a small budget ($10 - $30) behind your daily posts. You can select targeted audience to be people who like your page, making sure that this content will pop up in their feeds even if it is not something they often engage with.

Like Ads: If community growth is a primarily important for you in 2018, like ads are the perfect solution! These ads specialize in growing your community and generating more "likes" for your social media page. It gets even better when you consider you have the ability to select the exact public that you want to follow your brand. Select an age group, location, demographic, or interest to ensure that the new followers you receive will be engaged with your content and ultimately becoming brand advocates. We suggest spending anywhere from $300 to $2,000 a month on these ads.

Lead Ads: What if you could use Facebook to poll your audience on a daily basis and learn about their shopping places , preferences, and even question them about new product ideas? Well, forced ads make it possible to gather consumer intel like these examples and more. Instead of directing audiences to an external landing page to submit a form or survey, lead ads collect this same info through Facebook. Once the ad is clicked, audiences will be able to answer the questions asked and easily submit them in a matter of few seconds. An extra sweet feature to these ads is that Facebook automatically fills in any basic personal information (such as name, birthday, email address, etc.) saving users time and keeping audiences from navigating away before completing. When it comes to the right amount to spend, ask yourself: how much would you spend to get this sort of information from a specific group? The sky's your limit.

Conversion Ads: If you read my recent post on the Facebook Pixel, you know that conversion ads are another treat that I can't live without. These ads are perfect for tracking the success of a promotion and helping to see exactly how your landing pages are performing. If I notice a high amount of clicks on my ad but not many people submitting forms, I know that the landing page is not performing well, due to copy, design, or content. Through these ads, I am able to make changes mid-promotion to ensure that I gain as many submissions and/or leads as possible.

Before you dive into one of these advertising approaches, it's important to remember these Facebook advertising best practices. Once you've got these down, you'll be ready to harness the power of Facebook ads in your favor.

How To Set Up A Campaign

Creating high-converting Facebook Ads isn't actually as difficult as it sounds. Because many brands and small businesses prefer Facebook's Ads Manager to the more intricate Power Editor, I am going to use the Ads Manager's Create an Ad process for this Facebook Ads guide.

1. Develop Your Strategy First

Before you can even start looking at the Ads Manager, you need to have a strategy in place. Without this, you absolutely will get confused by all the options and you'll end up creating an ad campaign that doesn't actually target anyone useful because you're creating an ad for no one in particular.

For each campaign that you're going to create, you need to ask yourself:

- What product or services am I specifically promoting?

- Who am I targeting?

- Will they be a cold audience or a warm audience?

- How will they use the product?

- What is their pain point, and what objections will they have?

- Which stage of the funnel are they in exactly?

- What is the goal of the campaign?

- Do I want leads, brand awareness, site traffic, sales, or something else?

If you don't have a strategy with a goal of what you want to accomplish, you won't be able to create strong ads. Develop your game plan first.

2. Choose Your Objective

The very first thing you should do when creating your campaign is to choose your objective. It is important to choose the right one, because Facebook will optimize ad placements based on your objective of preference . In times the right objective can lower your CPC and improve your results. You can choose from the following objectives:

- Brand awareness

- Reach

- Traffic

- Engagement

- App installs

- Video views

- Lead generation

- Messages

- Conversions

- Catalogue Sales

- Store Visits

You want to select an objective that most cohesively aligns with your underlying goals. If, for example, you're running a video campaign that's designed to drive sales, choose the "conversions" option instead of the "video views" choice. Sure, you do want video views, but not at the expense of more conversions.

417

3. Target Your Audience

You should start making your ad campaign with a strong idea of who you want to target - now's your chance to flesh that out.

You can use:

- Custom audiences, which target specific users from your email list, or users who have taken certain actions on your site, your Facebook, or your Instagram's marketing profile.

- Lookalike audiences, which replicate qualities from your custom audience

- Demographic targeting

- Location targeting

- Interest/behavior targeting

- Connection targeting, which determines if you want your ads to be shown to users who are or are not connected with your brand

4. Choose Where You Want Your Ad To Be Displayed

Next, at the ad set level, you'll be choosing what placements, apps, and devices you want your ad to be shown on. You can choose mobile only, desktop only or both desktop and mobile. You'll also have multiple options on Facebook, several on Instagram, and the audience network. You can run ads with almost all placement options selected (unless you choose to run an Instagram Story Ad, in which case you can only use that placement), or you can disable or enable only certain ones. You can read an extensive resource on ad placements and their pros and cons here.

5. Set Your Budget

In the next section, you'll be able to choose your budget, schedule your ads, and select an optimization method. You can choose a lifetime budget or a daily budget and you can either have your ads run indefinitely or be scheduled to start and end on certain dates. You can even choose to use dayparting, which allows you to run your ads only at certain times or on certain days of the week. At this stage, you can also choose if you want to optimize your ads. For those who are wary of this, Facebook automatically has things set up for you and I'd only recommend going in and manually updating them if you're familiar with the platform and have reason for doing so. That being said, you can choose to change what you're bidding on (like link clicks or impressions), if you want to spend your ad budget as quickly as possible or spread it out over time, and if you want to set a cap on your bids.

6. Choose Your Ad Format

There are several incredible ad formats on Facebook. You can choose from:

- Single image ads

- Video ads

- Carousel ads, which allow you to show several videos and/or pictures

- Canvas ads

- Collections, which open up to be a full-screen mobile experience.

Each ad type as it's own unique benefits, but video ads and carousel ads (with or without video) typically have some of the highest engagement and CTR rates.

7. Don't Forget the Details

At the very bottom of the creative section, there's a lot of small details that are easy to miss. These include multiple sections where you can put copy, along with things like CTAs and URL descriptions. Take advantage of every single one of them. The CTA button will help drive conversions, and using the right copy in the right places will make a world of difference on your campaigns.

8. Monitor Your Ads Carefully

After you've started your campaigns, monitor them carefully. Some campaigns may start to see increases in CPC after the frequency gets too high and others may start out at a significantly higher CPC than you'd expect. Others may just not be performing the way you'd like. Facebook's Ads Manager will show you the details of all of your active campaigns. Watch the CPC, frequency, relevance scores, and number of actions taken particularly carefully. These are the most crucial metrics.

Create The Business Page

A Facebook Business Page is a free opportunity for businesses to increase brand awareness and generate sales on Facebook. To create a Facebook Business Page, simply log into your personal Facebook account, click "Create a Page" from the drop-down menu, and then follow the steps to build out your business profile.

Follow These Steps To Learn How To Create A Facebook Business Page:

1. Register for a Facebook Business Page

Facebook business pages are created using a personal Facebook account, so you'll need to first log in to your Facebook account. In the right-hand side of the blue toolbar, find and click the "Create" button. A drop-down list will appear after clicking "Create." Select the first option, "Page," to create your Facebook Business Page. You will have the option between two page categories—a "Business or Brand" or "Community or Public Figure." Most for-profit businesses will want to choose Business or Brand.

2. Enter Your Business Information

Tell Facebook what you want the name of your business page to be. This should be the same as your actual business name. Then, choose a business category that best represents what your business offers. For example, a clothing brand could enter "Clothing," which will then pre-populate a list of related options for you to choose from.

3. Upload Your Profile Picture & Cover Photo

Next, choose a photo to upload as your business page profile picture. Businesses commonly use their logo as a profile picture, but you may use any photo that represents your business and your business' branding. Be sure that your image is clear and doesn't get cropped. If you don't already have an image in mind that you'd like to use, or are in need of a new one, it's worth checking Fiverr. There you can find freelance experts who can design a professional profile picture for you, whether it's a logo another image, at an affordable price. Click here to browse freelancers.

Next, consider uploading a cover photo. A cover photo is the background image that appears on your Facebook Business Page, similar to your personal Facebook account. You want your cover photo to be visually appealing and representative of your business. Your cover photo should be at least 400 pixels wide by 150 pixels tall. If you are having trouble finding a cover image, you can create one for free using Canva. It includes many Facebook cover templates that you can easily customize without any graphic design skills or knowledge.

4. Invite Friends to Like Your Page

Facebook will prompt you to invite your current Facebook friends from your personal account to like your new business page. Existing Facebook friends can provide a good initial base of likes for a new Facebook Business Page, so it is advised to go ahead and do this. Either click the pop-up prompt, or invite friends from your "…" button from your business page as illustrated below.

5. Include Additional Business Details

In the left-hand menu, find and select "About." This is where you will input information that tells readers about your business, from ways to contact you to your products or menu. Enter all pertinent information, such as your website, hours, and contact information. It's not uncommon for a business' Facebook page to rank higher in organic search than their website, given Facebook's domain authority. Keeping this in mind, it's important to complete all information, as it may be a potential customer's first point of reference for your business.

6. Add a Button to Your Page

After you have input all of your important information into your Facebook business page, you will want to add a button to your page, which will appear in the top right-hand of your business page below your cover photo. This acts as your Facebook page's call-to-action (CTA) and is free to use. Including a relevant one to your business can help generate more leads, and in return, increase sales.

To do this, click the blue "+ Add a Button" option on the left-hand side of your page below your cover image. You can choose from the following types of buttons: Book with You, Contact You, Learn More, Shop, or Download. Select the button type that best suits your business. For example, a hair salon would likely want to use the Book with You option, whereas a brand selling products would find the Shop option a better fit.

7. Market Your Facebook Business Page by Being Active on Facebook

Creating a Facebook Business Page is only the first step to marketing your business on the platform of Facebook. You will need to be active on Facebook in order to market your page and grow an public . For example, you will not only want to be persistent in posting on your page, but you will also want to actively take part in relevant groups where your target audience is likely spending their time.

How to Grow Your Business with Your Facebook Business Page

For a Facebook business page to serve as an effective marketing channel for your business, you will need to promote your page. You can do this by taking advantage of Facebook opportunities from Facebook Ads to get your name out there by participating in relevant Facebook groups.

Here are different way you can get started promoting your Facebook Business Page:

Link Your Facebook Business Page to Your Website - Be sure your Facebook business page links to your website. You can do this a number of ways, from including your URL in the About section to adding a button to your page that links to your site. You can also post content on your page with links to your website.

Advertise on Facebook - Once you create a Facebook business page, you're all set to advertise on Facebook. Facebook advertising is not only an affordable advertising platform where you only pay for the clicks your ad receives, but it is also unique because you can target an extremely specific audience through sophisticated ad targeting. Your ads are shown to precisely the people you need to reach, giving you the opportunity to land in front of the right people. If you are producing great posts and content on your page, another option is to use Facebook Sponsored Posts, which is a form of advertising that will put your post in front of your target audience. It is a very easy and cost-effective way of having your Facebook posts reach users outside of your Facebook network.

Get Listed in Google's Organic Results - Ranking on the first page of Google search results can be difficult for small business websites. The good news is that having your business listed on Facebook (and other online directories like Yelp and Google My Business) increases your chance of your business ranking high in search results.

Market Your Business Online for Free - If done right, you can also see results from marketing your Facebook page without having to pay a dime. You can do this by sharing content like videos, blog posts, and images that will garner your audience's attention. We have an article on how to get free Facebook likes that will teach you what types of posts will get you more fans. If you own a seasonal shop like a food truck or pop-up shop, and you don't have a separate business website, you can also use your Facebook page as your main online presence.

Connect with Your Customers - When people like your page, you can tell them what's new with your business, share interesting articles you think they would enjoy, and respond to their posts on your page. Remember to regularly respond to comments and questions from your followers and build a relationship with them. This is a great platform for a local business that relies on local patrons to keep their business booming.

Build Awareness Through Facebook Groups - Facebook groups can be a great opportunity for businesses to increase their exposure and build brand awareness. Find relevant Facebook groups and actively participate in them. Keep in mind that your participation should generally be with the goal of connecting with new people and helping others, not offering a sales pitch, so refrain from using it as a platform for selling your product or service.

How to Optimize Your Facebook Business Page

Optimization involves changing one element of your Facebook page at a time to test the performance of the change. For example, you may change different aspects of your business page from your profile picture or cover photo to the type of call-to-action button you use. It's beneficial to optimize this way because it leads to higher engagement, following, and ultimately, sales.

Optimization also help your Facebook business page in the short-term as users are notified when you update your profile, making your page appear in their news feed. Gauge performance by tracking likes, views, and interactions of the posts you've optimized. For example, if your previous profile picture had 72 likes and 13 comments, but your new one gets 144 likes and 24 comments in its first month, you can assume the newer image is better. Another good way to do this is by using heatmap software to track how and where users engage on your Facebook business page. Hotjar is a great heatmap tool with a free forever plan that can be used to track what users do on your Facebook business page.

LinkedIn

With a rapidly growing user base of 500 million professionals, LinkedIn provides organizations with unique opportunities. Beyond being a prime place to share content and showcase thought leadership, LinkedIn performs almost 3 times better than Facebook or Twitter for generating visitor-to-lead conversions. Creating and maintaining an up-to-date LinkedIn Page is crucial for any marketing strategy. At a glance, running your LinkedIn Page might seem pretty simple. But growing an engaged following on LinkedIn is apples and oranges compared to any other social network. And given the platform's best practices and new slew of business features, there's perhaps no better time to revisit your LinkedIn presence for optimal engagement.

Below I have broken down the anatomy of the perfect LinkedIn Page whether you're looking to optimize your current profile or start from scratch.

Best Way To Set Up Linkedin Page

First things first: businesses need to cover the basics of their profiles. Although setting up your LinkedIn Page is straightforward, there are some important decisions to make in terms of optimizing your creatives and profile copy.

Choosing a logo and cover photo - Chances are you already have the creatives on deck for your logo and cover photo. In addition to your tagline, this is what users will see "above the fold" when checking out your business. Unlike Facebook or Twitter where you might use a cover photo of your team, clean and colorful imagery is your best bet on LinkedIn. When in doubt, keep it simple. The approach you take to your creatives is totally up to you, though I recommend coming up with a cover photo that's exclusive to LinkedIn for the sake of giving your profile some flavor.

Filling out your LinkedIn profile - Any given LinkedIn Page contains a series of subsections. Businesses should ideally fill all of these sections out 100%, with the exception of the "Jobs" section if you aren't hiring.

About - This section highlights your organization's basic information, including a brief "About" blurb and a place to list industry-specific keywords in the "Specialties" field. The information here is more akin to a Facebook "About" section versus a stylized Twitter or Instagram bio. Your LinkedIn "About" section highlights your company's mission statement as well as industry-specific keywords

Life - The "Life" section is an opportunity to show off your organization's culture. Here you can highlight your organization's values, provide a snapshot of your workers' day-to-day lives and explain what separates you from other organizations in your space. LinkedIn's "Life" section is the perfect place to highlight your company culture and values

Jobs - If you're hiring via LinkedIn, this section will aggregate and house your job listings. LinkedIn allows businesses to post job listings

People - The "People" tab will populate based on which workers have your organization listed as their employer. There's also a brief demographic breakdown based on your employees' location, education, roles and skills. This section is valuable for potential prospects and people interested in reaching out to your organization.

Best Practices To Maximize Your Linkedin Engagement

Now that you have an idea of how to fill out your LinkedIn Page and what to post, it's time to think about how you're going to maximize your profile's reach. Want more followers? Looking to attract the attention of industry players and influencers? Here's how you do it.

Get your employees involved - Okay, this is the big one. Employee advocacy is the absolute best way to grow your LinkedIn presence and exponentially increase your content's reach. Think about it. When you restrict your organization's content to your Page, you're only being seen by your current crop of followers. But let's say you have a few dozen employees with a couple hundred followers each. Even if there's some overlap between your page followers and theirs, this enables your posts to be seen by thousands who'd otherwise miss out on them. Rather than manually have employees post organization content, platforms such as Bambu or LinkedIn Elevate allow organizations to curate and amplify social content within a single platform. This encourages a uniform approach to sharing content that ensures that as many eyes are on your organization as possible. Bambu's employee advocacy platform makes it a cinch to share company content through individual profiles.

Prioritize video content - Video content is quickly taking over social media itself and LinkedIn is no different. LinkedIn released its video capabilities in 2017 and has been stressing the importance of video ever since. It's no surprise that video content is among the most popular and LinkedIn and appears to be prioritized by the platform's algorithm. From educational video to commercials, organizations should step up their video production ASAP in an effort to stand out on the platform.

Come up with a consistent content calendar - Based on our data regarding the best times to post on social media, good engagement appears to shift between mornings toward the late-afternoon throughout the workweek. It is not rare that we see most organizations post at least once daily, although we encourage businesses to experiment with frequency. Having an understanding of your timing and determination can help you put together a comprehensive content calendar specific to LinkedIn. With the help of Sprout, you can then publish directly to your LinkedIn Page and schedule your content alongside your other types of social profiles.

Stay tuned for opportunities to connect and engage - Whether your content strategy focuses on posing questions or sharing thought leadership, your public is expecting to hear from you. 55% of buyers say that liking or responding to a consumer's post on social media helps brands connect with consumers. Now with "real-time" notifications for comments in the Smart Inbox, it's easier to create connections with your consumers with more contentment . Think: shorter response times when cultivating conversations or answering questions directed towards your brand/business . Acting quickly in those moments inspires more engagement from your public.

Understand your analytics - According to Sprout's 2018 Social Index, audience insights and data-driven strategy should be the top priority of any organization looking to thrive on LinkedIn. In other words, you need robust analytics. What posts are your top performers? When are you scoring the most shares and followers?

LinkedIn Groups

The best way to place your company in front of your customers is to create a group that is relevant to your field. In this group, you can start discussions, and create an open forum for your customers to share their opinions, suggestions and concerns. However, you cannot just create a group and leave it at that. You must actively participate in those discussions and address your customers's opinions or concerns.

Other than creating a brand new group, you can also consider joining other groups and communities that are related to your business's niche. This way you can listen to what your target audience is talking about and the kinds of problems they are facing. Address these problems in those groups and propose solutions that your company can offer. If you develop a connection with a potential customer in the group, you can send them a message via LinkedIn InMail and start building a stronger relationship with your customer.

Organic Growth

While you might understand the importance of an established LinkedIn company page for your business, it can be more difficult to determine what best practices to follow in order to grow your page organically. By employing these tactics, businesses everywhere can expect substantial increases in the value of their LinkedIn business pages:

1- You should make sure that all employees complete their profiles on LinkedIn and add your company to their profiles as employees are automatically followers of their Company Page.

2- Motivate your employees to share your content with their many connections. This will raise your brand perception and increase the engagement including the likes, comments, and shares. Remember that employees on average, have 10 times the connections as their company has followers on LinkedIn and so when they share your content with their connections, this will increase the popularity of your brand.

3- Follow other businesses and influencers in your industry and engage with them so that you can use their reach to grow your following as well.

4- Post updates consistently that your followers can like, share, and comment on. When they engage with your content, their followers will also see your own updates. According to LinkedIn, B2B prospects engage with 7 pieces of content on average before making a purchase .That's why Top performing Companies will post several pieces of content each week, and some even post daily. Content often published on LinkedIn include images, infographics, posts from the company blog, leads to events, webinars, ebooks, and many more. So drive higher quality leads by featuring a good mix of upper funnel and lower funnel content, including tip sheets, eBooks and case studies you should take in consideration.

5- You could Post high-quality Content. Your content should focus on teaching others how to solve a problem and establish you as a thought leader in that particular area. According to LinkedIn, 74% of prospects choose the company that was first to help them along their buyer's adventure. So sharing perspectives on industry news and trends, helpful product how-to's and articles that reflect your company's vision will definitely establish you as a though leader in your own industry.

6- Post and share rich media like engaging visuals, videos, and infographics that capture the audience's interest.Based to LinkedIn, adding rich media to your LinkedIn Sponsored Content can increase CTRs by as much as 39%!

7- Engage with your network by responding to comments, liking or sharing other posts, and engaging in relevant groups for your industry. Also, joining groups that are relevant to your target audience will enable you to know what your audience is talking about and communicate with them. You can also create groups to share your content that your audience will be interested in and demonstrate your expertise while at the same time ensure that no competitors get in.

8- Add social sharing buttons and links to your Company Page on your website and other social media platforms. Add them on all of your blog posts and website content to allow users to quickly share content as updates.

9- Update your Career Section frequently with job postings so that people looking for jobs will find your page in search features or through connection suggestions and will hopefully follow your Company Page to stay updated with new openings and future opportunities.

Paid Advertising

With LinkedIn Targeted Ads, you can target the right people at the right time with LinkedIn Advanced Targeting Features. LinkedIn targeting is unparalleled since it provides you with targeting options that aren't available in other social media platforms like Facebook. The Demographic Targeting is exceptional where you can target people specifying the company name they work in, their job function, their seniority level, the industry they're operating in, the company size, the degrees they've acquired, the education level, the groups they've joined, and many more. This targeting method is what makes LinkedIn Advertising Cost higher than other platforms, but at the same time the leads acquired through LinkedIn Ads are more qualified and valuable leads which makes the Conversion Rate higher.

LinkedIn Dynamic Ads now available in the Campaign Manager are great to get new followers. LinkedIn Dynamic Ads are divided into three parts which are the Followers Ad, the Spotlight Ad, and the Content Ad. The Dynamic Followers Ad allow you to expand your page followers similar to Facebook Page Likes Ad, a new feature that wasn't available for us before.

Also, LinkedIn Sponsored Content helps you to publish relevant content and reach a targeted audience of professionals beyond just your LinkedIn Company Page Followers. You can promote and advertise the company's content through Sponsored Content Ads to target a niche audience, increase visitors and generate sales leads. You can also choose to add a "Follow button" to your Sponsored Content if your goal is actually to acquire followers.

You can also add a "Follow button plugin" for free to your website so people can follow your Company Page from your site. You can request the "Follow Company Plugin Generator" through this link.

Also, promote the company's content through other types of LinkedIn Ads like Text Ads, or Dynamic Ads to target specific audience and generate awareness, increase traffic, and generate qualified leads. Another type of Ad is Sponsored inMail where you send a personalized message to LinkedIn members' inMail box and with a CTA feature asking them either to subscribe, sign up, download, and many more.

Remember to identify your target public clearly and determine who you're trying to reach and who are the people you want to be your Company Page's Followers before starting your Ad Campaigns by answering the following questions:

- What is their job title and what are the functions?

- Where are they actually located?

- What industry do they work for ?

- What is their advantage ?

- What are they interested about ?

- What kinds of content they follow?

- What kinds of questions do they ask ?

- What are their weak points?

Youtube

When people talk about social media, they rarely mention anything about YouTube. This is sort of surprising since YouTube is the second ranked search engine of choice by volume actual used. Now, more than ever, YouTube users can up being just as valuable, if not more valuable, than traditional social media followers for the matter.

While the userbase makes up the heart and spirit of all social media platforms, a subscriber on YouTube is much more important than a follower on either Facebook or Twitter. Organic Facebook followers are much harder to reach than they used to be, and Twitter followers see a cascade of tweets by the hour, making it likely that your tweets go unnoticed. Unlike any other social network however, nearly 80% of adults consider themselves a "regular" systematic YouTube user. In addition, it is very easy to use, since a Gmail account is all someone needs to create their own playlists, vote on videos, use the comment system, or become a subscriber.

The ease of use, combined with the gift to create so many different social signals, makes YouTube an important part of any social network marketing strategy. These users are going to see your new videos, they are going to pay attention to the message in the videos, and they can even help attract new subscribers and also comment.

How to Create Videos for YouTube

Making videos that people enjoy can be challenging, especially if you are just starting out. Most people like to do things at their own speed, which makes it even more crutial that your video is good, or people will not want to waste their time with it. In a article from the Huffington Post, companies seeing the greatest YouTube success ranked different types of videos by their importance and effectiveness. Below, I cover these videos as ranked in the article.

Before you brainstorming for, filming, and editing your videos, take into consideration this list of video types.

Customer testimonials. Customer testimonials are short interviews with satisfied customers. Customer testimonials can help build company and product credibility.

On-demand product demonstration videos. Demonstration videos are short pieces of content showing the benefits and proper use of a specific product .

Explainer and tutorial videos. Explainer videos are in-depth videos explaining how to use a product or various parts of a certain product or service. Tutorials can be used to answer customer support questions or explain a new product feature and evidence the use of purposes of it.

Thought leader interviews. Interviews with experts or thought leaders can help deepen your company's credibility in an industry.

Project reviews and case studies. Project reviews or case studies revalueate a successful campaign or project and often include statistics and results.

YouTube Live. YouTube Live allows users to broadcast

live content to viewers online . Live video allows you to easily share unfiltered moments and lets your audience participate with real-time comments and reactions with emoji. Live videos on YouTube are recorded and appear like any other video uploaded . To Go Live from your YouTube channel by clicking the camera+ icon in the top right corner and choosing "Go live".

Video blogs. Video blogs are daily or weekly videos documenting daily life or activities. You could also record a video that list or highlights a blog post so your audience has multiple ways to digest the content.

Event videos. Event videos feature in-person experiences at a conference or expo and can be a great way to show the excitement of a group.

How to Promote Your Videos

Once you have your first video ready to go, you need to promote in a proper or it may end up being completely unnoticed by the YouTube community. This can be done by:

Give it a good description – The title and description for your video can help bring in search traffic both on YouTube, and through search engines. This is incredibly important, especially when you are just starting out, since the value of an individual viewer or subscriber is much higher when there is a low number of them in the first place. Think about what people might be searching for and if your video would be a good fit for them. Throw a couple of those keywords into your title or description, and you should be ready to upload it.

Comment on related videos – While this might seem a little "spammy", it is still one of the best ways to get your video in front of a targeted audience. There is a good chance that if a viewer is interested in the video that you commented on, and it is at least somewhat relevant, they may be interested in yours as well. This is best done while your channel is still young and you do not have a lot of subscribers. Building up a healthy subscriber base is crucial to your success, and you will probably gain a few subscribers with this method. Doing it too often though, and doing it when you already have a fair amount of subscribers, will lead to diminishing returns.

Use your existing social media accounts to promote your videos – If your other social media accounts already have a decent number of followers, you can use your videos as posted content. This gives your other social media accounts some variety, since you are posting a video, and it will direct people already interested in your business or website to YouTube, where they may become subscribers there as well.

Keep people on your channel with in-video links – Having a link to another one of your videos come up when people are almost done watching their first video will keep people around longer. This increases the chance that they will perform an action which can cause your video to become more popular. They might become a subscriber, give it a thumbs up, or even share it off-site. The longer you keep someone engaged, which can be easy with an in-video link, the more valuable that person becomes to you.

For those of you starting out with YouTube, you will probably find that promoting your videos is going to be the hardest part. Over time, as long as you keep adding quality videos, it should become easier as your success starts to build upon itself. The most popular YouTube stars do not have to worry about how they are going to promote their videos, they are going to get hundreds of thousands, perhaps millions of views no matter what specifically because they are already wildly popular. You on the other hand will need to keep promotion in the forefront of your mind.

There are so many different ways that YouTube users can increase your social media presence, and by extension your main website or business. You don't really see the same kind of versatility with other social networks, but the tradeoff is that you absolutely need to keep users engaged more than with just written content. If you make good videos, and you promote them the right way, you will probably have a lot of success building a YouTube following, which can end up giving you a big return on your social media budget.

Organic Growth

With so many subscribers, channels and viewers on the podium, increasing traffic on YouTube has become a challenge for brands. We've listed the following tips to boost organic reach of your YouTube videos.

1. Conduct thorough keyword research

YouTube's conclusion takes into account keywords in the channel description, video titles, video descriptions and tags. Ask yourself: what is my public searching for on YouTube? Now take that knowledge and research how your public is looking for that content. Are they typing in "How to" or looking for something more specific and detailed?

YouTube auto-suggest is a great place toto begin. Let's say your video is about styling ripped jeans. YouTube auto-suggest provides insights into what people constantly search and you can get a pretty good idea of what to title your video, too. You should also take a more analytical path to.

2. Optimize your videos (before and after uploading)

This is easily the most important part. Optimization is key to both before and after uploading to successfully increase views.

Tips for optimization before uploading

- Shoot high-quality video and use premium type editing

- Use a primary keyword to name your uploading file

Tips for optimization and filters uploading

- Write clear, natural titles with max 1-2 keywords

- Write titles no longer than 70 characters ca.

- Use high-volume, low-competition keywords in the descriptions

- Try to Keep video descriptions between 100-200 words, using a primary keyword throughout

- Upload a custom thumbnail to show off in search results

- Include relevant, on-topic video tagging

- Keep information natural to set realistic expectations for your viewers

3. Fill out the about section

Your company's YouTube profile section is prime real estate for not only telling your brand story and describing your channel, but also great place to implement market keywords. Fill in as much information as you can, including social profile links and your company website. You should also utilize keyword meta tags to describe your channel, which you can found under "Advanced" in channel settings. Channels with complete information stand out and rank higher.

4. Follow a consistent upload schedule

YouTube recognizes active channels, and the more videos you will upload, the stronger your channel will appear. This might mean posting once or twice a week or maybe biweekly. Upload schedule should remain frequent and posting should happen when your particular audience is most active on the platform.

5. Find smart ways to engage your viewers

Lastly, find unique ways to attract your viewers to keep them engaged longer. As stated above, YouTube strongly ranks videos on whether or not people are watching them. High view rate and public retention are major factors in organic performance.

A few other tricks to keep your audience engaged:

- You should request that they subscribe

- You should Add end screens and cards to direct viewers to another video

- You may Organize videos into playlists

- You may also Hold engaging contests

Paid Advertising

Are you ready to develop your first ad but unsure on which format you should use? I am not surprised. There are three types of YouTube ads - all of which have their own requirements, benefits and also use cases.

Pre-Roll Video Ads - This type of YouTube video ad is shown before a video, and runs about 30 seconds. They're charged per click, meaning you only pay for the total number of clicks generated, rather than the number of video views. Since these ads are charged per-click, they're usually the most cost-effective for campaigns focused around on-site conversions such as link clicks or to grow your subscriber list.

In-Stream Ads - If you've selected TrueView ads to form the basis of your YouTube advertising campaign, your videos will be shown to users before they view a normal video. You'll be charged per view for these ads and there's no upper time limit.

But here's the catch: Whoever's viewing your ad has the opportunity to skip your video after five seconds. Although you've got more space to play with, you've got less chance of encouraging someone to watch the entire video, especially if the first five seconds don't grab their attention. That's why these ads are usually best for generating brand awareness.

Bumper Ads - If you don't fancy creating longer videos to promote via YouTube ads, don't worry. You're able to use the bumper ad format to show a six-second, non-skippable clip before a regular video:

You might not think that six seconds is enough time to grab your audience's attention when running video marketing campaigns on YouTube, but Google found just the opposite: in 300 bumper campaigns, 88% drove a significant lift in ad recall - making them a fantastic format to use if you're looking to boost brand awareness.

In-Display Ads - If you don't want to advertise within the video itself, in-display ads are your best bet. Charged on a per-view basis whenever someone clicks the link, in-display YouTube ads are shown on the right-hand side of a user's screen.

Despite the name, in-display ads aren't the most prominent type of YouTube ad. Users are able to bypass your advert altogether if they're only interested in watching the video they're currently viewing, but they're a good option if you're looking to boost conversion rates. The person who's clicked on your in-display ad has done so by choice, meaning that they're already interested, and therefore potentially easier to convert.

How to Produce the Perfect Creative for YouTube Ads

Now that you've selected the suitable YouTube advertising format for your product or service, it's time to think about the overall video, which is often referred to as one of the most important aspects of your entire campaign. Creating a video that's enjoyable to watch is the good   basis of any successful YouTube video campaign. After all, you can't expect to see results if you aren't prompting   people to listen to whatever you're saying.

Here's the list you'll need when nailing the creative of your video ad:

- Make the first 5-8 seconds alluring. After this point, people may   decide if they want to skip your ad or continue watching.

- Replicate the language, cinematography and

447

personality of the industry you're looking to advertise to so you can tailor and develop it to what they want.

- Design a thumbnail for your YouTube ad that fits this industry as well.

- Focus on explaining one key point to avoid annoyance within your viewers.

- Tell a story to attract your audience, but make sure it's relevant and fits within the time you've got.

Other Tips and Tricks

I have created a comprehensive YouTube marketing strategy 2019 including all the tips and tricks to ace YouTube marketing. Follow these tips to master the YouTube marketing strategy 2019:

1. Build your YouTube brand channel

Your YouTube channel should spin out your brand's story to the people. From your channel icon to channel description, everything should speak your brand's voice. Add your brand's logo to the YouTube channel icon. Add a custom YouTube banner as well, with social media icons leading your audience to your social media handles across platforms. In the 'About' section of your YouTube channel, add a brief description of your brand. Your description should introduce every new visitor to your brand and reflect your brand voice. Put calls to action leading to your website or any other pages you want to lead your audience to. Finally, divide your videos into different playlists. You can create branded playlists with names unique to your brand. Categorise playlists into webinars, behind the scenes etc., depending upon your video content.

2. Consistently create and add compelling videos to your channel

Create video content that gets your audience talking. Most importantly, use YouTube videos to bring out your brand's story.

Are you a B2B brand? You can create YouTube videos that complement your blog or website content. Bring your customers to give quick reviews of your brand. Ask them to share the experience of using your products, working with your brand and so on to take your YouTube marketing plan to the next level. Create and run a separate Video blog channel for your brand and interact with your audience using the platform regularly. Interview industry professionals, seniors and subject matter experts. Informative video content is most popular with the audiences. Post step by step videos and tutorials on how to use your products or services. At the same time, keep posting videos consistently on your channel. Find out the right time to post content, when the audience is most active on the platform. Add videos to your channel accordingly.

3. Leverage YouTube tools and features

YouTube has a host of tools and features that can help you enhance your YouTube marketing strategy 2019. Use end screens and cards to add your desired calls to action. Shared a video on how to assemble a product? Lead your audience to other videos on how to use the product and other similar content from your playlists. Add transcripts your videos. Make your video content universal by adding closed captions. It cuts out the language barrier and makes your content consumable by audiences across borders. At the same time, you can reach out to the disabled with this YouTube video feature. A keyword-optimized video transcript helps enhance your YouTube SEO as well. These incredible tools come as a part of your YouTube channel. Make the most of these, to level up on your YouTube Marketing strategy.

4. Optimise your YouTube video description and thumbnails

Since your YouTube video thumbnails and description are the ones that provide a glimpse into your content, optimize these for better results. Your YouTube thumbnail should push YouTube users to click and watch your video. The most important elements of a good YouTube thumbnail image include a picture and a caption. Add a popping image and caption that draws the attention of your audience. Use facial-closeups for best response. The idea is to create a visual representation of the video content in the thumbnail. Equally important in your YouTube marketing strategy 2019 is your video description. Make all your YouTube video descriptions keyword optimized to enhance YouTube SEO. Also, make sure that your YouTube video descriptions align and complement your YouTube video content. Apart from using keywords, use catchy phrases that push the users to hit the play button on your videos.

5. Add YouTube stories to your YouTube Marketing Strategy 2019

After Instagram and Facebook, YouTube hops on to the stories' bandwagon. YouTube now has the stories feature which allows for you to add short, mobile-only videos that expire after 7 days. YouTube offers this feature to creators with more than 10,000 subscribers on the platform. Easily create YouTube stories in a matter of seconds with the tap button on your profile and then edit them. Trim your YouTube stories and add filters, music, text, stickers, and even links to your videos. As a creator, this tool allows you to diversify on your content on the platform. With this new feature and the tools that come along with it, you can build a strong relationship with your community. It will also help you boost engagement. Create compelling stories that generate interactions with viewers. Respond to all the comments and expand your community.

6. Optimize Video Titles For YouTube Voice Search

Enhance your YouTube SEO by optimizing title for YouTube voice search. People use YouTube voice search to find videos quickly, without having to use their fingers to type out the video titles. Since voice search is an easier, hassle free way to get YouTube video results, you need to ensure your videos appear before your audience.

Most importantly, optimize your YouTube video title to make it SEO friendly. Imagine yourself using YouTube voice search for your videos. Would you go for a longer YouTube video title or a shorter one? Most people will use a small number of keywords to describe their YouTube query. So, frame a YouTube title that includes important keywords, is short and simple and has a conversational tone. This will improve your YouTube SEO to a great extent and eventually increase your views on the platform.

7. Influencer Marketing On YouTube

Include Influencer marketing as a part of your YouTube marketing strategy 2019. There are 3 main important benefits of partnering with an Influencer:

- Access to a bigger audience

- Access to another person's skills

- Assortment of your content

And all these advantages add up to bring more engagement for your brand. Find out alcove Influencers. Someone whose niche may aligns with your brand. Using Unbox Social's social media analytics tool, impress different Influencers from your niche. The business feed feature on the tool dashboard allows you to track as many Influencers as you want and get regular updates about them. Monitor their activity and stay on one Influencer. Engage them and bring them on board. You can use Influencers to shunt great quality video content. Weight their content creation skills and influence to your best. Ask them to do product reviews, feature on your channel for account takeovers, or make them your brand agents. There are many ways in which you can use Influencer marketing as a part of your YouTube marketing plans . At the same time keep track of all the trends and watch out for outdated Influencer marketing practices that you may be nourishing in.

8. Use YouTube Ads

Paid content will continue to be an important part of a good YouTube strategy 2019. A sure way to make your videos appear before your audience is through the advertising option. YouTube Ads come in 6 different formats- skippable TrueView in-stream Ads, 6 second bumper Ads, sponsored cards, overlay Ads, display Ads and Trueview Discovery Ads which shows on the homepage, alongside search results and next to related videos. If you aren't using YouTube Ads to market your brand, you may do it now and check out the results for yourself.

9. Monitor your Competitors

Monitoring your competitors is an essential part of every business and marketing strategy. Competitor analysis can easily be done by visiting their YouTube channel as well. Identify their videos with most views to identify content that most people engage with. Use that content to draw inspiration for future video posts. Skim through their comments to find out any mentions or naming of your brand. If you spot your brand mentions, make sure to respond to each of the comments. Also find out if any of their Ads are featuring on your videos. If that is the case, you may block these on the Google Ads manager.

10. Track and report on important metrics to learn from them

An important part of YouTube marketing strategy 2019 is to track your performance and watch out for extensive metrics. You may Use a social media analytics and reporting tool such as Unbox Social. With this tool, you can track all important social media metrics and then generate customized reports of the same. Use Unbox Social to monitor metrics like watch time retention, top videos, video-wise engagement. Monitor your audience metrics along age, gender and even location. Target audience fragment accordingly.

11. Keep up with industry trends and updates

To be on top of your game in any industry, it is necessary to keep track of industry trends and updates. The social media industry is a potent one in itself. New features and trends in the Business as well as on the platform will inform your YouTube marketing plan. Use Unbox Social's personalized feeds to derive information and daily updates on your industry from your connections. Get an edge over the others by always staying on top of news, trends and updates in your business.

A great YouTube marketing technique involves leveraging all the tools and features at your disposal and employing them to build engagement. It also involves keeping watching on the industry as well as your competitors.